TO ALCATRAZ, DEATH ROW, AND BACK

Memories of an East LA Outlaw

Ernie López and Rafael Pérez-Torres

UNIVERSITY OF TEXAS PRESS, AUSTIN

Copyright © 2005 by the University of Texas Press

All rights reserved

Printed in the United States of America

First edition, 2005

Requests for permission to reproduce
material from this work should be sent to:
Permissions
University of Texas Press
Box 7819, Austin,
TX 78713-7819.

∞ The paper used in this book meets the minimum requirements
of ANSI/NISO z39.48-1992 (R1997) (Permanence of Paper).

Library of Congress Cataloging-in-Publication Data
López, Ernie, 1922–
To Alcatraz, death row, and back : memories of an East LA outlaw
/ Ernie López and Rafael Pérez-Torres.— 1st ed.
p. cm.
Includes bibliographical references.
ISBN 0-292-70660-x (cloth : alk. paper) — ISBN 0-292-70683-9 (pbk. : alk. paper)
1. López, Ernie, 1922– 2. Recidivists—California—Biography.
3. Death row inmates—California—Biography. 4. United States Penitentiary,
Alcatraz Island, California—Biography. 5. Hispanic Americans—California—
Biography. I. Pérez-Torres, Rafael. II. Title.
HV6049.L59 2005
365'.6'092—dc22 2004028383

This book is lovingly dedicated to Vivian Ledesma,

to whom I am forever grateful.

I have always counted on her to be in my corner

through all the hard times.

No words can express how much her care

and support have meant in my life.

E.L.

CONTENTS

PART THREE **SURVIVAL**

INTRODUCTION

RAFAEL PÉREZ-TORRES

The story you are about to read reflects a world where crime follows punishment and persecution shades into injustice. The life that Ernie López has led seems like a cross between a Dickens novel and a potboiler. But the events recounted here are real.

Born into poverty in East Los Angeles, a young boy finds himself committing petty crimes because he fears the abuse of his father. Subject to harsh beatings if he doesn't bring home money to contribute to the family's expenses, the boy learns to survive as best he can through petty criminal activity. As his misdeeds escalate, he gets committed to a brutal youth camp after a harmless joy ride through the streets of Los Angeles. His criminal involvement leads ultimately to incarceration in three infamous prisons: McNeil Island, Alcatraz, and San Quentin. Though dramatic and powerful, the events told here are conveyed as accurately as possible. These events, related during hours of interviews, form the basis of this first-person narrative in which I have attempted to convey in writing the flavor and tenor of Ernie's vivid stories.

Why read the story of a man who has spent the majority of his life in prison? What significance is there to the life of a career criminal? My own involvement in the writing of this book is due entirely to the sense of humanity that fills the story. After years of brutal incarceration, Ernie conveys a strong sense of humor, a firm code of his own ethics, and a burning sense of defiance. The U.S. prison system is designed to break men of their will. Ernie has refused to succumb. Though one might not envy or approve of Ernie's choices in life, there is much to learn from his example about self-reliance and fortitude in times of adversity and suffering.

The grace, irony, and humor Ernie demonstrates are somewhat characteristic of Chicano culture. The stories Ernie tells reflect the wry, often understated humor that marks one way Chicanos express themselves. A kind of gallows humor proves useful when approaching the inevitable trials and setbacks that life deals. So while Ernie's story is interesting because it offers an insider's picture of Alcatraz and San Quentin, it also shares qualities found in other aspects of Chicano culture and storytelling. Ernie's history is one of struggle and survival, of endurance and triumph. The philosopher Walter Benjamin says that the history of the underclass is a story of suffering and defeat told with "courage, humor, cunning, and fortitude," those qualities that bring to our lives refinement and spirituality (254–255). An attentive reader may find these qualities evident in this story.

The events recounted here are ones few of us are likely to have shared. While it is, unfortunately, becoming more and more common for people in the United States — especially among its racially and ethnically subordinate populations — to experience incarceration, few men have endured the kind of inhumane treatment meted out to Ernie López. Fewer still have responded with such burning ambition and fiery defiance. Finally, few have survived with their integrity and humanity intact. Ernie has. As these pages will reveal, at every turn possible Ernie sought to beat a system of justice and punishment that seemed out to destroy him. No matter how one may feel about the things he has done, his survival is a testament to the will and the power, both light and dark, of the human spirit.

WALTER DUNBAR,
~~RICHARD A. McGEE~~.
DIRECTOR OF CORRECTIONS

EDMUND G. BROWN
GOVERNOR

STATE OF CALIFORNIA

Department of Corrections

CALIFORNIA STATE PRISON
SAN QUENTIN. CALIFORNIA

F. R. DICKSON. WARDEN

October 1, 1963

ADDRESS ALL CORRESPONDENCE
TO THE WARDEN

ATTENTION OF: D B FRADY

PLEASE REFER TO LOPEZ, Ernest
FILE No.
Barragan
#A65453
(Condemned)

Mr. Lawrence B. Lopez,
3343 E. 3rd Street,
Los Angeles 63, California.

Dear Sir:

We are very sorry to write you regarding the following, but
you will appreciate the necessity for such communication.
The judgment of the court against your brother Ernest
has been upheld, and date of execution has been set for
Wednesday, December 11, 1963.

As you are listed as Subject's nearest of kin, we should
appreciate an immediate reply from you as to whether or not
you intend to claim his body, or designate another to do so.
This will be at your expense and it will be necessary for
you to make tentative arrangements with a mortician of your
choice. We should be notified immediately regarding the
name of the mortician and receive authorization to release
the remains. If you or any other member of your family
cannot claim the body, we make disposition through State
facilities, in which case the remains would not be claimable.

In the event that judgment is carried out, please advise us
if you wish to be notified. If we can be of service to you,
please let us know.

Yours very truly,

DALE B. FRADY, Associate Warden
Administration

Vs.

If you wish us to write your mother, at 3822 E. 1st Street,
Los Angeles, please advise us, as she would be the nearest of
kin. However, our records indicate he wishes you to be notified,
about this matter.

PART ONE EDUCATION

THE JUDGMENT AGAINST ME

I suppose my childhood was very much the same as that of any other kid who was born and raised in East LA, particularly during the Depression years before World War II. I was born April 5, 1922, the fourth boy and seventh child. Everyone I came to know in East LA had the same things in common: we were all poor, from large families, and doing everything we could to survive. By the time my two younger sisters came along, I had five sisters and three brothers as well as my mother, Dolores, and father, Jesús. Eleven of us had to be fed and clothed. Store-bought children's toys were an unheard of luxury and—starting at the age of seven—my after school hours were spent on a street corner selling newspapers. This was the beginning of the Great Depression, and often people just didn't have enough change to buy a paper, and many times I would walk along and coax or badger pedestrians to buy a paper so I could sell out my stack. This was one step away from outright begging, which I couldn't bring myself to do.

Often I would start selling newspapers at 2 in the afternoon and wouldn't come home until 8 or 9 p.m. because sales on my corner went so slowly. Saturday and Sunday were even longer days. There were times when I just couldn't sell papers to anybody, and on days like that I felt I had to do something to come home with some money. My father would accuse me of sloughing off if I didn't sell out the entire stack, which meant on a very good day bringing home eighty or ninety cents. Usually I brought home less, on average fifty or sixty cents, and my father would accuse me of having gambled the money away. The reality was I simply had had a slow day selling papers. I couldn't explain to him that people

just didn't *want* to buy papers. So when I had bad days I would make up for it by stealing whatever I could get my hands on.

I really wanted to please my father, but I found I rarely moved him, no matter what I did. He never knew how many times I stole money to make him think that I had sold all my papers. I hated selling papers. On those occasions that I was able to steal enough, I relished tearing up my stack and stuffing them in the sewer gutters.

Whenever I failed to live up to his expectations, my father was quick to give me the strap. So I found it easy to steal when I had to because I had such a strong desire to please him and avoid his punishment. By contrast, my mother was as loving and tender as my father was strict and unfeeling. She could see how hard I was trying and would attempt to make my father understand, but though she tried to defend me, she never argued with him. He was sole master of the castle.

I spent hour after hour standing on my street corner selling news-papers. There were times I would leave my corner to deliver a paper to a regular customer. One was an old man who had a little store a short way down the block from where I peddled my papers. He sold cigarettes, cigars, gum, all sorts of little things. The store was so small that the man didn't even have a cash register, just a little drawer where he kept his money, which was usually just change anyway. He had a little bell attached to the inside of the door that rang when a customer came in.

Every once in a while, the old man would come shuffling out of his little store holding his hands behind his back, looking at the window displays of other stores. When he did shuffle out, he would slowly make his way to my corner to buy a newspaper from me. He usually came around noon when the intersection at the street corner was busy with traffic and people walking to go home or to some small diner for lunch. But there were other times that I would walk down to his store to sell him a newspaper, which is why I knew about the little bell inside his door. When I would take him the paper, he would pull open the drawer of change and pay me.

Another one of my regular customers worked at a hardware store about a block away from my corner. Every afternoon I would deliver a newspaper to him at the hardware store. When I went to go make my delivery, I would stack all my newspapers against the side of the corner drugstore building next to where I sold papers. Sometimes while I was gone people getting off from the yellow streetcar would take a paper and drop their money on top of the stack.

One early afternoon I had gone on a delivery and left some money on top of the stack as usual so people would know to leave their change when they took a paper. Returning from the delivery I found all the money on the stack and almost all my newspapers gone! Right away I suspected that some of the kids who used to hang around the corner shining shoes were the culprits. Everyday I would see them come and go with their shoeshine boxes strapped to their backs, calling out to passersby if they wanted a shine. They used to charge five cents to shine a customer's shoes. Like me, these were poor kids from the neighborhood, hustling for what little money they could earn. But now they had gone and taken all the money I had earned that day.

Though it was still early, I had nothing to show for all my hard work, and I even owed the newspaper boss money for the papers that had been stolen. Since I didn't have enough money to pay off the boss, let alone have any left over to take home, I figured I was going to be beaten but good.

In desperation, I decided to steal some money from the old man's store down the block. I waited until he came out from his little store, tottering very slowly as he always did toward the corner. With my newspaper apron on and a couple of papers tucked under my arm, I crossed the street very quickly, trying my best not to act suspicious. I walked across the street from the old man heading in the opposite direction, passed the man's storefront, crossed the street as casually as possible and made my way back to his little store.

Very slowly I pulled the door open, making certain that the little bell didn't make any sound. I went directly to his money drawer and quickly stuffed as much money as I could into my apron pockets. My heart pounding, I rushed back to the door and peeked out to see how far the old man had walked. He was just halfway to the corner. Mindful that the old man couldn't see me, I came out of the store with my newspapers under my arm, looking around to make sure that nobody else was eyeing me. I crossed the street again, scurried back to the end of the street, and casually crossed to my own corner. With his slow shuffle, the old man hadn't even reached my corner yet. As I tried to look as nonchalant as possible, the man finally came up to me, bought a paper and turned back to his store just like normal.

As soon as I could, I counted out the change I had scooped from the drawer. It was the most money I had ever seen. There might have been about $35 or $40, which was a good amount of money for those days,

especially for a little boy. I felt pretty clever for just having grabbed the money, sneaking out, and getting back to selling my papers before the old man even turned around.

Well, now I had a new problem: I didn't know what to do with all that money! My best friend at the time was Alberto Silva, whose father owned a butcher shop on the corner of First and Rowan where I sold papers. His father was just like my father when it came to using the strap freely, so he understood the kind of torment I went through at home. I told Alberto about stealing the money, even offering him some of it, though he wouldn't take it. We put our heads together to figure out what was best to do next.

"I want to give my father some of it," I told him.

"Oh, no, Ernie," he said. "Don't do that. Hide it somewhere where nobody knows about it. Everyday, give him a little of the money and that way you won't get in trouble."

This seemed like a smart plan, so every day I'd take a bit of money from my stash and bring home eighty or ninety cents.

On these days, my father would look down at me and say, "Hmm, ahora se portó bien"—today you behaved well. I would just nod, and accept the compliment I was so hungry to hear.

"Vaya a comer. Tu mamá tiene algo pa' ti." So off I would go to my mother and get something to eat, happy that my father was treating me so much better.

The next day I would do the same thing, and the day after again. Between using the money to fool my father and buying small treats for myself, the day finally came when I ran out of money. I had little by little used up everything I had hidden. Then the same old pattern started up again when I brought home less than the full amount he wanted. He accused me of keeping the money for myself or gambling it away, and he took to whipping me every night.

Given the circumstances, I had to come up with another plan.

Down the block from First and Rowan, about halfway down from my corner and only two doors away from the old man's store, was a little restaurant called Joe's Hot Dog Joint. Behind the counter there was a wall with an open window for clean dishes to be passed through once they were washed. In that window, Joe kept a big tip jar full of quarters and nickels. The bathroom for Joe's was out behind the restaurant in a little driveway that came to a dead end. It was always locked up tight with a padlock, and anybody who wanted to use the toilet had to ask Joe for the key.

The bathroom had an old fashioned toilet, the kind with the water

box above the toilet. You had to pull a long chain that hung from the box whenever you wanted to flush. Above the water box was a rusted screen that was so old it was corroded and disintegrating. The screen connected the bathroom to the back storage of Joe's restaurant, a small dusty room that was practically empty and always dark.

Joe's stayed opened until late at night, and one evening I made my way to his restaurant. With the little money I had, I ordered myself a hot dog. I asked Joe for the key to the bathroom, as I had done many times. But instead of relocking the door, I left the padlock open, went back to the counter, and returned the key to Joe.

Later that evening when it was good and dark I returned to the unlocked bathroom. Once in, I climbed on top of the toilet and started to work the decomposing wire screen back and forth. I could hear the late-night crowd ordering their food and chattering noisily just on the other side of the storage room. I managed to push a hole in the screen large enough for me to climb through, and I carefully lowered myself into Joe's back storage room.

My plan was to make my way slowly from the storage room to the front where the clean dishes were piled in stacks next to the tip jar. With any luck, the dishwasher would be out collecting dirty dishes and Joe would be busy with the bustling crowd. It was dark in the back, and with all the people eating in front, the little restaurant was pretty noisy. I was going to reach around through the window and grab the large jar, slowly creep out through the storage room, pull myself up with my loot into the bathroom, and snap the padlock shut as I left. Unfortunately, things didn't exactly work out as I had planned.

Just as I was about to jump down into the storage room, I unintentionally made a loud noise. Joe started hollering, "Who's back there? Who's back there?"

I got scared and leaped back into the bathroom. As I was doing that, the money I held in my newspaper apron fell out and scattered on the floor. I stumbled and hit my head on the wall, cutting myself just above my eye.

I managed to hightail it out of the bathroom before Joe came running down the alley, but now I had less money than when I started! It was already 7:30 at night and I would have to go home empty-handed. I was tired, bleeding, and dispirited. Instead of walking directly home down First to Indiana, the way I always went, I turned left on Townsend Street toward Third. As soon as I made the turn on Townsend where it was dark, I started crying.

Just then I noticed an old lady walking toward me—well, at least I

thought she was old. She must have been about twenty years old, and she was actually very pretty. I wish now I had been about ten years older. In any case, she was walking along with her husband and stopped when she heard me crying.

"What's the matter kid? Is something wrong?"

I don't know why, but I said, "I got robbed. They robbed me right over there by the house on the corner with the hedges."

The lady knew me from sight and told her husband, "This is the kid that sells papers over by First and Rowan." She bent down to comfort me and told her husband over her shoulder, "Call the police."

The poor guy had to go house to house until he could find somebody who had a phone, a utility not so common in East LA back then. I think he went to about three houses before he found one with a phone. The whole time, the woman held on to me, hugging me, trying to console me.

Pretty soon a squad car came around with its spotlight shining on all the yards of the houses. They finally got to where we were standing, and two cops with uniforms and badges and flashlights got out of the squad car. I had never seen a policeman like that in my life. One came over and the woman started explaining that I was walking home from selling papers when some kids behind the hedges jumped me, hit me, and took my money. That explained the cut I had over my eye.

The cop said, "Sounds like they were waiting for him." Then he turned to me, "Do you come this way every day?"

"Well, not often. But I do come through here sometimes."

"Yeah, they were waiting for you," the cop said with finality. "Don't worry, we'll catch 'em!"

He offered to take me home, and the lady insisted that she accompany me. We got into the back seat of the patrol car and were driven to my house. My father answered the door with my mother standing behind him. The police explained how I was robbed and hit over the eye, how the thugs were waiting to ambush me, but not to worry, they would catch the guys. My poor mother started crying and hollering. "If he doesn't get beaten up here at home, he gets beaten up in the street. He can't win. My poor boy can't win! I don't want him selling any more papers!"

She was going on like that for some time when the next thing I knew the truck from the *Herald Express*, which was the paper I sold on the corner, pulled up to my house. These men with cameras and notepads came out and knocked on the door.

"Who's little Ernie? Ernie, I wanna see you. You little Ernie?"

I said yeah.

"Aw, they robbed you, huh, kid? C'mon over here, I wanna take your picture."

They took me to the front lawn and were taking pictures of me, asking me to put on the Herald Express apron, to hold a paper up like I was hustling it on the street, taking one shot after another. It came out in the paper the next day that the newspaper boy from First and Rowan got robbed the night before, and the story got picked up by *La Opinión* and other papers. My mother collected all the clippings and kept them for years.

I thought to myself, "Jesus, what did I get myself into?" I swore I would never tell anyone about what had happened. In fact I never did say one word about it until years later when I got to Alcatraz. I told the story to one of my best friends, who was celled next to me.

He laughed when I finished and said, "Ernie, you're just a born criminal."

When you're little, you think that the fact your father whips you and ties you up is a normal part of life. You don't know why he's doing it; in fact, you don't even wonder why he's doing it. To you, it's just the way things are. Only later, when you're older and start thinking about these things, do you start to question what was going on. All I knew was that I hated my father with a passion.

He was a well-educated man from Mexico and had been married there with many children, though I never knew any of them. He used to read all the time and was able to talk about almost any subject. I remember people would come over and talk to him about all sorts of topics.

He was especially interested in talking about religion, because he was strongly anticlerical. He had gone to Catholic school as a child, and one of the priests had molested him. This drove him to read all about religion. He learned about the Inquisition and the garrote and other tortures, and read about the popes and all the power they had. He knew the history of seemingly anything you wanted to talk about. That was his life, reading, and he would read everyday, all day long, up until midnight.

He fled the Mexican Revolution in the 1910s and seemed pretty bitter at the world after that. With me, I always thought that he just hated me, that maybe I shouldn't have been born. I was not allowed to have

friends over and was never permitted to play in the yard. Over time, he got it in his head to teach me Spanish. I think this was really just a pretext to figure out another reason to punish me. He didn't behave like a father who really wanted to teach something to his son. He had absolutely no patience, and everything had to be done his way. Whenever he was going to teach me a lesson, the first thing he did was to pick up a stick or his belt. Then he wrote down words in Spanish for things like "dog," "cat," "house," etc. I had no idea what the letters he scribbled on the paper meant.

He would point to a word and ask me, "What's this?"

When I got the answer wrong, he would hit me. My sister saw me going through this torment and she pulled me aside.

"Listen," she told me, "the next time he calls you for your lessons, look here. See this right here? This word means 'house.' I'm going to put a little roof over the word. Remember, that's 'house.'"

She would faintly trace a little roof over the word so I would remember what it meant.

"And see this right here?" She would point to another word. "That's 'cat.' See the little ears I'm putting here? That's 'cat.' And this over here is 'dog.' And this is 'mouse.'"

I must have been six years old at the time when he called me for these Spanish lessons. He would hold his belt in one hand and the piece of paper in the other. He'd stand over me and point to a word.

"¿Bueno, qué es esto?"

I would see the little roof my sister had traced and remember it was the word for "house." "Casa," I would say.

I think he was a little surprised I knew the word, but he grunted his approval and then pointed to the next one. On that one I could see the little cat ears, so I said, "Gato."

After a while he became suspicious and started to figure that there was something amiss. He looked carefully at the paper where the words were written.

So he said, "Okay, now we're going to do this without these little marks here." And he got an eraser and rubbed out the little signs my sister had lightly traced in.

Well, I couldn't read those words to save my life. First he whipped me for lying, and then he whipped me for not knowing the lesson. He called me all kinds of names: *sinvergüenza, baquetón*—shameless, rotten. All kinds of names.

When I was even younger he used to put me in the highchair and tie

me up tightly with a rope. Then he would get a small funnel and pour castor oil down my throat. I would sometimes vomit the awful oil out, which made him even madder. He would hit me, slap me on the face, call me all sorts of names. My mother caught him doing this one time, and she tried to put a stop to all that.

I wasn't the only one who suffered my father's abuse. He used to whip my two little sisters, Florence and Sophie, as if they were dogs. He couldn't control himself and didn't know when to stop. My sisters were not older than seven or eight at the time. My father would whip us if he caught us playing in the backyard, something he prohibited. He never worked, as far as I can remember; but he never took us out any place, not even around the block for an evening walk. Instead he spent his whole life, as I said, reading from morning to night. He wanted all of us to stay inside the house, as he did, which is something that is very hard to do for a small child full of energy.

Every once in a while my father would leave the house for the day, and while he was gone we would go out to the backyard and play baseball. We couldn't really play baseball because we didn't have a baseball bat or a real ball. Instead my sister Florence would make a ball out of old torn socks that she sewed together using needle and thread. For a bat we used a stick we'd find in the yard. We would place a rock on the ground for home plate, and another for first base. When we hit the ball, we had to hit it far enough so that we could run to first base and back to home plate. Otherwise we were out.

Up on a hill about half a block away was an apricot tree. From there, when he was on his way home, my father could spy down into the backyard and see if we were playing against his wishes. He was such a mean bastard that he would intentionally sneak around the apricot tree, keeping out of sight, to catch us playing in the yard. When he did catch us, he would come home, change his clothes, get out his strap, call us all together and whip the holy hell out of each one of us.

He would be shouting in Spanish that he saw us. "¡Los miré, los miré!" he would scream over and over.

I remember seeing the fear in my four-year-old sister's face while he whipped us. She would run behind an old heavy piano and hide, trembling and trying to escape punishment. When the whipping was over, I would go behind the piano and hug my little sister and put a cold towel on her little face because she was crying and trembling uncontrollably from fear. I would calm her as best as I could, but I was only a child myself, and I didn't really know what to do. The terror in our house

was so great that I hardly ever saw my three older brothers and older sister because they stayed away from home as much as they could. They were almost never there.

If my father was my torment in my young life, my mother was my salvation. She had been a teacher in Mexico, but she ended up owning a nursery in Los Angeles because she loved plants and knew a great deal about how best to take care of them. In fact, she started the nursery because she had seen an old man who owned one near our house. She had given him advice about when it was best to transplant some shrubs and how best to prune back some bushes. He was so impressed with her skills that he left the nursery to her when he died. She ran the nursery until she passed away in 1967. Then my oldest brother took it up. He still runs the nursery today.

After selling newspapers all week long, I would sometimes get ten cents from my mom on Sunday to go to the show. The money we earned, my brothers and I, on the paper route was for the household. But on Sunday I could try to get away to see the show at the Muni Theatre, which was my only recreation. Even then, many times my father said that I had not behaved properly during the week and took my ten cents away as punishment.

My mother was always kind and gentle with me. When she came home from work, I would go out into the backyard and work in the garden with her so that I could be near her. At night I would help her baking or cleaning up or helping in whatever way I could. I was small, but I used to pick up and help her with things around the house. My father didn't like that. He used to call me *pegajoso*, meaning I stuck around too much.

My mother would get mad at that. "Why do you call him like that? What are you bothering him for?"

She had many arguments with my father on account of me. She used to go out onto the porch to talk with him. I would sit right behind the bedroom window, listening to everything they said.

She would ask, "Why do you treat him that way? What has he done? Tell me! If he's done wrong, I'll punish him myself."

He would call her an *alcahueta*, meaning she pampered me. "He's spoiled on account of you!"

"But what does he do? Tell me!"

He could never explain to her.

The mistreatment went on. Sometimes he would lock me in the closet

and feed me boiled beans. If I didn't want to eat, again he would whip me. "You're not the boss around here!" he would yell. Sometimes I was left in that cramped, dark closet for hours. In fact, when I got to Alcatraz and was threatened with being put in the dark hole, the lightless isolation cell, I just laughed.

"This ain't nothing," I taunted the screws. "I've spent my whole life in the hole."

It seemed I was always out in the street doing something to supplement the family income. There were many times I was awakened at midnight to get dressed and go stand in line at the local bakery door to get the bread that hadn't been sold the day before. I had to get there in the early morning hours since the line would be long by 3 a.m. The bakery door never opened before seven, and I was often the first one in line. On those mornings, I would spread out a newspaper and lie down to sleep and wait. The bakery rarely had enough bread for everyone in line, and sometimes only a few people were lucky enough to get what was left over. My job was to be one of those lucky few.

When things seemed too unbearable for me, I would run away from home. I only ever stayed away for three or four days at a time. The first time I ran away, I was nine years old and I had no place to go, so I just wandered around town until dark. Later when I would run away, I would sleep at night in the restroom of a gas station or sneak into an all-night movie house. I couldn't stay away too long without money or food, and when I returned home my father couldn't wait to punish me for having made my poor mother worry so much. I guess the times I ran off just made things worse between my father and me, and he became more distant. I found that no matter what I did, I just couldn't please him.

In 1934, when I was twelve, I got arrested and booked into juvenile hall on a charge of burglary. A Buster Brown shoe store had been burglarized about 1:00 a.m., and a bunch of shoes had been stolen. I had known beforehand that the store was going to be burglarized, and I was actually supposed to be in on it. The store was only about a mile from my sales corner.

On the day of the robbery, I didn't wake up in time to join the others, and so I assumed that they would postpone the job until they could find out what had happened to me. By this time my paper job had changed hours from evening to early morning, so I got to my corner at about 5 a.m., after the heist, and had just begun unbundling my stack

in preparation for the day. I didn't know that the burglary had taken place, that the police had already picked up some neighborhood kids, and that one of them had implicated me in the burglary. He was also a paperboy, and he had known about the planned burglary but didn't want any part of it. He knew that I was supposed to be in on it, so he gave the cops my name when they picked him up. The cops were already waiting for me when I showed up at First and Rowan that morning.

The juvenile authorities didn't believe me or the other guys who said that I wasn't part of the burglary, and I was kept in juvenile hall for three months. That took away a lot of my passion for mischief for some time.

When I finally returned home, I attended school and worked at odd jobs to help make ends meet and make up for the trouble I had gotten into. Nevertheless, at thirteen I was again arrested, this time for auto theft and joyriding. What had started out as an afternoon of fun, just riding around in a stolen car, turned out to be damn near a life-and-death situation.

There were five of us who had managed to hotwire a car. I drove as we cruised around town for a few hours. A police car spotted us and made a U-turn to come in our direction. The only thought I had was to get away so I wouldn't have to go back to juvenile hall. I stepped on the gas and made a run for it. What I didn't anticipate was the police reaction to this move. As soon as I sped up, they turned on the siren and red lights, which had a very frightening effect on all of us.

When I didn't pull over, the cops pulled out their guns and started shooting. Later they said that they were only trying to disable the car, but from where we were sitting, those bullets were aimed at our heads. There was just no way I was going to stop now. I wasn't even going to slow down. After leading three squad cars on a high-speed chase all over Los Angeles, we finally managed to elude them.

That was enough excitement for one day. We ditched the car and ran home, trying to act as if nothing had happened to us that day. The cops scoured my neighborhood all evening and into the night and finally apprehended one of the boys. He told them where everyone else lived, and late that night I was arrested while at home in bed.

The cops were furious, and when I was taken down to the jail the arresting cops gave me a good working over. I was hit and pushed among them, one throwing a punch, one shoving me against the wall. Finally one of them threw a swift kick to the pit of my stomach. That wiped me out, and I wasn't even able to stand up on my own. I was eventually

taken to a hospital, where they discovered I had a ruptured appendix. They rushed me to the operating room for emergency surgery. I stayed in the hospital for a few days until I was able to walk, but my recovery only meant that I was brought before a juvenile court for disposition of the auto theft and joyriding charges.

Because I had been the driver, the authorities claimed I was the ringleader. At the age of thirteen I certainly wasn't any leader of that bunch, and in fact I wasn't as old as most of them, which is a big thing among kids at that age. But the judge had his mind made up and handed down the punishment the way he viewed the situation. Three of the boys were given probation, one was sent to Whittier School for Boys, and I was committed to the Preston School of Industry, a state reformatory at Ione, California, which was used to house hardcore juveniles.

My family was very upset by the judge's decision, especially my mother, and we were all stunned that I had received such a sentence. Even my probation officer was surprised. He had argued on my behalf that I was not a "hardcore" juvenile delinquent, showing the judge evidence that I helped support my family by working at odd jobs after school. He also brought some employers to court to testify to my character and that I was a hard worker. This was a lot more than the other boys had going for them, since none of them worked and they couldn't make a claim that they were any more disadvantaged than I was. Still, I got the severest sentence by far, which seemed to set a pattern that held up throughout my life whenever judgment was pronounced against me.

MY FORMAL EDUCATION

The year was 1935 and I was thirteen years old. Even at that young age, I had heard many bad things about Preston, and I dreaded the idea of having to go. Early in the morning on the scheduled day for the transfer, a police officer in civilian clothes came to my cell and waited for the officers to unlock the door. As he waited, I could see him looking me over, probably to determine if I was big enough to give him any trouble. At that time I stood about five feet two inches, if I stretched a bit, and weighed 120 pounds after a full meal.

After a moment he grinned at me and said, "Well, Ernie, are you ready?"

I just shrugged my shoulders, since I was very shy when it came to talking to people. My door was unlocked and, despite my small size, he put a pair of handcuffs on my wrists. He led me to his car and had me climb into the back seat. We headed out of LA to make the trip up north. Since he told me that it would be an eight-hour drive, I stretched out and got as comfortable as I could, considering my hands were still cuffed together.

After we had driven for a short while, he said to me, "Listen, Ernie, we're in Pasadena right now, and I'm going to make a short stop here and pick up a friend."

As we pulled up in front of a house, he turned to me and said, "Now look, if I take off your cuffs, can I trust you not to try and run off?"

I nodded my head up and down, and he seemed quite satisfied that I wouldn't try anything funny. He removed the cuffs and walked a few feet from the car where the steps led up to the front door. I really had

other thoughts, but the car was a two-door sedan, and I didn't think I could push the front seat down, open the passenger door, scramble through, and get very much of a running start before he could leap down the stairs and be on me. So I just sat and waited to see what else would develop.

He rang the doorbell and looked back in my direction just as the door opened. Inside stood a young, good-looking woman. She gave him a quick hug and a kiss, and he spoke to her for a few moments before picking up some luggage she had waiting by the door. As they walked toward the car, I saw him point at me, and I strained to hear what he was saying. He was telling her about transporting me to Preston. She listened intently, nodding her head. It was obvious to me he was romancing her. I believe he had taken off my cuffs to impress her how he had everything under control. Maybe he just didn't want to look like a guy who had to act tough around a thirteen-year-old.

He opened the passenger door for her, and when she saw me, a look of surprise came over her face. She almost squealed with delight when she spoke.

"Oh, he's just a little fellow, isn't he?"

Because Preston housed many young men in their early twenties, her image of a Preston internee was quite a bit different from whom she found looking at her from the back seat. I probably seemed no more than a child to her. As the officer introduced her to me, she gave me a wide smile like an adoring mother and said to him, "Gee, he's a cute little guy."

She was just about cooing by then.

We left Pasadena around 3:30 in the morning and the woman turned to the officer. "Why don't you stop and get some candy bars for the little boy?"

He didn't seem too thrilled with the idea, but he drove us to an all-night restaurant. Instead of getting out, he started blowing his horn until a waiter came out to the car. He asked the waiter if he could bring out about five assorted candy bars. The waiter brought them out to the car, and I munched on the candy as we made our way to Bakersfield. Pretty soon I fell asleep in the back seat.

I woke up as we were nearing Bakersfield, and I heard them discussing various restaurants they thought would be a good place to stop and have breakfast.

When the woman saw that I was awake, she said to me, "You've been a good boy. You slept all through the mountains."

It was still dark out, and she said, "We'll be in Bakersfield in about fifteen minutes, and we'll get breakfast because you've been a real good boy."

We pulled up in front of a downtown restaurant, but the officer wanted me to stay in the car, and said he was ordering the food to go. I watched him go to the door and open it. Meanwhile his girlfriend opened her door and got out so she could stand up and straighten out the wrinkles in her dress. As she was standing by the front of the car with the door wide open, I saw my chance to make a break. All I had to do was push the seat rest forward and run for it.

The officer had just barely entered the front door of the restaurant when I jumped out. His girl was still bent over, tugging on the hem of her dress, as I shot by her.

I was in full stride when she looked up and tried to shout to him, "Whoops, there he goes!" I had all the head start I needed, and in just seconds I was running along back alleys and climbing over fences.

That was my first escape, but it represented a basic urge to flee from fear and the unknown. I was driven by my overwhelming desire to be free.

That day I hid underneath a house until it got dark. I made my way to Route 99, the old main highway in the Central Valley, and waited at a four-way stop. When a truck hitching two trailers made a boulevard stop, I hopped aboard the second trailer. The first was filled with straw, the second with cows. I huddled between two cows for warmth, and the truck eventually took me back to LA. I stayed hidden at the homes of various friends for a little over a month. My luck ran out when the father of one of the boys decided to call the police and tell them where I was staying. The cops surrounded the house at 2 a.m. and once again were able to catch me asleep in bed.

I was taken to the main jail this time to await transportation to Preston, and I knew I wouldn't get another chance at escape. Three weeks went by before I was told early one morning to get ready; a police officer would be there shortly to transport me. Soon my cell door was unlocked, and there stood the same cop I had run away from almost two months before.

He wasn't grinning this time, and when I came out of my cell he grabbed my arms and pulled them around behind my back while he put the handcuffs tightly about my wrists. He was angry, but didn't do anything right then because there were other cops standing around. When we were outside by the car, before I had a chance to enter the back seat,

he stopped and placed a pair of leg shackles around my ankles. After I crawled in the back and settled in, he reached over the front seat and punched me full in the face—for good measure, I suppose.

"You made me look pretty bad, kid. If you try anything this time, I'll kill you!"

I couldn't do anything if I wanted to, given the way I was chained up. This time we drove directly to Ione, with no stop for romancing along the way.

When we arrived at Preston, my heart just sank at the sight of the place. It looked like a medieval castle standing alone in a remote mountainous area. It was too late for me to escape now, although I wanted to more than ever. He didn't waste any time before telling them the details about my escape, and I was immediately treated like a captured public enemy number one. They housed me in "G" Company, which was a section of the reformatory reserved for troublemakers.

Everyone at Preston was required to work eight hours a day, but when they came around to assign me a job, I refused because I was still in pain from the appendix operation. It didn't matter to them, and they placed me in isolation for refusing to work. While I was in isolation, I had tear gas shot in my face at point-blank range more than a few times. To say that we were mistreated at Preston would be an understatement. I was beaten too many times to try to count them. Not only did the guards mistreat us, but they also recruited inmates to serve as enforcers in return for favorable treatment. You never knew where the next attack against you was going to come from.

We were forced to march everywhere we went, from our cells to the shops, from our shops to our meals, from our meals to the showers. We had to be absolutely silent during these marches. Any slight infraction of the smallest rule would be met with a beating. At thirteen, I was one of the youngest inmates, who were mainly eighteen, nineteen, and twenty years old.

After a few months I felt my time there was a simple matter of survival. My fists and my speed helped me avoid any serious assault from the older inmates, and I was not kidding when I said that I would have killed anyone who tried to mess with me. My whole outlook on life changed. I began to see things as those around me did, older boys who were already bitter and criminally sophisticated way beyond their years. I spent fifteen months in Preston before I was released on parole, but I went out a hell of a lot different from the way I came in.

I had arrived frightened and heartbroken, but I left feeling that nothing could ever frighten me again. My youthful spirit was gutted, and my feelings and emotions had been pretty much torn out. My keepers had not shown me any kind of human compassion, and at that age those effects are lasting. The whole experience caused me to feel alienated from the rest of society, and I have to say society has done little to make me feel any different.

Within a year I was returned to Preston for a technical parole violation: associating with known delinquents. Those "delinquents" were about the only friends I had. Having met them in Preston, I felt we understood each other much better than we did other youths my same age. My parole officer felt that it was all right for me to associate with them while I was in Preston, but not out on the streets of the free world. So I was returned to Preston, where I associated with known delinquents for another eight months before being released on parole again.

All the time I was at Preston, my father never visited or even wrote me. We didn't have much communication during the best of times anyway. By now my family lived in a different house, and I was about fifteen when I moved back in with them.

The tension between my father and me continued until one day when everything came to a head. I wanted to throw a football around on the playground that was close to my house. I loved football and was one of the best players on the high school team. Football was about the only reason I went to school. I was fast and fairly strong for my size, and, more importantly, I could hit and take a hit pretty well.

As I was coming down the hallway with the ball, my father barked out, "Where are you going?"

I had just returned from my second stay at Preston, and I had changed a lot as a result. I hadn't taken any crap from the guards, and I sure wasn't going to take any from my father. I had no plans for letting anybody, not even my father, control me. That part of my life was all over.

He started to get aggressive, and I told him, "You know what? I'll kick your ass. I'm not that little boy you used to put in the closet. I'm not that little baby you used to tie in the highchair and feed castor oil. I'm not the little boy who used to be whipped and watch his sisters get whipped."

I told him, "No more! I'll beat you, and I'll beat you to death if you try any of that."

I had plans to kill him when I was small, and now I had the power

to do it if I wanted to. I told him that he didn't know how lucky he was that I didn't kill him when I had the chance.

He just looked at me. My mother was crying and moaning, "No, no, no . . ."

I never talked to him again after that. Even after I was married and had a little son of my own—a son my father doted on when he thought no one was looking—the only thing I wanted was to have him out of my life forever.

Eventually even football was not enough of a lure to stay in school, so I quit and went to work at my brother-in-law's tire shop. As things got better for me, I took on another responsibility, and in 1938 at the age of sixteen I married my high school sweetheart, Mary. We moved into a small apartment of our own, and within a year she gave birth to our only child, Ernie Jr. In the meantime, my parole officer was contemplating the idea of violating my parole and returning me to Preston for getting married without asking his permission. However, he changed his mind when he learned that my wife had just given birth to Ernie Jr. Shortly after, he mistakenly thought that I was to turn eighteen, and he told me that I would be discharged off parole. My true age was sixteen, and I would soon turn seventeen. I didn't correct him, because I wanted very badly to be discharged off parole, and a short time later I received my official discharge papers.

During that time, my little son and I were very close. I used to take him everywhere with me. I would take him to the bakery and kneel down next to him, asking him what bread he wanted to buy. I would work it so that he chose the bread that we needed, but it made him feel good to believe he had made the decision. I would let him proudly carry the bread home to his mama.

He would often wait for me to get home from work. It seemed that he could distinguish the sound of my car motor, and when I was due home, he would sit in the front room listening to the cars passing. He would hear one and perk up, before realizing it wasn't the sound of my motor. Then another car would pass, but that wouldn't be it either. Finally, he heard my motor, and he would jump up and run to the front door yelling, "Daddy! Daddy! Daddy!"

I never hit my boy. Never. The worst thing I could do to him when he did something wrong, the thing that would make him feel real bad, was for me to tell him, "I'm mad at you. I don't want to talk to you." Then I would turn my back to him and ignore him.

He would stand there with tears in his eyes. And I couldn't stand it, so I would turn around and hug him and kiss him. He was a good kid, and he never really bothered me or did anything really bad. Those were happy times.

About four months after being discharged from parole, I was arrested along with five associates and charged with a series of armed robberies. Since my juvenile records indicated I was eighteen, this time I was taken to the main jail and brought to court to be tried as an adult. My wife went to my ex-parole officer and told him that I was only seventeen, but he refused to intercede. My bail was set at $25,000, making it impossible for me to post bond, and I spent the next six months in jail fighting the charges.

The first trial resulted in a hung jury. Since the reputations and criminal records of most of my codefendants were hurting my case, I managed to get a separate trial the second time. Things were a lot different under that situation, and after a short trial the jury acquitted me of all charges. All the other five were found guilty at their second trial and sentenced to state prison.

I returned home to my wife and child and went to work at another tire shop, which was owned by a friend of the family. Being married young with a child to support is normally difficult for anybody, but the events that happened put an added strain on my wife and me. This inevitably led to marital spats and arguments.

One day after a rather heated argument, my wife took the baby while I was at work and went back to her parents' house. When I came home, I found the house empty and—assuming that she had gone to her folks' home—drove over to my in-laws to bring her back. Her father told me she wasn't there. I insisted, he kept denying, and soon her father and I were fighting in the front yard. I really didn't want to hit him, so I just grappled with him in an attempt to wear him out. Meanwhile, his neighbors came running to his rescue. Suddenly I was fighting not only him but four of his friends too. The police were called in, and I was arrested for disturbing the peace.

On court day I stood before the judge's bench to receive my sentence. Out of the corner of my eye I saw two men watching the proceedings with more than a casual interest. The judge sentenced me to fifteen days in jail. But before he had even finished pronouncing sentence, the two observers came over to my side and placed me under arrest for burglary.

It seems that, while I was in jail, the police had searched my car and found a spray gun for paint they claimed had been stolen from a hardware store during a burglary. I told them that I had bought it from an unknown person, which was the truth, but I had to go to court anyway. After a jury trial, I was acquitted. When I returned home, my wife said that she regretted she had run home to her folks after the argument, and she blamed herself for all the trouble that resulted from the fight and my subsequent arrests.

Time wore on, and World War II broke out. Because my record made me unsuitable for the draft, I found a job working in the shipyards and made the best of it to support us. Because the war was on, a sense of urgency seemed to fill everyone. For over a year after starting work at the yards, I had no trouble to speak of.

It was right about this time that I succumbed to what I thought was a once-in-a-lifetime opportunity to provide my family with enough money to live comfortably for the rest of our lives. The war had caused considerable limitations in various commodities, one of them being gasoline. The government had established an Office of Price Administration (the OPA) in an effort to enforce, among other things, gas rationing. If an individual worked and owned a car, he was entitled to a specified number of gas coupons, which were issued in the form of a small book of stamps. It was virtually impossible to obtain gas without these coupons. Offering to purchase gas with currency was useless because the stations were required to redeem the stamps in order to obtain gas from the oil companies.

An OPA office was located not too far from where I lived, and I struck upon the idea of investigating how to obtain some coupon books in order to sell them to certain interested parties with a lot of ready cash. After casing the building, I saw the opportunity to enter the OPA office. With the help of an acetylene torch, I cut through the thick-as-a-bank-vault safe where the coupons were kept. It was a considerable haul. I was able to gather a few boxes containing thousands of "B" and "C" coupon books.

Having these books was better than having cash money, because the average citizen could only get "A" coupons, which allowed for about eight gallons of gas a week. The "B" and "C" types were for people involved in working for defense, and allowed for much more gas. In short order, by virtue of the stamps, I found myself being introduced to many celebrities from all walks of life, including politicians, motion-picture

stars, professional football players, directors, and nightclub owners. Errol Flynn and his director, Raoul Walsh, would invite me to the Warner Bros. studio to watch their movies being made. I remember sitting on the set of Flynn's 1943 movie *Northern Pursuit* in which he plays a Canadian Mountie who poses as a traitor in an attempt to infiltrate a Nazi spy ring. In between takes, Flynn and Walsh would come over to chat with me behind the cameras.

Several years later I saw Flynn when he came for a VIP tour of Alcatraz prison. In the company of a number of officers, he looked startled when he turned the corner and saw me sitting in my cell. I could tell he recognized me, and I subtly lifted my chin. He gave me the slightest nod of acknowledgement before moving on. Needless to say, that was the last time I ever saw Errol Flynn.

I received all kinds of special treatment from a number of important people. They were all overjoyed to help share my treasure and didn't mind in the least throwing money my way in return for a few books. I made sure to buy plenty of life's necessities (including much-needed home repairs) for my mother and even my brother-in-law. I also bought a few luxuries, and my wife and child got plenty of new clothes and many nice gifts that we had previously been denied. I suppose I gave away and loaned too much money to friends as well, but at the time I was in the position to do so.

I bought two new automobiles as gifts for myself, and made a number of trips to Las Vegas to splurge. I spent a lot of time driving, since all my gas was free. Things couldn't have been happier at home during this time. Although my wife was curious about how I always had large sums of money and was able to buy so many nice things for us, I managed to convince her that I was gambling a lot and doing very well at it.

In fact I did attend the racetrack a number of times and always managed to come away with quite a bundle. Mary was not the inquisitive type anyway, and I discouraged her from probing into my affairs in order to protect her from the authorities in the event anything should ever happen to me. Soon enough, something did.

To begin with, the cops had arrested someone who had a large number of stamps in his possession. The police and Secret Service managed to get enough information out of him to launch an investigation against me as the main source of the stolen coupons. Without any knowledge that things had gone sour, I continued to do business as usual. One of

my regular stamp customers was a big-time local bookie by the name of John Tudisco. As I was to find out later, Tudisco was in considerable debt to members of the underworld and was reselling the stamps to the patrons of his bookie operation for a profit. He was apparently getting quite desperate for money. My first tip-off should have been when he tried to whittle down our established price for the coupons so that he could make a larger profit when he resold them.

When he suggested a new price to me, I refused, and made him stick to the agreed $25 a book. We finally made a deal for 1,200 books, which came to $30,000. As usual, I personally counted out the number of books and went along with a partner to meet Tudisco for the exchange. We drove over to the side street as arranged, and I watched as my partner approached Tudisco waiting in his car. I saw them both walk into a side entrance of a barbershop, and after about ten minutes my partner exited carrying a small shoebox. He walked hurriedly back to the car where I was waiting.

As soon as he reached me he said, "Tudisco only gave me $22,000. He says we're short the rest of the balance."

I had told my partner not to let the stamps out of his sight, but he had let Tudisco go into a back room by himself to count the stamps and get the money. I knew goddamn well how many stamps were in the bag he received, and I told my partner to go back and tell Tudisco that I wanted to talk to him.

While he was inside with Tudisco, I pulled the car around and parked directly across the street from the barbershop. Tudisco came out of the door first and was surprised that I had come along, since he was under the impression he would be dealing with only a runner. From across the street he told me in a deeply sincere voice that he hadn't burned me. I leaned out the window, told him that I had personally counted the stamps, and told him either to pay the full amount or return the bag of stamps. We got into a loud argument during which a couple of his friends came out of the shop to watch the scene.

Tudisco finally made a move as if to cross the street and come at me. When he did, I opened the door of the car and sprang out with an ice pick in my hand. He stopped dead in his tracks, and the rest of his friends started getting very agitated because they thought I was going to stick him. When he backed away, I told my partner to get back in the car so we could leave. But Tudisco was the type of guy who couldn't sleep nights if a person left angry at him after a beef, and he quickly changed his tone in an effort to plead his case before I drove off. The son

of a bitch had burned me, and I told him that I would get the money from him one way or another.

The following day, John Tudisco was found murdered. He had been strangled to death, his body stuffed into the trunk of his car. The police interrogated his associates — including those present during my argument with Tudisco — to try to find a motive. But none of them knew who I was, and their description of me didn't amount to much as far as the cops were concerned. However, the unknown person who had argued with Tudisco became a prime suspect.

Tudisco's brother Angelo went through John's house two days later to sort out his deceased brother's belongings. In the garage Angelo found the gas stamps I had sold John, stuffed in some empty two-gallon oil-cans. He turned them over to the police. Since the cops were already investigating me as the main supplier of stolen stamps, I was connected to the murder. After they showed Tudisco's friends my picture, they identified me as the person who had argued with Tudisco and threatened him. The police were positive I was the killer.

The heat was on, and unbeknownst to me, the police were gathering evidence and information implicating me in the Tudisco case. About five days after the murder, my wife happened to look out the front window.

Mary turned to me. "Ernie, I think there are police parked across the street."

I took a look. They were plainclothes cops, and I thought they were on my trail because of the stamps. I hadn't read about Tudisco in the papers, so I had no idea that they could have other motives. I decided to get out of the house by the back door, and I walked three miles to my brother-in-law's house. I had left my car parked in front of the house in plain view of the cops.

I asked Benny, my brother-in-law, if I could borrow his car and drive over to my partner's house. When I got to my partner's house, I explained that the cops were snooping around in front of my house, and I asked if he could go over and try to find out what they wanted. We drove close to my place and parked where I was able to watch the front door of my house. My partner went inside. After waiting about fifteen minutes, I decided to drive to a nearby restaurant and eat a fast breakfast. When I returned, I parked in the same spot and waited for a long time, but my partner did not come back out.

I drove back to Benny's place and told my brother-in-law that I was

concerned because the cops were at my house. Could he go over with me? I gave him the keys to my Buick and told him to get Mary and the baby and drive them to his tire shop, where I would meet them. I watched as Benny went in my house, then I drove away to give them time to get ready. On returning, I noticed that my car was gone, and I assumed that Benny had taken Mary and the baby out of the house and over to the shop.

I headed to the tire shop to meet them, but when I turned the corner where the shop was located, I saw police cars everywhere. I felt I had driven into a trap. There seemed to be some confusion as I slowed to a stop. Benny's brother Joe seemed very excited, hollering, "Here comes Benny! Here comes Benny!"

It seems that a slight emergency had developed at the shop. The steam boilers were overheated, and nobody knew how to turn them off before they blew. When Joe saw me driving up in Benny's car, he thought I was Benny arriving just in the knick of time to save the shop.

That threw the cops off a little. I knew the shop well because I had worked there about a year or so before, so I went to the rear of the shop and turned the steam boilers off. That seemed to assure the cops that I was Benny. But they had opened the trunk of the car anyway, and were giving it a thorough search when suddenly more police cars careened around the corner and skidded to a stop. One of the cops seemed to recognize me right away.

This cop would later turn out to be my most cowardly enemy, a true sadist hiding behind a badge. He took great pleasure in beating a man who was wounded or in handcuffs, and he never missed the opportunity to shoot a man if he could pass it off as being "in the line of duty." His name was Harry Freeman, and at that time he was assigned to the homicide detail of the LAPD.

Some years later he was busted in connection with a classic case of police brutality, the infamous event referred to in the papers as "Bloody Christmas." James Ellroy features these beatings in the opening scenes of his noir classic, *L.A. Confidential.* On Christmas Eve and into Christmas Day 1951, Los Angeles police took turns beating and torturing a number of Mexican American prisoners who were thought to have hit a cop while being arrested. A couple of the officers involved were eventually sent to state prison as a result. Freeman, originally indicted with the rest, managed to avoid prison time. He was, however, removed from the Homicide Division and demoted to radio dispatcher. All this took place eight years down the line.

For now it was Freeman who recognized me from my police mug shot, and he rushed over to where I was standing and started cussing and throwing punches at me. We were near Benny's car and I jumped into the back seat to keep him from being getting a good swing at me. He got a firm hold of the roof and jumped up swinging his feet through the window into the car, kicking me and kicking me until the other cops finally pulled him away. I was handcuffed and taken to jail where I was booked on suspicion of murder.

THE FEDERAL CASE

Immediately after being booked, I was taken into a room and interrogated about the Tudisco murder by Detective Harry Freeman and some of the other cops from Homicide. There were Secret Service agents present in the room as well, waiting their turn to ask me about the stolen stamps.

Freeman started off right away. He punched me in the left eye while I was still handcuffed, but I refused to make any statements until my attorney was called. I didn't know it at the time, but my attorney was on his way over to get me released on a writ of *habeas corpus*. When the cops got word he was coming, they removed me from the old Central Jail and took me to the Newton police station. Freeman kept up his rough stuff in an effort to force me to confess to Tudisco's murder, but after a while he gave way to the Secret Service agents who were patiently waiting to ask me questions. Again I refused to answer until my attorney could be present. I was finally taken to a cell, where I fell asleep, exhausted from the beating and the long interrogation.

The next day they started again. After about three hours, I heard one of the cops say in a loud voice, "Let's get this son of a bitch out of here quick. That goddamn shyster is here to spring him."

So they hustled me out a rear entrance and took me back to the old Central Jail on First and Hill in downtown LA. There they placed me in a cell that had been wired with microphones, although I didn't see them at first because it was too dark, and it took awhile for my eyes to adjust to the dimness.

I was surprised to find my partner in the adjacent cell, but later I

figured this was all intentionally arranged to get us to shout back and forth to each other and so have our conversations recorded. At any rate, they never obtained any incriminating statements. They did succeed in recording nine tapes of useless jailhouse banter before I spotted the wires hidden in the cracks of the cell wall and yanked them out.

They kept me hidden in the old Central Jail for a week before my attorney finally caught up with me and had me released on a writ. Although I was out of jail, my problems were only beginning. The Secret Service had arrested a man by the name of William Summers, also for possession of stolen stamps. Summers had been introduced to me by another man, to whom I had occasionally sold stamps, named Burt Oliver.

Oliver had been reselling his stamps to Summers and other friends. When Summers got a chance to talk to me, he asked me to sell him stamps directly because Oliver was asking for too much money. I denied that I was Oliver's supplier, but I did tell Summers I would pass the word on to the right person.

Now that Summers had been picked up by the Secret Service, he offered to help them set a trap that would catch me red-handed dropping off the stamps. A few days after I got out of jail, Summers approached me about buying fifty books of stamps. We arranged to meet in Boyle Heights on a poorly lit street. He would be waiting for me across the street from the telephone company.

Unknown to me, police officers and Secret Service agents had hidden themselves in the front porches of the houses across the way. We had agreed that I would meet him in front of the fifth house from the corner of Velasco and Fourth Street. The row of houses across from the phone company was very dark since there were no streetlights set up on that block. I was supposed to drive up to the fifth house, and Summers would walk over to the car and exchange the money for the stamp books. I would have driven into a trap had I made the drop as planned. However, by pure coincidence, another car pulled up to the fifth house and paused momentarily before driving away. The cops, thinking it was me, came out of their hiding places and gave pursuit until they stopped the car several blocks away.

Just as this was happening, I drove up with Mary—we were on our way to the show. I had to put the stamps in a paper bag to hide them from Mary, explaining that I had to drop something off for a friend before going to the movies. When I handed Summers the bag, I motioned for him not to hand me the money right then. Mary didn't know any-

thing about the stamps, and I had never said a word about them to her. I drove off thinking nothing unusual was afoot and planning to get the money later. All of a sudden two cars full of cops pointing revolvers, rifles, and shotguns pulled up along both sides of me.

When I looked over to my left, I was staring right into Freeman's face, twisted with anger. He was pointing a .38 almost through my car window and shouting for me to pull over. I slowed down and pulled up alongside the curb. The cop cars screeched to a halt all around, making any escape impossible. Out leaped Freeman and charged wildly at me like a maniac.

I got out of my car very calmly and very confidently because I knew that I had nothing in the car and that I was clean. This seemed to infuriate Freeman even more. When he reached me, he called me a son of a bitch and took a swing at me, but I managed to partially deflect the punch. Then my wife jumped out of the car and started raising holy hell because she didn't know what was going on or who these men were. Some of the other cops restrained her and finally placed her in one car and me in another. Both of us were taken to the East LA substation. I was detained, but Mary was released immediately.

I was taken into a room, and the Secret Service and the LAPD commenced to question me once again. They seemed pretty angry about the situation because they had fouled up the trap they had so carefully set by speeding off after the wrong car. Not a single law officer had witnessed the drop.

Freeman and his partner, a cop by the name of Gillian, were in the room, and they were *determined* to get me to confess to the Tudisco murder. They fashioned a rope into a noose and slipped it around my neck. They used it to drag me around the room while I was still handcuffed as several cops took turns beating and kicking me. Then Gillian pulled on the rope to force me to stand up. When I got to my feet, Freeman landed a solid kick to my groin. The force of the kick actually knocked me backward over a chair. Someone was still holding onto the rope when I was kicked, and as I flew over the chair the noose closed tightly around my neck. I started to strangle.

I fell to the floor in terrible pain and tried to act as if I had lost consciousness. Freeman got a bucket of water and doused me with it. When I began to move, he swung the heavy metal pail at me a number of times, landing blows all over the upper portion of my body. Again I was made to stand up. I saw Gillian give Freeman a type of handcuffs I had never seen before.

They looked more like pincers than handcuffs, and they were placed only part way around the upper portion of my hands instead of around my wrists in the normal manner. The opened ends were carefully positioned to dig into my hands just below my knuckles in the soft spot between my thumb and first finger and in the joint between my little finger and ring finger. A key was inserted into a ratchet-type lock, and the cuffs were tightened so that the pincers dug into the joints in the back of my hands.

The pain that shot through me was unreal, and I hollered at the top of my lungs in the hope that somebody would come into the room to see what was going on. I heard Freeman say, "Let's take the son of a bitch up in the hills and shoot him!"

He was joined by Gillian, who offered, "Yeah, we'll say he was trying to get away." There were at least ten cops and federal agents in that room at the time, and I thought for sure that one of them would say something. Not a single word of protest came from the bunch.

Pulled along by the handcuffs, I was led out to a car. As they were about to shove me in the back seat, I noticed some people walking on the sidewalk near the driveway entrance of the alley. I hollered as loud as I could to get their attention, "Help, help, they're going to kill me! They say I'm trying to escape!"

Freeman had been walking away toward his car, and when I shouted he spun around and made a flying tackle, knocking me off my feet. When we were on the ground, he muttered under his breath, "You dirty son of a bitch, I'm gonna blow your brains out first chance I get."

By then there was a large crowd of people standing on the sidewalk trying to see what the commotion was all about. That was exactly what I had hoped for, and to this day I am convinced that this was the only thing that saved my life.

So instead of being taken to the hills and shot, I was driven to the old Central Jail, where I was booked on federal charges: conspiracy to possess and possession of stolen government property. I was processed and taken to an isolated section of the jail, where they placed me next to one of the occupied cells. I was surprised again to see that the occupant was my partner. He told me that he had just been arrested that same day while down at the pool hall. He said the cops were on him about taking a lie detector test to determine if he had any knowledge of the Tudisco murder. I told him right away not to take the test. There had recently been a big scandal involving cops who had used a polygraph

examination to try to frame a guy; the suspect's attorney found out that the cops had given the man a rigged-up test.

At any rate, my partner succumbed to all the pressure and submitted to the test. When it was over, he came out positive — he was telling the truth. This still didn't satisfy Freeman. My partner later told me that after the test Freeman punched him in the stomach and told him, "You son of a bitch! The only reason you came out positive is because you have high blood pressure."

Next it was my turn to be dragged down to the polygraph room. It was a small room with some heavy curtains hanging from a doorway leading into another room. When I sat down in the chair, I told the operator, "Look here, don't waste your time hooking me up because I won't take the test under any conditions."

After it was clear that the test wasn't being conducted, Freeman and Gillian stepped out from behind the curtains where they had been hiding.

Freeman asked the operator, "What happened?"

The operator said, "He refuses to take it."

Freeman rushed at me and punched me in the jaw. He was obsessed with the idea that I had killed Tudisco and was determined to elicit a confession from me. After punching me a bit, he finally gave up, and I was taken from the old Central Jail to the LA County Jail.

At this point the investigation was turned over to the Secret Service, and things started getting really sticky for me. They took me from the jail to the Federal Building, where they interrogated me about the stolen coupons. I listened very carefully to every question asked of me and took a great deal of time before answering, wanting to make sure I didn't offer any more information than the absolute minimum. One question that really surprised me was when they asked if I knew a fellow by the name of Raul Cruz. I knew Raul very well. He was a hardworking and honest man, and I couldn't imagine why the authorities would be interested in him. I had never had any dealings that could possibly have implicated him in the possession of the coupons. However, I later learned of some of the details that caused the cops to suspect Raul.

During the time that I was conducting gas-stamp transactions with various individuals, a small-time hood from East LA by the name of Joe Loco was following me. He wanted to find out where I had stashed the haul of coupons so that he could break in and steal a few thousand books for himself. On one occasion he followed me over to Raul's house

when I dropped by for a social call. Raul was watering his front lawn when I pulled up, and Loco must have seen us talking and ratted to the authorities. This was how Raul become a suspect, though he was only an innocent victim of circumstance. Fortunately, he was soon dropped from the list of suspects.

Joe Loco had a few years earlier been involved in a stolen-car racket as a result of which a number of men were sent to San Quentin prison. Loco was never even brought to trial. The word spread around LA that Loco had ratted on the rest in return for a deal to drop the charges against him. I knew about Loco's reputation, so when he had approached me for stamps, I tried to make out as if I was only an intermediary in the operation. Apparently he wasn't convinced. When I was arrested the first time for the Tudisco murder, my wife went with our son to stay with her folks. Loco took the opportunity to break into my house. There weren't any stamps to take, but Loco did steal some furniture and other items in which he thought I might have hidden the stamps. His plan was to tear the things open to see if I had stuffed the stamps inside. In his rush, he overlooked about $5,000 that I had casually thrown on top of a chandelier hanging in the bedroom.

Evidently Loco had given the cops Raul's name as a possible contact of mine so that he could burglarize Raul's house too when the police took him down to the substation for questioning. But it didn't work out that way. The Secret Service took me over to Raul's place, and they conducted their interrogation at his home. He knew he had nothing to hide, so he permitted the federal agents to search his house without a warrant. Then a most unbelievable coincidence occurred.

In the basement at the rear of the house the agents discovered a suitcase containing 900 books of stolen coupons. I saw trouble for Raul. It was a good thing I was there because I started talking real fast. A few days before, an acquaintance of mine named Frank Rodella had asked me if he could leave a suitcase filled with clothes at my house because he and his wife had just had a marital spat. I told him that since my house had recently been burglarized, he might want to leave it in a safer place, so I referred him to Raul, whom he also knew. I had no idea that Rodella had any stamps in the suitcase, and to this day I don't know where or how he came across them, though they were definitely part of the stolen bunch that I had taken from the OPA office. Even stranger, I had seen Rodella get killed in an accident the day before my arrest while he was riding a motorcycle over to my house. It happened only a block away from my home, and my wife and I had witnessed the accident while we were walking toward the intersection.

An ambulance was hurrying to cross an intersection before the light turned red. Rodella had just turned into the intersection from a cross street and didn't notice the ambulance coming up behind him, because its siren wasn't on. Watching the accident, I didn't know it was Frank who had been hit. But I did recognize some of his friends who had been following behind on their own motorcycles, and I walked over to see if it might be someone I knew. When I came to where the body was lying, they told me it was Frank. Since he hadn't worn a crash helmet, there was no way I would have recognized him if they hadn't told me who he was.

When the agents opened the suitcase and I saw the stamps, I realized that Raul was going to be an automatic suspect. I knew he had no idea that Rodella had stashed the stamps in the suitcase, so I told the agents that Rodella had asked me for a place to leave his suitcase, and Raul verified the story. Although this got Raul off the hook, it served to incriminate me because the coupons still had the covers with the serial numbers on them, which allowed the agents to identify them as the stamps stolen from the OPA office.

The agents sent word to have Rodella picked up. I didn't say a word about Rodella's fate as they led me back to the car. I noticed that Freeman had been tagging along, and I watched him confer with the agents. After he was briefed on the developments, he took off to locate Rodella. I was taken back to jail, where I waited for the bomb to hit when Freeman discovered that Rodella had been killed the day before.

About two hours later an officer led me into the interrogation room. No sooner had the door shut than Freeman attacked me in another fit of rage. He was convinced that I knew about Rodella's death and so had made up the story about Rodella and the suitcase. I did my best to sound surprised that Rodella had been killed, and I asked Freeman how he had died.

Freeman was furious. He wouldn't tell me the cause of death, but yelled, "You know goddamn well how he died. That's why you made up all that bullshit!"

He was angry because Raul corroborated my story about the suitcase, which was really true anyway. With Rodella dead, the cops could not link me directly to the stamps, much less to the Tudisco murder. Freeman ordered the other cops in the room to take me away, and I was returned to my cell.

About three days later Freeman had me called to the attorney room. When I arrived, I was surprised to see him sitting by himself, waiting

for me. He looked at my left eye, where he had hit me earlier in the week; it was still black and swollen.

"How's your eye?"

I stared straight through him to the wall and didn't answer.

"Listen, Ernie, I was wrong about you, and that's why I want to talk to you." He then apologized for all the beatings and mistreatment he had given me, and went on about how he was wrong for doing such things.

Then he said, "I've been doing some investigating, and I found out a few things that will help you out of this mess. Now just listen to what I have to tell you, all right?"

I knew he had something up his sleeve, but I listened to him to get it over with.

"I found out that Tudisco was planning to kill you, Ernie, and I've got witnesses to prove it. The way I understand it, Tudisco was at the barbershop getting a shave when he got a telephone call. The people in the shop said he was arguing with somebody on the other end, and they heard Tudisco threaten to kill the other party. When he hung up he was pretty mad, and he said he was going to kill the son of a bitch. It was right after that that he went outside and threatened you. I see now you didn't have any choice but to defend yourself. When he came at you with a stiletto, the only thing you could do was kill him in self-defense. Isn't that about how it happened, Ernie?"

I looked at him a long time. Finally I spoke.

"I don't know what the hell you're talking about."

Freeman got real empathetic and said, "Ernie, I swear to you, and may God strike my son dead if I'm lying to you, if you'll just help me clean this mess up, I promise you that we'll get you off with self-defense, and I've got the evidence to prove it."

By then I thought Freeman had gone completely insane. Here he was trying to use psychology to get me to confess to a murder that I didn't commit and knew nothing about. But that was how obsessed he was with the idea that I had killed Tudisco. I think he could have easily won an Oscar for his performance.

Even while I was leaving the room, he continued pleading with me to think it over. Except for a few times during my trial, I did not see Freeman again until nearly a year later, when I found out how treacherous he really was.

At the trial, Oliver and Summers — the men who had helped the Secret Service set a trap to catch me — were the main prosecution witnesses

linking me with the drop of the fifty books. That charge amounted to only a misdemeanor because there were so few books and their covers had been torn off. This made it impossible to connect them with the thousands taken in the burglary of the OPA office. However, the books found at Raul's house still had the covers and serial numbers, which made them easy to trace to the burglary. Still, there was no way to legally connect me with the books left by Rodella at Raul's house. Evidently, Rodella had obtained the books from somebody whom I had sold them to, and he had probably been reselling them on his own. I know that many other people who had bought books from me were doing just this.

At any rate, the prosecuting attorney managed to work the jury up enough that they returned a verdict of guilty on the charges of conspiracy to possess and possession of stolen government property. I received a sentence totaling seven years, five years for possession and two years for conspiracy. The judge never considered probation, and in fact he stipulated that I be sent to a penitentiary to serve my sentence. My partner, who was indicted with me, had a different judge, who sentenced him to six months on the county road camp.

It so happened that at the same time I was on trial, the chairman of the local OPA Board, Winston Anderson, was also indicted for possession and sale of stolen government property. He had been caught stealing gasoline coupons from his own office and selling them to others. He was convicted one day after me, and he received a sentence of thirty days in the county jail.

The only difference that I could see between our two cases was that Judge Baldwin Campbell sentenced Anderson and Judge Leon R. Yankwich sentenced me. Looking back on the trial now, I can see plainly that my attorney was extremely incompetent — or else he was in cahoots with the prosecution. At the time I was not aware of the many legal defenses available to me, so I never made much of a protest. But after this conviction I made it a point to study the law, a practice that many years later saved my life.

After a wait of about two weeks, I was transported along with three other men to McNeil Island, a federal penitentiary that lies in Puget Sound near Tacoma. The island is surrounded by choppy, freezing water channeled into the sound from Alaska. We were bused to Seattle, then taken to the island by a boat that docked within walking distance from the front administration building. It was September 1944 and I was twenty-two years old. I would not turn twenty-three until April.

I was thoroughly disgusted with the whole situation, and I felt even worse when people told me that I had gotten a rotten deal from Yank-

wich. Even the court clerk had told me that he felt bad about the decision. "Everyone is trying to connive for stamps," he had told me. "Including me."

The two U.S. marshals who transported us to McNeil echoed the same sentiments. After I had been in prison a few weeks, nearly half the convict population personally offered their condolences to me. I was given a nickname right away. Since I had violated OPA laws, the men tagged me with the handle of O.P.Appo (as in Oh-pee Ah-poh).

It is only natural for most men to think about escape when they're first locked up in a place they don't want to be. The overwhelming desire to be free grows very strong when your freedom has been taken from you. I tried not to give it too much thought, but after I had been at McNeil a couple of months, a fellow by the name of George Dillon approached me with the idea of escape.

Dillon was about forty years old and had been around the joints most of his life. He had also successfully escaped from Walla Walla prison in eastern Washington and from a prison in Texas before that. Impressed with his resume, I put a lot of trust in him. My hopes for escape soared sky-high.

We set about making plans for the best method and route to get away. Since I didn't approve of many of his ideas for our escape, it wasn't long before I began to feel disappointed in his judgment. I let the idea cool down for a while until I could get more familiar with the prison and its daily routine. I knew that if I wanted to escape, I would have to rely on my own wits rather than Dillon's experience.

In the meantime, I made a friend of a prisoner who worked in the captain's office. He told me something that set me thinking very seriously about escape again. In the captain's office there was a board hanging on a wall with mug shot pictures of the men in McNeil who were thought to be a high security risk. There were about twenty-five pictures on the board, and one of them was mine. My friend decided to go through some of the office files to see why I was considered such a desperate character. He showed me a typed FBI report that identified me as a suspect in two murders and some other gangster-type activities, and I realized that the parole board would make me do time on the "silent beefs" even though I was innocent of the allegations.

I didn't like the idea of doing all seven years in prison on account of some false report, and I saw my chances of gaining an early parole fly out the window. I started making plans in earnest to break out. After

a few months I learned all I could about the surrounding islands and coastal territories from the books available in the library. When I figured I was ready, I met with Dillon and told him my plan. He approved of everything, and we set a date to leave when we figured there would be no moon out and the night would be dark.

On November 4, 1944, we were prepared and waiting for the sun to go down. After supper that night, Dillon and I sneaked from the dining room into the back of the main kitchen. There we had another friend help us hide in the elevator shaft, which led down to the basement under the kitchen and up to the bakery on the second floor. The rest of the men had filed out of the dining hall and returned to the cell house to wait for the evening movie. The movie scheduled for that night was *Escape from Devil's Island.*

We planned to wait in the elevator shaft until darkness fell and then to climb out of a bakery window on the second floor where I had had a friend of mine previously cut the bars and carefully fit them together with sooty soap. To the unwary eye, the bars appeared perfectly normal.

When we thought we had waited long enough, Dillon and I clambered up the shaft and over to the bakery shop. It was deathly quiet as we climbed up on top of a bank of large bread ovens directly in front of the window bars we had cut. Looking out, we saw that it was still too light, so we decided to wait about another half hour for darkness to fall. Just then we heard a noise, and since we knew that everyone was supposed to be at the movie, we figured it must be a guard snooping around.

Dillon and I hid under a heavy canvas tarpaulin atop the oven to hide from the guard. I heard him walking around the bakery and moving things about. Apparently he was searching for home brew, which prisoners occasionally made in the bakery. The bakery regularly used yeast — a necessary ingredient for fermenting the brew — and there were numerous places to hide the stuff among the pots and pans.

By now it had grown dark, and I heard the guard click on the light switch. We had to wait until he finished searching before we could climb out the window. Just then he got curious about the lumps under the canvas he saw on top of the ovens, so he grabbed hold of the window bars behind the ovens and climbed up. He came over to where we were hiding and picked up one corner of the canvas to take a look underneath. When he did, he saw my shoe. We had been found out, and we hadn't even set foot outside the cell house.

ESCAPE

I figured I had to do something now before the guard sounded an alarm, so I shot up quickly and told him not to move a muscle. It turned out to be a guard named John Harris. A terrified look came over his face, and he began hollering, so I knocked him off his feet with a flying tackle I had long practiced on the football field. I told Dillon to cover Harris's mouth while I found something to tie him up with. He tried to cover Harris's mouth with his hand, but Harris managed to bite down hard on his thumb. Now both Dillon *and* Harris were screaming.

The only thing I could think was somehow to force Harris to let go of Dillon's thumb. I hit him in the stomach with my fist, but he still wouldn't release his bite. Both men continued hollering. I spotted a long wooden paddle, resembling an oar for a rowboat, used to place the bread into the ovens. I grabbed the paddle by the handle and thrust it forward in the direction of Harris's jaw, hoping to jar his mouth open when it struck him. I missed his jaw, and the paddle glanced off his forehead. He let go of Dillon and fell over.

While all of this was going on, another guard patrolling outside the building heard the commotion and looked up to the second floor. With the lights on behind us, we were clearly visible through the bakery window, and he spotted us struggling with Harris.

He recognized me, and I heard him shout "Let him go, Ernie, leave him alone!"

"Fuck you!" I shouted down.

He tied the police dog he had with him to a steel handrail and ran as fast as he could to phone for help. He had no idea that we were trying

to escape; he just assumed that there was some kind of trouble in the bakery.

I felt I had no choice now but to get out. Meanwhile, Harris was pretending to have some kind of fit. I knew I hadn't hit him hard enough to knock him unconscious, but he shook his body and began flopping around like a fish out of water. Dillon bent over Harris and pulled a long sliver out of his forehead where the paddle had struck him. Harris must have wanted us to think he was nearly done for so that we wouldn't hit him again. At any rate, he didn't realize how close he was to the edge of the oven bank, and after flopping around some more, he fell off the edge and landed with a thud about eight feet below. He immediately picked himself up and ran out of the bakery, through the kitchen, and into the main dining hall, which by now was completely locked up.

We didn't bother to chase him, since we had to move quickly now that the other guard was already calling for help. I yanked out the bars we had had cut, climbed through the window, and dropped onto a small roof that sheltered the doorway on the first floor from rain. From there I jumped to the ground, and Dillon followed right behind. The guard dog tied to the rail cocked its head and, instead of barking, looked at us with curiosity.

We ran to the cyclone fence topped with barbed wire and clambered over it to get out of the prison grounds. Another guard, also with a dog, was patrolling the fence perimeter, but he couldn't get the dog to look in our direction, so we were able to run to the wooded area of the island without the dog chasing us.

It was very dark, and it had started to rain rather hard, which slowed our progress through the trees and heavy underbrush. We heard the bloodhounds off in the distance, and that prevented us from stopping to catch our breath. Finally we came to the edge of a cliff overlooking Puget Sound. The beach was about fifty feet directly below us.

I started climbing down the cliff ahead of Dillon, but the rain was causing me to slip, and I was afraid that I might fall. I climbed back up, angling toward another direction and hoping to find a part of the cliff that sloped down at a more gradual angle. Dillon was following me, and I could hear him wheezing and gasping for breath. The search party was getting closer by the minute, and I was beginning to feel desperate that we weren't going to make it to the water. Finally I thought I saw a trail that might lead to the bottom of the cliff, and I told Dillon to stay right behind me because we couldn't see more than two or three feet ahead in the pitch-black night.

As I started down the cliff, I suddenly slipped. The mud gave way, and I found myself tumbling head over heels down the side of the cliff. The underbrush was so thick that it served to cushion and slow my fall, and when I finally came to a stop, I was down on the beach lying on the sand. I was a little shaken up from the sudden fall but otherwise unhurt.

I couldn't see Dillon, but I knew he was still up near the top, and I tried not to holler loudly as I told him to just throw himself onto the brush and roll down. He didn't answer, but I could sense his reluctance to tumble headlong down the cliff—brush or no brush. The dogs were hot on our trail, and they were barking louder than ever.

Finally I heard Dillon come crashing down the side of the mountain, and the next thing I knew he was at my feet. I helped him up, and we ran as fast as we could along the beach to get away from the bloodhounds. We got about three hundred yards down the beach before I turned and looked back in the direction of the cliff. I could see flashlights, and I watched the search party make their way down the cliff where we had first attempted to climb down. They must have seen where our footprints led back up, because soon we saw the whole search party make their way back up the cliff and then disappear completely.

The dogs could not pick up our scent from the spot where we had fallen, and the guards must have assumed that we had changed our direction and climbed back up to the top again. They were obviously confused, and the dogs were leading them around in circles.

In the meantime, I found two large pieces of wood and tied them together so we could have something to hold onto during our long swim to Fox Island. I got in the water first and held the wood with my right arm circled around it. With my left arm I stroked the water to get us moving. Dillon grabbed the other end of the wood with both hands and used his feet to kick for more propulsion.

The water was frigid and very rough, and the going was torturously slow. After about a half hour the night sky lightened as the heavy, dark rain clouds moved away, and it was possible to see a considerable distance. It was still raining, but not as hard as before, and I could see Fox Island off in the distance ahead of us. It still looked to be about a mile away. Behind us I could see McNeil and, occasionally, a light flash here and there.

Dillon's kicking made a lot of noise, and I couldn't help but think that somebody on McNeil must be able to hear us. With the clouds gone and the night still, the noise could tip them off, and they might pos-

sibly see us. I expected a bullet to hit us at any second. About this time Dillon began complaining about how tired he was, and we were both near exhaustion. I prodded him to keep kicking while I stroked with my left arm, and I was sure we would soon hit the shore of Fox Island.

It seemed like forever before we got close enough to the island that the water was shallow enough for us to stand and walk. Dillon let go of the wood and swam toward the shore, leaving me adrift.

I let go of the wood and tried to swim ashore after I saw Dillon had made it to the beach, but I couldn't move my legs. I hadn't realized that the freezing water had paralyzed my legs to the point that they wouldn't respond to my efforts to move them; they were just dead weight. When I let go of the wood, I sank straight to the bottom like a rock. Fortunately the water wasn't too deep near the shore, and when I hit bottom I was able to spring with my feet back up to the surface, where I gasped for air. Immediately I sank again, even though I tried desperately to stay afloat by flailing away with my arms. My wet clothes and dead legs were like anchors pulling me down. In the end, it was the waves washing up against the shoreline that eventually saved my life. Every time I bobbed up for air, another wave thrust me forward a little bit closer to the shore. After continuously sinking and bobbing, I was finally swept up to the shore, where I crawled out of the water.

I was so exhausted that I just collapsed on the beach until Dillon came over to help me up. When I tried to stand, my legs would not hold me. Dillon didn't have any problem with his legs because he had been kicking the whole time, keeping his circulation going. My legs, dangling motionless in the frigid water, had frozen to the point that I couldn't move them or feel any sensation.

I kept struggling to get my legs moving, and slowly I began to perceive the slightest tingle, which then turned into a terrible pain as the sensation began to course back through my body. After a while I was able to stand up and walk on my own, but the pain increased to an indescribable agony. After I had walked along the shore for a considerable distance, the pain began to fade as life returned to my legs. Soon we saw a small cabin that looked deserted, and we went inside to get out of the rain and to rest. We were both shivering uncontrollably from the effects of the freezing water, but there was nothing we could do to start a fire because Dillon had lost the matches that we had wrapped in cellophane.

In the cabin we found a number of mattresses but no blankets, so after removing all our clothes, wringing them out, and hanging them

up to dry, we crawled between two mattresses to try to get warm. I found that I couldn't sleep because my legs were still aching too much, but after about an hour I dozed off from pure exhaustion.

When I awoke in the morning, I was very hungry and cold but anxious to get out in what little sunlight there was and start walking. I woke Dillon up, and we went over to where our clothes were hanging. We began dressing but found the clothes still wet. We had no choice but to put them on, and when I placed my leg into my pants, it felt as if I was sticking it into a sack of ice cubes. I had never felt anything so cold in all my life.

After dressing, we walked about the island looking for food. We had packed some Hershey bars for energy, but lost them along with the matches when we tumbled down the cliff. Luckily, the island had many types of berries, which we picked and ate until we lost our hunger pains. In the meantime we walked about the island to see if we could find some dry clothes. We traveled by night and slept during the day, and the rain continued to pour down the whole time.

On the third day we found a small rowboat, and late that night we left Fox Island. We rowed over to the mainland portion of Steilacoom. When we landed, we gave the boat a push, and the tide caught it and took it miles away from that spot. We hiked up into the hills, and when the sun came up the next morning we could look down into the peninsula and see the surrounding landscape.

Down below us was the boat dock for the service that ferried the residents of Steilacoom across Puget Sound to Tacoma, but we knew that they would be looking for us if we crossed over that way. We decided to head up into the hills in a northerly direction because the law would least expect that of us. We roamed around the hills for two weeks, and during this time all we ate were apples and carrots from the several farming areas we stumbled across. Finally we made our way down to the two-lane highway that ran along the coast of the peninsula, and we walked along the road during the night.

The next day we approached a house that had been partially remodeled into a roadside restaurant, and Dillon asked me to go in and buy some hamburgers with the money we had, which came to twenty dollars. I didn't want to go inside a restaurant that was this close to McNeil, but Dillon insisted that everything would be all right. I was young, so I would look less suspicious walking in and ordering food. Rather than argue with him, I walked in while Dillon waited in a nearby orchard.

Stepping through the front door, I spotted four men sitting at a booth. Each wore a red jacket and cap and had either a rifle or a shotgun on his lap. When I walked up to the counter, I saw them look at me.

I heard one of them say in a low voice to the others, "Hey, look at that guy. He might be one of the guys that escaped."

Then another one said, "Yeah, look at his shoes. They're all muddy."

I wanted to get out of there, but I also didn't want to look suspicious. Slowly, and in a voice loud enough for them to hear, I ordered some hamburgers, but the woman behind the counter told me she served only cold sandwiches.

"All right," I said. "Change my order to ham sandwiches. And could I have four, please?"

I sat down to wait for the sandwiches and continued making small talk with her.

"I'm having trouble with my car. I left it down the road a ways with my wife and two kids still inside. If I can push the thing this far, do you mind if I use your driveway to try to work on it?"

She said I was welcome to use the driveway if I needed to. I quickly paid her for the sandwiches and walked out. As I closed the door, I noticed that the hunters were again paying attention to their food and not looking at me anymore.

When I got back to where Dillon was waiting, I told him, "As long as we're in this area, never ask me to go inside one of those places again."

I told him about the hunters and what they had said.

Dillon didn't believe me. "Aw, you're being paranoid. It's all in your head."

I let the matter die.

We made a wide circle around the restaurant and continued along the highway in the same direction. As we left the area, I noticed a sign with the name of the nearest town, Gig Harbor. We walked on for another day until we came upon a small farmhouse. In the driveway was a car that looked to be in running condition. I got inside and pressed the starter, and the car started right up. Since there didn't seem to be anyone around, Dillon jumped in, and we drove off in the direction of Port Orchard.

We drove for about an hour. It grew dark, and as the highway turned and entered Port Orchard, we saw a large barge full of sailors crossing the bay. It was a town only four or five blocks long, and we drove just past the main section, which was brightly lit, and turned off the road into a vacant lot between a block filled with saloons and one filled with old rundown apartments overlooking the bay. Dillon again talked me

into going into one of the cafeterias to buy food. I really didn't want to take any more chances, but we were hungry. I decided to try one more time; it was quite late, and most lawmen wouldn't be on the lookout this time of night.

As I walked around the corner of the lot and onto the main sidewalk, I noticed a car parked at the curb just in front of one of the saloons. When I looked over at the driver's side, I noticed a man duck down so low behind the steering wheel that I could barely see his head. That had to be a cop, but I didn't want to run and make myself conspicuous. It was possible that he was just checking me out and didn't know for sure who I was.

I stopped at the doorway of one of the saloons and pushed open the door as if I were looking for somebody in particular. I could see from the corner of my eye that the guy in the car was watching me like a hawk, so I walked toward his car very casually and crossed the street as if I hadn't seen him. I walked to the front door of a cafeteria and did the same thing I had done at the saloon, very casually looking about as if I just couldn't find whom I was looking for. Then I started walking toward where I had parked the car, only I was across the street.

I noticed there was a gas station on the corner, and I tried to act very nonchalant as I neared it. Approaching as leisurely as possible, I saw that the station was right on the corner, allowing me to cut across while out of view of the guy watching. As I turned into the darkened station, I broke into a run and ran up the road for a short distance. The road climbed a steep hill, and I jumped off a high bank on the other side and found myself in the back lot of a row of stores.

Just as I landed, I heard the sound of a car racing its motor, and I saw the headlights turn onto the steep road and disappear up the hill very quickly. I ran a ways behind the storefronts, went through an opening between stores, and came out onto the main road, which was rather dark at this end of town. I ran across the road where the shabby apartments stood and headed back to the car by walking under the pier. Finally I got to the car and Dillon without being seen.

I told Dillon what had happened, but again he told me it was only my imagination. By now I was getting burned at Dillon. I saw some more cars drive up the steep road and park, and I told Dillon to see for himself. Men got out of the cars with flashlights and began looking around the bushes and under a few houses.

We stayed put for about a half hour until the men gave up. Once they were gone, I drove the car off in the same direction we had come from

because I was afraid the guy in the car had seen us drive into the town. He would know what direction we were headed in. We laid low for a day, then resumed driving north, again hoping to throw the cops off our trail, since they probably figured we would be heading down south toward LA. Dillon and I made plans instead to go to Vancouver.

After a few more days of driving, we arrived at Vancouver, where we abandoned the car in the back of an apartment complex. The car was undiscovered for a month. We walked to the bus station and bought tickets for the first available bus to Portland.

When we got to Portland, we decided to split up and try to get some more clothes and money. We agreed to meet at the city library at eight that evening. I walked around town looking for a place that wouldn't be too difficult to burgle after the sun set. Finally I spotted a beauty salon that had the type of spring lock on the front door that I could easily undo.

When it got dark, I slipped a thin piece of celluloid between the doorjamb and the lock. I pushed, and the door flew open. I found about seventy-five dollars in the cash register. Then I opened the barbershop next door and found another twenty-five dollars. It was now about 6:30. Since I had some more time to kill, I headed for a dry cleaners I had seen earlier. I noticed that it had a spring lock also. I made short work of the door, and quickly ducked in before anyone could see me.

Inside there were many racks of clean clothes, and I spent quite awhile looking for a suit that fit. I eventually found three suits, about five shirts, plus ties, socks, and even a pair of shoes that fit me perfectly. Before I left, I shaved with a razor I found in the bathroom. Then I changed into a snappy suit and tie, put on a nice overcoat, and walked out the back way, leaving the door unlocked so I could bring Dillon in the back entrance.

Arriving at the library, I saw Dillon reading a newspaper at one of the tables. He was pretty easy to spot since he was the only bald man in the room. He was very absorbed in what he was reading, and didn't pay any attention when I sat across from him. I opened a book I had taken off one of the shelves. In a low voice I called his name. He lifted his head, but he looked right past me, instead looking around with a puzzled expression for the person calling him.

I had the book in front of my face so he couldn't see me, and the clothes I had on fooled him completely. Finally I lowered the book, and his face lit up in surprise.

"Ernie! Where'd you get all that?"

I motioned for him to lower his voice and then told him about the dry cleaners.

I asked him, "How did you make out?"

He looked down at the table and told me sadly that he hadn't found anything.

We left the library and returned to the cleaners. Inside Dillon went wild, and soon he had a bundle of clothes that he had selected from the racks. He shaved and changed into a nice suit, and we wrapped the extra clothes in some paper and departed. We decided we needed another car, so we walked around town until we came to an auto service center. After casing the area, I scaled a wall and climbed through an unlocked window into the building. Dillon waited outside to warn me if anyone approached.

Inside I found three new autos. I settled on a Buick, which looked like it had been serviced and was ready for pick up. The keys were in the ignition, so I unhooked the garage door and started the car. More luck! I noticed that it had a full tank of gas. After I drove out, Dillon closed the garage door behind me and jumped in the car with the packages.

We headed out of town and toward the California state line. After driving for some time, we spotted a roadblock just ahead of us. It was too late to turn the car around without looking suspicious, so we decided to tough it out and take our chances.

We drove up, dressed to kill and in a brand-new Buick, and did our best to act like two wealthy and upright citizens just passing through. Dillon rolled down his window as one of the cops came over to his door, and I did the same when another cop came over to my side. Before we could even think of something to say, they both stuck their heads in the car as if looking for something in the back seat.

Dillon asked if they were looking for hitchhikers, and the cop on his side replied, "Yeah, possibly. We're looking for a couple of escapees." My heart stopped. Then he quickly added, "Okay, you can go." It seems that just the day before two men had escaped from the Salem State Penitentiary, and the roadblock had been set up as part of the search for them.

I drove off as calmly as I could, but it felt like my heart was pounding nearly through my rib cage. I was not happy that Dillon had spoken to the cop, and I told him not to say a word unless they asked him a question. He just couldn't keep his mouth shut. I guess my nerves had worn a little thin during the three weeks since the escape, and increasingly I

didn't have much faith in Dillon. With each passing day I viewed him as a growing liability.

The car broke down just after we crossed the border from Oregon into California, so we took a bus the rest of the way to LA. Once in town, I bid Dillon farewell and we went our separate ways. He was caught about two weeks later in some small town in the Southwest. Later I found out that the cops had had no trouble getting Dillon to tell them where he had last seen me. Again the heat was on me in LA, although I didn't know it at the time.

FREEMAN'S REVENGE

Newly arrived in town, I found a small apartment that I liked and rented it for a month, until I could get myself situated. Not long after Dillon was caught, I was walking down a sidewalk with a couple of friends when I spotted a cop car slowly cruising down a sloping street in our direction. My instinct told me that I had been spotted, and I told the others to keep walking while I lagged behind. I stepped over to the curb and tried to hide behind a telephone pole.

The squad car came to a stop about a hundred feet from where I stood, and a cop with a pistol drawn jumped out of the car and ran in my direction. I turned and started running, heading for a vacant lot that led to a construction site where large drainage ditches had been recently dug. Before I could turn into the lot from the sidewalk, the cop fired a couple of rounds at me. The bullets missed me and hit the corner of a house that sat at the entrance of the vacant lot.

I stopped and pulled out a gun of my own. I whirled around and returned two shots in his direction. He looked surprised that I had a gun, and I watched him dive under a parked car for cover. Later I found out he had hurt himself rather badly in the dive and had to be taken to a hospital. I managed to run ahead and jump into a large drainage ditch. I ran, hidden from view, for quite a distance.

Fortunately I wasn't living in that neighborhood, so it was easy enough to avoid the area all together. Not long afterward I saw my picture on wanted fliers at the post office and various other places around town. I left LA and went to Juárez, Mexico, to let things cool down for a while. After about three months I went back to Southern Cali-

fornia and rented an apartment in Wilmington near San Pedro, south of LA.

At this time I was introduced to a guy named Sandy Serna, who people said was a good burglar. Serna said he used to work at a place where the owner ran an operation repairing jukeboxes. He knew that the owner kept a lot of money locked up in a safe inside the office. A few nights later I met Serna at his girlfriend's house, and we drove over to the shop in a stolen car that I had just hot-wired.

The shop was a low building on a corner near a residential area. We climbed a wooden fence and dropped into the alley next to the shop. Sticking a crow bar into the doorjamb, I broke the lock open. As we went inside, I happened to look through the front windows. On the street I spotted a police car turning toward where our car was parked. I warned Serna, and we left by the alley. I noticed a ladder leading to the roof of the building, and I told Serna to follow me.

He had been running toward the fence, and wanted to go back to the car, but the police had stopped across the street. Serna came to a sudden stop and turned back toward the ladder. As I was climbing onto the roof, I thought Serna would be right behind me. After I leaped onto the roof of the neighboring building, I turned to look for him, but he wasn't in sight.

I continued to run across the rooftops of the other store buildings until I came to the end of the block. I climbed down and walked around the block until I came near where our car was parked. I was hidden between two houses, and could see everything the cops were doing. They had Serna in the back seat of the police car and were searching the stolen car for any merchandise from the shop.

I remained hidden until they left, taking Serna with them. The next day I found out they had taken him to Huntington Park jail, which I got to know very well. I cased the jail and found that it had an alley running alongside the section where the prisoners were housed.

Late the next night I went to the window where the cells were located and whispered Serna's name.

I heard him ask in a hushed voice, "Ernie, is that you?"

I told him that I would be back to get him out, but first I needed to get some tools. He was very happy to see me, and I had to reassure him a number of times that I would be back to get him out.

There were a few other prisoners in the cells next to him, though there were only three cells in this substation. I'm sure the other pris-

oners didn't believe for a second that anyone would really try to break a guy out of jail. I left to look for the necessary tools, and I ended up burglarizing an auto mechanic. I went back to the jail with a hacksaw and a set of wire cutters. Making four separate cuts, I was able to remove the bars on the window. The screen was easy to cut through with the wire cutters, since only the top and bottom were welded to the window frame; the sides were not secured. That took care of the window, but Serna was still locked up in his cell, which was across the hallway that led out to the front booking desk. I asked him if he wanted the hacksaw, to cut his way out of his cell, but he said he would wait until morning when the cops opened the cell doors for the exercise period. We agreed that eight the next morning would be the best time to break out, and I told him I would return then.

I had stolen another car, and didn't want to drive all the way back to my apartment. Instead, I stayed at a friend's house. I told him about the plan, and he said he wanted to help. I agreed to take him along in the morning, and we got up about seven, had breakfast, and headed for the jail. I was in one car, and he followed behind in another. We parked about a block away from the substation. I walked over to the alley while my friend stayed in his car, waiting for the signal to drive down the street and pick us up.

I walked down the alley to make sure everything was all clear. Just then I noticed some people in a nearby parking lot watching me as I neared the window. I tried to act as nonchalant as possible, and when I was directly below the window I called out for Serna. I didn't get an answer. I turned around, walked under the window again, and took a quick peek into the jail, but I saw that everybody was gone.

I took off immediately. I jumped in my friend's car and told him to drive me to my apartment in Wilmington. On the way I told him what had happened, and that I had a hunch that something had gone wrong. I made up my mind to get my belongings out of my apartment and find another place, since Serna knew where I lived. If he had been snagged trying to escape, they would make things hard on him unless he told them who had cut the bars.

When we pulled up to my place, I took my gun out of my coat and put it in the glove compartment. I got out of the car and, instead of going directly inside and down the hall to the door of my apartment, walked around the back to my bedroom window. I tried to look through the curtains to see if anything was amiss, but I couldn't see much through

the glare against the window. I started to walk toward the hall entrance. Just as I took a step, I thought I heard a noise from within my apartment, so I stopped and placed my ear next to the window to hear better.

The next moment a loud crack from a gun sounded, and I ducked below the window at almost the same instant that a gunshot blew through it, showering glass and leaving a terrific ringing in my ear. Two more shots followed, but they hit the pavement just beyond me. I ran in the opposite direction from the car in the hopes of shaking off whoever might be on my trail.

As I got to the far end of the apartment complex, a short fat man came barging out of the hallway, hollering my name: "Ernie, stop or I'll kill you!"

I ran even faster and turned into a plowed-up oil field. When I turned, I saw the fat man stumble and fall in the plowed dirt. He was completely out of control, and he churned up a lot of dust. Right behind him were hordes of policemen, and they were running after me like a posse in hot pursuit.

Later I found out that there had been seventeen cops assigned to stake out my apartment complex. They were still quite a distance from me, and I was sure that I would be able to get away if I could make it to the end of the open field and into the surrounding neighborhood. Just then I heard what seemed like hundreds of shots being fired, and I saw dirt flying up all around me. Most of the shots seemed to be coming from rifles, so I knew I would have to dive for cover.

I ran to some houses I saw at the end of the field. I ducked underneath a house through an open cellar, catching a glimpse of an old woman with a dish towel in her hands who was coming out onto the rear porch of her house to see what all the shooting was about. I knew she saw me run under the house, so I quickly took out all my fake ID cards, tore them into little pieces, and stuffed them into a small hole in the ground.

All this happened a minute or two after the first shot rang out from my bedroom. I was trying to catch my breath before I made another run for it. As I breathed in, I heard a gurgling sound deep in my throat, but I didn't know what was causing the noise. I looked down at my chest and noticed a lot of blood soaking my shirt and the inside of my coat. When I reached with my right hand to open my coat, I noticed blood coming from underneath my coat sleeve and running down my hand.

When I pulled up my sleeve, I saw a hole on the top of my wrist where the blood was pouring out. On closer inspection I saw that a bullet had

passed completely through my wrist. When I opened up my coat, I saw a bullet hole over where I thought my heart would be. I tried to see if I had been hit anywhere else, and then felt a pain under my right armpit. When I felt it, I found another bullet hole.

Even though I had been hit, I still felt like I had enough strength to run. I crawled out from beneath the house and got up to run again. As I looked to my left, I saw the police running across the field about fifty yards away. On my right was a residential street, and as I began to run I saw my friend pull up some distance away. He was motioning to me with his arm to run over to the car. I started in his direction, but just as I took a few strides, I collapsed to the ground and found it difficult to breathe. I lay there gasping for air while a few more shots kicked up the dirt around me. As the cops ran up to where I was lying, I started to lose consciousness.

I saw them pointing their guns and rifles at me, and I heard the old woman holler, "Stop shooting at him! Can't you see he's wounded!"

I felt somebody kick me, and then I heard lots of voices shouting in anger.

I had run into a Mexican neighborhood, and the shots and noise had attracted the neighbors, who wanted to see what all the commotion was about. They saw that I was down and bleeding, and I heard them cussing the cops and shouting at them to leave me alone.

The old woman shouted a second time, "Don't kick him! You're supposed to be policemen, not animals!"

The other bystanders joined in, "Yeah, don't kick him! Call an ambulance!"

Mostly they were just shouting obscenities at the cops.

Then one of the cops bent down and spoke to me, "Just hang on, Ernie. We'll have you out of here in no time." It didn't seem to take the ambulance very long to get there, and we were headed toward the hospital in a matter of minutes.

On the way I kept drifting in and out of consciousness, and the next thing I knew we were pulling into the emergency entrance of a small hospital. A doctor came running out of the front doorway and placed a stethoscope on my chest just as the gurney hit the sidewalk. They had pushed me only a few feet when the doctor ordered them to put me back in the ambulance and take me to Seaside Hospital in Long Beach.

I passed out again, and when I regained consciousness I was being wheeled inside the Seaside Hospital corridor and into a room. A nurse put some ice to my lips. Later she told me that I had been asking for ice and complaining that it felt like I was burning up inside.

Everyone was scurrying around, getting me ready for the treatment room. I passed out again, but regained consciousness when I heard someone running down the hall in the direction of my room. Even through my heavy eyelids I could still see the doorway.

Suddenly I saw a man in a suit run in the room. Nearly out of breath, he asked, "Is the son of a bitch dead yet?" My eyes focused on his face, and I saw that it was Harry Freeman.

What in the hell was Freeman doing in the hospital room only fifteen or twenty minutes after I had been shot? Was it possible, I wondered, that he had got himself involved with the stakeout squad? It had been nearly a year since I had last seen him at the county jail, and now here he was, all excited, asking questions of the hospital staff. I heard one of the attendants tell him that it was unlikely that I would make it, and Freeman left the room.

It was becoming very difficult to remain conscious, although I struggled to stay awake. I passed out again, and when I came to I saw my wife near my bedside, standing next to a priest. I felt some water being sprinkled on me, and I muttered an objection so that someone would stop the water. I don't know how long I had been there, but it must have been a couple of hours because the police had notified my wife. Since nobody thought I was going to make it, she had gotten hold of a priest to have me baptized. I'm not religious in any way, but my wife was, and she had often tried to talk me into getting baptized. I had always refused, but now she was finally getting her way.

Then the pain in my chest became excruciating, and I hollered out for a doctor. My wife ran out into the hall and did the same. He came running into the room to see what was wrong, and my wife told him that I was in terrible pain.

The doctor tried to reassure her. "I don't want to give him any more shots because it might weaken him."

Then he bent down to examine my chest. I saw him frowning as he looked at the bandages wrapped around my chest.

"Who put this on?" he asked in an angry voice.

He grabbed hold of one end of the tape firmly and yanked the bandages off my chest with a quick pull. As he pulled the bandages off, I saw a thick stream of blood squirt up in his face and another squirt hit his shirt collar and tie. At the same time I felt a tremendous relief from the pain in my chest and a very cool sensation run down through my body, starting from my forehead and moving into my lower stomach.

Whoever had taped me up after cleaning the bullet holes had applied the bandages so tightly that the pressure built up in my chest cavity and

prevented me from breathing. It seemed now that a cool, gentle breeze was blowing across my body. The doctor walked out of the room, and I could hear him raising hell with a couple of nurses or interns down the hall.

The priest spoke to me. "Ernie, you're not going to make it. You better confess now and tell us why you killed Tudisco. I think God will understand."

As he spoke, I noticed three cops stand up from where they had been sitting just out of my view and come over to my bedside with notepads and pens. They were waiting for me to make a statement, and had obviously primed the priest to ask me that question. I don't remember exactly what I said to him, but I do know that I cussed him out and spat at his face. I was too weak to reach him with force, and most of the spit fell to the floor.

My wife hollered at him, "You're no priest—you're a policeman! Get out of here and leave us alone!"

They all left the room without another word.

Soon I was placed in another ambulance and taken to the old LA County Hospital. I was put in Ward 110, the high-security section of the hospital where prisoners are kept while they recover from their wounds or injuries. My wife rode with me in the ambulance, and I remember that she slept in the ward in a bed next to me the first night, when they didn't think I would live. After the second day, I started showing signs of recovery, so my wife wasn't allowed to stay over anymore.

After about five days I decided to get out of bed to see if I could walk, since my strength seemed to be returning quickly, and I already had ideas of escaping. County Hospital is located on Morango and Mission Road, which was in my neighborhood, and the familiarity only heightened my desire to be free. Ward 110 was separated from the rest of the hospital by a barred door that closed off the main hallway from the high-security section. A deputy sheriff was assigned to unlock the door for hospital staff who needed to enter. Otherwise, he guarded the patients in the jail section.

I figured if I could get through that door, there was nothing to prevent me from running down the hallway, to the courtyard, and through the gate of the iron fence surrounding the hospital. That gate, the emergency entrance for the ambulances, was always left open. I saw a young kid exercising in the hallway and asked him to get me a pair of pajamas, which he did. I put them on in place of my hospital gown.

When I tried to get out of bed, I found I couldn't swing my legs around, so I rolled over the side of the bed and placed my feet on the floor. I kind of slipped off the bed like a snake. I didn't realize how weak I was until I tried to stand and was unable to straighten up. I had to shuffle my feet in an effort to walk. I was stooped over like a feeble old man, and I asked the kid to help me walk to the bathroom. After I used the toilet, he helped me walk back to my bed.

Just then the doctor happened to come into the room, and he gave the kid hell for being in my room and helping me walk around. He ordered the boy out and threatened to lock him up if he caught him in my room again.

The doctor said to me, "Ernie, do you know that you've had one hemorrhage already? If you get another one, you might not survive." I told him that I didn't like to use the bedpan. He assured me that he would let me start walking in a couple of days if I would agree to stay in bed until then.

We talked about my condition, and finally I asked him about my bullet wounds. He explained how I had been shot and the angle the bullets had traveled through my body. When I had placed my ear up to the window, I had raised my arm up and away from my body so that I could cup my hand around my ear to hear better. The first bullet had entered my right armpit, which my raised arm had exposed, and angled toward the front of my chest, exiting just above my heart and puncturing my lung in the process.

The second shot had hit my wrist after I had ducked down below the window and grabbed the windowsill for balance. I had been shot twice in rapid succession at nearly point-blank range. Because of the closeness of the weapon, the bullets had passed through my body very cleanly, which is why I did not know that I had been shot until some minutes later.

In a couple of days I was permitted to walk, so I left my room and walked up and down the hallway. I used this time to case a possible escape route and get familiar with the guard's routine.

I had been at the hospital about a week, and was getting anxious to put together an escape plan. I now knew that I could be transferred from the hospital to the main jail at any moment. About this time another patient was brought into the high-security ward, and I watched the attendants carry him on a stretcher into the room directly across the hallway from mine.

His door was locked after he was put inside. Later I talked to him

through a small screened opening in the door. I learned that his name was Angel and that he was on parole from Folsom prison. As I talked to him, I saw that his face was bruised and pretty badly cut. He told me that he had got caught pulling an armed robbery and that the cops had beaten him up during the struggle. I figured he might be a good candidate to help me break out, and I told him about my intentions. He seemed very willing, and agreed to team up with me since he would be returning to Folsom if he didn't think of some way to get out of the ward.

A few days later they permitted Angel to exercise in the hallway. When he was up, I went down the hall where the shower room was located. While Angel acted as a lookout, I grabbed hold of the showerhead and began pulling it off the wall. The exposed shower pipe was attached to the wall with two small brackets, and my plan was to break the pipe just at the elbow joint. That would leave a two-foot length of pipe. I would then be able to work on the connecting joint nut and separate the showerhead portion. However, it broke off beyond the elbow joint and past the regulating valves, and water began spurting out all over the floor. Fortunately, the young kid in the room across the hall was watching every move I made, and he told me that I could shut off the water in a closet right next to the shower room.

After I turned off the water, I went back in and started twisting the connecting nut just below the showerhead. It was too tight to move, so I stuck the other end of the broken pipe into the floor drain and used the hole for leverage. Soon the rust loosened up, and I was able to disconnect the showerhead portion. This left me with a curved piece of pipe about seven inches long. When I held the nozzle end in my hand, anyone looking quickly at the pipe might mistake it for a handgun.

It was early evening, and our plan was to leave that night. I connected the showerhead back to the other pipe where it had broken off beyond the valves. I replaced the metal brackets around the pipe and attached them to the shower wall, just as they had been before I tore the pipe down. When I finished, it was impossible to tell that the shower pipe had been tampered with, unless someone pulled on the pipe or turned on the water.

Before I left, I placed a small piece of a match in the break of the pipe: if anyone touched the pipe and moved it even slightly, the match would fall inside the shower wall, alerting me that the guards had discovered my actions. I went back to my room because it was close to 9:30, lockup time.

There was only one patient to a room, so everybody got locked in separately. Once the guard locked your door, he would hook a padlock that hung on a short chain into the hasp attached to the door. Since there were no sinks or toilets in the rooms, you had to summon the guard if you wanted to use the bathroom after lockup time. By pushing a button near your bed, a red light would go on outside your door, and the guard would come and talk to you through a small screen window before unhooking the padlock. In my case, they had orders not to unhook my lock or let me out of my room after I was locked in for the night, so they provided me with a bedpan. But Angel and I had made a plan that would get me out of my room during the night.

At midnight, the guards changed shifts. There was only one guard on duty after midnight, and he had a habit of taking his coffeepot down to the other end of the hall to a small kitchen so that he could make his coffee and bring it back to his office next to the hospital entrance. The entrance was blocked by two doors, one a heavily barred door and the other a wooden one that they usually kept closed with only a latch.

My room was two doors down from the guard's office, close to the hospital entrance. From my room I could observe the guards' daily and nightly routines and habits. From my observation, I knew that the guard on the midnight watch carried the key to the front entrance in his back pocket. I knew that there was an extra key hidden in the office as well.

I found this out because one day the midnight-watch guard came to visit the day guard. I heard the two in the office talking. Before long the day guard walked to the small kitchen at the other end of the hall to make them both some coffee. Just then a matron who worked upstairs with the women prisoners came to the hospital entrance door and rang to be let in.

The night guard obviously knew her well because he talked to her at the door for quite a long time. The day guard stayed in the kitchen all this time, and the matron seemed impatient to be let in. The night guard went back into the office, and I could hear the sliding sound of a filing cabinet drawer being pulled open. He reappeared with an extra key and waved it in front of the matron.

"Don't let anybody know I let you in with this key." He opened the door and let her in. After he went back to the office, I heard him slam the filing cabinet shut. So I knew there was an extra key if I ever needed it.

I planned with Angel that as soon as the midnight guard started down the hall toward the kitchen with his coffeepot, Angel would push

the button to light the red light outside his door. We knew that the guard would unlock Angel's room and then prepare his coffee while Angel went to the bathroom. As he was making his way to the bathroom, Angel would come over to my room and unhook the lock on my door. When we were both out, we would go to the shower room and remove the showerhead and nozzle. We could then catch the guard in the kitchen by surprise, whip out the small pipe from under my bathrobe, spin him around, jam the barrel of the pipe against his back, and take the key from his back pocket. We would next simply unlock the front entrance and disappear into the night. The guard was an older man, so we figured he wouldn't put up much of a fight.

I realized there was a chance it wouldn't work, but I figured that with Angel helping me we could overpower the guard, take his keys, lock him in my room, and flee the hospital. After that it would be a simple matter of running out of the courtyard and across the street to the brickyard, which would take us to a nearby friend's house.

I waited for midnight. Soon the guard arrived for his watch. After a short time he came out of his office with the coffeepot in his hands as usual. He passed my room on his way down the hallway, and I saw the red light outside Angel's room go on. I saw the guard talk to Angel and then unhook the lock on his door. He continued toward the kitchen as Angel stepped out of his room. I saw him come over to my door, and I waited for him to unhook the lock. But he didn't. Instead he whispered to me through the screened hole that the guards knew about the escape. He said a nurse had told him earlier in the evening that they knew about the pipe in the shower and were expecting something. We called off the plan and decided to try to think of another way out.

I wasn't especially worried that they had found out, but I felt terrible that my chance to gain freedom had gone up in smoke after all the planning I had put into it. Nobody came to my door all night, and after a while I began to wonder if Angel was telling me the truth or if he had just gotten cold feet and lied to me.

I couldn't get to sleep all night, and in the morning when the guard unhooked my door, I headed straight for the shower room to confirm my suspicions about Angel. I took a careful look, and everything was just as I had left it. The match was still sandwiched between the broken pipe where I had joined them together. It was obvious that Angel had lied to me, so I knew that I would have to try the escape on my own. I was very disappointed because I had counted on him to help me.

As I walked out of the shower room, a guard called to me and told

me to get back into my room. I went in and sat on the bed, wondering why he had ordered me back inside. He stood at my doorway as if he were there to prevent me from trying to leave. Then I heard the sound of rattling chains.

Soon the other guard came into my room carrying a pair of handcuffs and a long steel chain. I knew for sure that the jig was up and that Angel had tipped them off about the escape plan. They handcuffed my hands behind my back, looped the long chain around each of my ankles one time, then secured the loops with a padlock for each ankle, thereby creating a makeshift set of leg shackles.

They were about to leave the room when the doctor came in and asked what they were doing. He insisted that they remove the chains because he wanted me to exercise, but one of the guards motioned for him to step out in the hallway, where the guard whispered something to him. Finally the doctor compromised with them, and they removed the handcuffs but left the chains padlocked around each ankle.

That day I exercised out in the hall by myself, and Angel did not come out of his room. There wasn't any question in my mind that he had ratted on me. During my exercise period, I managed to get a paper clip, and I also found a safety pin. I took them to my room when I finished walking up and down the hallway. A nurse told me that the next day I would be taken to the X-ray lab to have some X-rays taken of my chest. The lab was located just across the courtyard, and I knew that I would be walking outside practically free except for the chains around my ankles.

I started working on that problem right away by unfolding the paper clip. I inserted it just a fraction of an inch into a small hole in the cement wall and bent the end of the clip at a ninety-degree angle. It would become my lock pick. That evening, right after the change of the guard, I set about picking the large Yale padlocks by using the paperclip and safety pin as my lock picks, but I had to sit up in bed in a very uncomfortable position in order to reach the padlocks on my ankles. It took me over four hours to finally unlock one of them, and by then my back hurt so much from bending forward that I didn't even try to unlock the other one. I tore a small piece of adhesive tape from my bandages and stuck it in the hole of the lock so that I could close the lock without it snapping shut.

I finally dozed off at about midnight. I was awakened in the morning by a man knocking on my door and calling out my name. It was

an orderly from the lab, telling me to be ready in fifteen minutes because we would be going over right after I ate breakfast. He turned and walked away. After I had finished eating, he returned and unhooked the padlock and opened the door. He was a tall black man who worked in the lab building across the courtyard. I slowly lowered myself off the bed and walked out into the hallway.

We were walking through the barred doorway when a guard told me to stop. He took out a set of handcuffs and placed them on my wrists, and I saw him give the key to the orderly. Now I wasn't sure what to do, because I hadn't planned on being handcuffed just to walk across the courtyard. The orderly looked too strong for me, in my weakened condition, to try to jump, so I began to feel miserable that my efforts at working on the padlock had been wasted.

As we walked across the courtyard, my eyes scanned the surroundings. I saw that the gate for the ambulance entry was wide open, as I had expected. We entered the building, walked a short distance down the hall, and turned into the X-ray room, where I was told to get on the examination table. A doctor stood by the table. A last-ditch idea came into my mind about how to get the handcuffs removed.

I edged up to the table and made it look as though it was impossible for me to climb on top with the handcuffs still on my wrists. After I tried a few times to climb on, the doctor asked me if I was having trouble, and I told him that I couldn't balance myself with the cuffs on.

The orderly said, "Oh yeah, I forgot." He unlocked the cuffs and took them off.

I slowly raised myself onto the table in a sitting position with my legs hanging over the edge, and the doctor left the room to do something. Meanwhile the orderly helped me swing my legs onto the table. When I saw that we were alone, I drew my legs up to my chest and kicked the orderly full force in the chest. He went flying across the room, landed hard against a wall, and crashed to the floor.

I quickly removed the padlock on my right ankle and was wrapping the loose end of the chain around my left leg when I saw him start to recover. I put my middle finger through the padlock, balled my fist around the heavy lock portion, and jumped off the table.

He was just getting to his feet when I swung my chain-wrapped fist, hitting him on the right side of his head next to his ear. He let out a scream and went down. I finished wrapping the loose chain around my left leg and ran down the hall, out into the courtyard, and toward the open gate. As I ran through, I heard the orderly shouting to the guards that I was getting away.

I ran out into the street and tried to stop a car so I could make a fast getaway, but when the drivers saw me outside the front of the hospital in pajamas and a bathrobe, they weren't about to stop. One guy swerved so far away from me that he almost hit the opposite curb. I ran across the street to a brickyard on Morango.

I had been able to see the large lot from the hospital window, and I figured that if I kept running in the direction I was heading, I would have a good chance to get away because the surrounding streets did not have access to the brickyard. The street on the left was an alley that became a dead end, and Mission Boulevard on the right ran at an angle away from the brickyard. So I had to make it past the dead-end section, then I would have a head start on anybody who chased me on foot.

As I ran across the brickyard, the chain came unraveled and started whipping at my legs, making it difficult to run. Suddenly I felt exhausted, and I realized that I was too weak to run anymore. I began to feel an anguishing sense of defeat. I fell in a heap on the ground next to a stockpile of old bricks. As I lay there, I saw a guard jump out of his car at the dead-end section of the alley and come running toward me. There was nothing I could do to get away, but I felt so desperate that I picked up a brick and threw it at him as he came upon me. The brick bounced harmlessly off his chest.

I pulled myself to my feet and tried to run one more time. As I tried to sprint away, I noticed a car parked in the yard facing the entrance road. I ran to it, opened the door, and jumped in. The keys were in the ignition, but I couldn't find the starter. The car was an unusual foreign make, and the starter was not where I expected it to be. I ran out of time looking for it.

Trapped in the car, I saw the guard running at me and two cop cars come to a screeching halt at the entrance road in front of me. I was surrounded. The next thing I knew, the guard opened the door and yanked me out.

He threw me to the ground, and all I could feel was the thud of fists pounding down on me and the sharp pain of a few hard kicks. I thought there were about fifty people stampeding over me. When they finally hauled me to my feet, I saw about eight policemen and the guard. One of them handcuffed my hands behind my back, and I was put in the backseat of a small coupe.

Just then I heard a man shouting as he came running up to us, "I'll kill you, you son of a bitch, I'll kill you!"

It was the superintendent of the hospital, upset because I had hurt

his orderly. The guard, who was sitting in the front seat, turned around and hit me in the head with the butt of his pistol. Guards were not permitted to have guns in the hospital, so he must have had it locked in his car. He was cussing at me as he hit me, and I could do nothing to protect myself.

He shouted at me, "Goddamn it. I got the best locks money can buy, and you went and picked them!" He punctuated about every other word by pounding my head with the butt of his pistol.

Finally he ended up hitting me very close to my left eye, making me suddenly jerk back as blood poured out of a deep gash. That seemed to affect him, because he stopped hitting me and looked rather concerned as he turned around.

He drove me back into the hospital courtyard through the ambulance entrance, followed closely by two other police cars that pulled up to a stop behind us. I was taken out of the car, and a number of policemen crowded around to escort me back into the hospital. We had started climbing the steps of the rear exit when all of a sudden I heard someone swear at me. When I turned my head to look around, I saw the superintendent of the hospital again. He grabbed the chains on my ankle and yanked me back so that I tumbled to the bottom of the steps.

The police lifted me to my feet, and we started to climb the steps again, but the superintendent grabbed the chain and yanked me off my feet so that I fell back down to the bottom once more.

He shouted at me, "Get up, you bastard! Get up, get up!"

He gave me a couple of swift kicks in my ribs while I lay on the ground. I couldn't ward off the blows, because my hands were cuffed behind me.

I hollered at him in response, "You fuck yourself! I'm not getting up! You'll have to carry me!"

Finally the cops told him, "All right, that's enough." They moved him away before he could kick me again, then picked me up and carried me back into the ward. I was placed back in the same room.

The hospital guard was searching the room for the key or lock pick I had used to open the padlock. After a few minutes he found the paper clip and safety pin at the foot of the bed where I had tied a knot in the sheet and tucked it under a corner of the mattress. I was chained spread-eagle to the bed frame for about five hours until some sheriff's deputies came to transport me to the old Central Jail later that afternoon.

They had three squad cars and put me in the middle one. We drove away in a small procession. Later I learned that they had had the notion

that a group was going to try to liberate me. I was still in my pajamas because the clothes I had been wearing when I was shot were so bloody they had to be thrown away. On the way to the jail they made a rather theatrical display of pulling over to a curb and stopping whenever a "suspicious" car drove by in either direction. On each occasion either the lead car or the car in the rear would radio the driver of our car to pull over. This happened about four times before we got to the jail.

I was taken inside and down some stairs to the portion of the old jail where the dungeon was located. The dungeon section had not been used in many years, and most people didn't even know that it existed. They removed the handcuffs and chains while we waited for a deputy to return with a key to one of the cells. When he returned, he selected a cell in the middle of the section. When he opened the cell door, I could see dust on the floor about an inch thick and cobwebs in every corner.

The floor was made of steel, and so were all the walls. The officers took away my shoes before locking me inside. After they left, I was the only soul down there, and it was very dark in the cell after they closed the main door. The only source of light was a small, dim bulb located some distance away.

The steel floor was ice-cold on my bare feet, and when I lay down I found it was impossible to get warm, no matter how long I stayed in one spot. They had not given me any blankets, and there wasn't a mattress to sleep on. So I spread out my hospital bathrobe and snuggled my head into the crook of my arm to sleep.

I remained there for nearly four days. I was never fed, and no one came back down until the afternoon of the fourth day, when two deputy U.S. marshals were escorted down to the dungeon by a couple of jail deputies. I was starving, and I felt extremely weak. Worst of all, the damp cold had caused my bones to ache something fierce. The marshals seemed a little annoyed that I was down there, and they could see for themselves that I was in pretty bad shape. The gash near my left eye was still covered with dried blood, and the hospital bandages on my wrist and chest needed changing because they were dirty from my sleeping on the floor thick with dust.

One of the marshals asked me how I felt, and I told him that I could use some food because I hadn't eaten anything since I had been there. He seemed very concerned. I didn't need to say much about my sleeping conditions, because it was obvious that I had no blankets or mattress and that the cell was filthy with dirt and dust. He told me that he

was going to see that I got fed right away and that he would be right back. He walked up the stairs and out of the dungeon. The other marshal gave me some khaki pants to put on and asked one of the jail deputies to get my shoes.

They didn't have a shirt for me, so I wore the pajama top when we walked out of the dungeon and into the main jail section. In a few minutes the other marshal joined us, and he told me that we were going across the street to a restaurant to eat before we did anything else. I was not handcuffed, and we walked across the street, entered the restaurant, and sat down at a table to order our meals. I ordered a plate of ham and eggs.

While we were in the restaurant, the marshal who had left the dungeon for a short while told me that he had gone to have a talk with the jail commander to find out why I had been placed in the dungeon without food or medical attention. Both marshals had picked up many prisoners from the jail over the years for transfer to federal prisons, but they had never seen anyone placed in the dungeon before. As he explained the details to his partner, he also revealed to me what had happened.

After my brief escape from the hospital, the superintendent immediately signed the papers authorizing my release from the hospital. He then called the sheriff's office to make arrangements for my transfer to the old Central Jail. Apparently the superintendent was anything but calm, and he told the sheriff that he wanted me taken to jail right away and that he didn't want to be responsible for me another minute.

He related the story of my escape to the sheriff, though his version was greatly exaggerated. He told the sheriff that I had been handcuffed and shackled around the ankles when I was taken to the X-ray lab, and that I had picked both the handcuffs and the padlock on the leg chains with a paperclip and safety pin prior to being escorted to the lab by the orderly.

He said that I suddenly removed the cuffs and kicked the orderly across the room while I was on top of the X-ray table. I then removed the padlock from my ankle and attacked the orderly with the handcuffs, hitting him with one end until he was nearly unconscious. I knocked the doctor down and ran out of the hospital compound and into the street, where I caused a motorist to have a wreck as he swerved to avoid hitting me.

He said I ran into the brickyard, and when the hospital guard caught up with me, I threw some bricks at him, hitting him so hard on the chest

and jaw that he was knocked to the ground. I then ran to the parked car and jumped inside. The superintendent said that I had just started the engine of the car when the police arrived and surrounded me with drawn pistols and shotguns. He said that I would have no doubt run over the police had not the brave hospital guard opened the door and pulled me out. He finally added that I was subdued with the help of eight other policemen.

The sheriff had called the jail commander, telling him that I would shortly be transferred to his jail. Then the sheriff related his second-hand information about me to the commander. By the time the story was told to the jail commander, it had been twisted all out of proportion. He was informed that I was a convicted felon who had been sent to prison for stealing government property and for murder, that I had escaped from McNeil Island, and that I had nearly killed a guard in the process. After returning to LA, I had shot at a policeman who had spotted me. The bullets had narrowly missed his head, but I had caused him to almost kill himself as he dove for cover under a parked car. Finally the story about the escape and the picking of the handcuffs and locks caused the jail commander to think that I was some kind of Dillinger and Houdini rolled into one.

Since I was to be his responsibility, it was no surprise that, after hearing all the distorted facts, he decided to house me in the old, isolated basement cellblock. It seems that he also issued strict orders that nobody, including the jail deputies, was to go down there for any reason without his approval. He reasoned that these tight security precautions would eliminate the possibility of an unscrupulous guard slipping me a paperclip or some other type of lock pick. Even my wife was not permitted to visit me during those four days. However, in his zeal for security, he failed to make arrangements to have me fed. In fact, very few people on duty at the jail were aware I was in the dungeon. And so I languished there for four days, filthy, thirsty, and starving.

RETURNED AND RESENTENCED

We went back across the street after breakfast and walked over to municipal court, where we took seats in the spectator section. The district attorney's office had filed charges against me for numerous burglaries and robberies. I was also accused of hijacking a truck containing $250,000 worth of cigarettes. I had supposedly committed all these crimes since my escape from McNeil. That was the reason the U.S. marshals hadn't come to pick me up right after my release from the hospital, because they were waiting for the disposition of state charges.

I had not been informed that those charges had been filed against me until that very moment when the marshal explained all the events. At any rate, the county seemed to be anxious to get rid of me, and had made arrangements that morning with the federal authorities to have me turned over to the marshals' custody. One of the marshals told me that as soon as the state charges were formally dismissed and the paperwork processed, I would be transferred back to McNeil. He walked over to the district attorney, had a brief conversation with him, and returned to where I was seated.

A case was already in progress when we entered, but as the marshal seated himself, the district attorney approached the judge's bench and interrupted the proceedings for a short conference.

The judge said, "We will continue the present case after a short recess. At this time the court will pass on to another matter. Is Ernest López present in the courtroom?"

The marshal asked me to stand up. The judge read the charges to me and asked the district attorney to enter any further motions.

The DA said, "Your honor, in view of the fact that the federal gov-

ernment has an indictment pending against Mr. López in the state of Washington, the people move to dismiss the charges in the interest of justice." The judge granted the motion, and the whole thing took less than two minutes.

We left the courthouse. The marshals placed me in their car and took me to LA County jail, where I was to wait for the completion of the paperwork and my pending transfer back to McNeil. I was now under federal jurisdiction, and the marshals assured me that I would receive much better treatment while being held in the county jail. They would also see to it that I was given medical attention. I was booked, allowed to shower, given some clean clothes, and taken to the medical clinic, where my bandages were removed and my wound cleaned up.

The hole in my chest was infected and draining, but they said there was little they could do about it. So a fresh bandage was placed over the area in the hopes that it would heal by itself. I was taken to the high-power section of the jail and placed by myself in cell 1. In a few minutes a jail deputy came back to my cell, wrapped a length of chain around the bars of the door, and put a padlock through the chain. The other prisoners in the adjacent cells got a big kick out of that, and I heard them talking back and forth, making comments about the chain on my door.

I laughed along with them as they offered such comments as "Hey, that guy must be a bad son of a bitch—the deputy just chained his cell door shut!" and "Hey, man, who are you, John Dillinger?"

Everybody was laughing because it was really a ridiculous thing to do. The section was designated "high power" because of its maximum-security design and location. Padlocking the cell was really just for show. I was there for two days, and during that time my wife visited twice. After the second visit, the marshals came to my cell to pick me up for transfer.

They got a big kick out of the chain on the door. By now they were beginning to like me, and one of them said in mock amusement, "Ernie, don't these people know by now that padlocking your door shut isn't going to stop you from breaking out if you want to?"

We laughed along with some of the other nearby prisoners, then left the jail and headed toward their car. As we were walking, one of the marshals drew my attention to a man in civilian clothes standing by the driveway exit, staring at us as we walked out of the jail.

The marshal asked, "Hey, Ernie, do you know who that guy is?" I didn't recognize him, so I said that I had never seen him before.

He added, "You don't know who he is? Come on, Ernie, you know

him." I looked again, but I was sure that I had never seen him before, and I shook my head.

The marshals told me, "That's the cop you shot at when he spotted you in your old neighborhood. He hurt himself pretty bad when he dove for cover. Now do you remember him?"

I said that I didn't know anything about it and that it wasn't me who shot at him. The marshal laughed and said, "Ernie, that guy's been calling my office every day wanting to know 'Have you caught the son of a bitch yet? When you gonna catch him?' " The cop was still staring at us as we drove away. I guess he received some satisfaction from knowing that I was being returned to prison.

Shortly after we left the city, the marshal sitting opposite the driver pulled an envelope out of his coat pocket and tore it open to read it. I heard him mutter, "Bullshit! I ain't going for this crap."

After a moment he turned halfway around in his seat and asked me, "Ernie, do you know what this is?"

I looked over the seat at the letter he was holding, but before I could make out what it said, he explained, "This is a bill for over a thousand dollars from the hospital for the treatment of your bullet wounds. And the assholes are billing the U.S. government. Bullshit! *We* didn't shoot you, Ernie. It was the LAPD!"

He gave me the letter and said, "Here, look!"

I took it and began reading it. I saw that it was on the Seaside Hospital stationery and that the letter was directed to the U.S. Marshals Office. It went on to itemize all the costs for medical services, medicine, room, and board. Attached was a photostat copy of the "Cause of Injury Report," and I read the brief explanation for the cause of the wounds. Then I saw the name of the cop who had shot me through the window, and it hit me like a bomb blast. It had been Harry Freeman!

I got a sick feeling in the pit of my stomach, which was immediately replaced with the most singular sense of hatred I had ever felt up to that time. If I could have managed to escape right then, I gladly would have given up my life just to go back and give Freeman a taste of his own medicine. I wanted to see if he had enough man in him to live through what I did, even with proper medical attention day and night.

Now it all came back to me. I was in the emergency room, and Freeman had barged in, out of breath, wanting to know if I was dead yet. He had gone out of his way to be on the stakeout team just so he could be there when the shooting started. The marshal noticed that I was visibly angry and asked what was wrong. I didn't feel up to telling him any-

thing about it, so I gave him back the letter and stared silently out the window as we headed north. It took two days for us to get to McNeil.

When I returned to McNeil, I was informed that Dillon and I would be going to court out in Tacoma to face charges of assaulting a guard and escape. In the meantime, I was housed in cell house 2. I wasn't placed in the isolation section of the prison, because the government didn't want to hurt its case against me by taking a chance that I would charge mistreatment. However, I might just as well have been in the hole because I was not permitted to leave the cell when the other men went to meals and to work.

A heavy iron boot was locked around the base of my cell door to prevent me from sliding my door open whenever the lock-bar was put in the unlocked position. Unlocking the lock-bar opened all the other cell doors. I was fed in my cell and was not permitted to participate in any kind of activity within prison, including taking a shower. My cell was the last one on the first floor, and each day many of the other prisoners would come to my cell either out of curiosity about the guy who had escaped from the island or just to shoot the breeze.

On these occasions I was able to get messages from other parts of the prison, and I learned some things that Dillon had been saying about the escape. When he had first been captured and returned, he was a big hero with the men around McNeil because he had managed to swim the icy waters after the break. Since he had managed to remain free for only a month, he gradually lost his glamour with each passing week that I remained free. By the time I was captured seven months later, he had completely fallen from favor, mainly from the things he was saying.

What turned the men against him most was that he tried to place the blame on me for the injuries that the guard, Harris, had sustained. He claimed he had had nothing to do with it. The men were not concerned over who had hurt Harris, but telling everybody it was me who had injured Harris was tantamount to being a stool pigeon. Even if it were the truth, Dillon was serving as both detective and main prosecutor by fingering me. Many of the men told him to just keep his mouth shut and say he didn't know how the hell Harris had got hurt. One of my friends told Dillon to say that Harris was perfectly fine when we last saw him and that, as far as he knew, Harris must have been beaten up by the warden for allowing us to escape. At any rate, Dillon became disliked by most all the prisoners. A few years later he was almost killed by another friend of mine because of his lies about the escape. I was

lucky enough to exact my own admittedly more gentle form of revenge a few years later.

Dillon did not try to come around to see me. I continued to get messages about the stories he was spreading about the assault on Harris. These stories were coming thick and fast since we were soon to be taken to trial on the charges. The whole thing made me mad because it was Dillon who had approached me with the idea of escape, and now he was trying to make himself blameless at my expense.

After I had been in McNeil a few days, the associate warden came by to tell me that right after our trial Dillon and I would be transferred to Alcatraz Federal Penitentiary. Alcatraz was notorious, and this certainly was not good news he had brought me. But I decided to face up to whatever came along and simply remained waiting in my cell.

I was in cell house 2 for about three weeks, until the day came for trial. During that time there was only one incident that happened, and it was a rather juvenile attempt at revenge by a guard who was close to Harris.

Lieutenant Kowskoski was on duty during the night, the time when the prison was buttoned down tight and all was quiet. It was a prison rule that all prisoners sleep with their head near the bars at the front of their cell to enable the guards to see "flesh," thereby eliminating the possibility of someone placing a dummy in their bunk during an attempted escape. At about two in the morning while I was sound asleep, this Kowskoski reached through the bars and grabbed hold of my hair with both hands, then quickly banged my head against the bars a couple of time. He ran like hell down the tier and out of the cell house before I could see who it was.

All I knew for sure was that I had been grabbed by a guard. I didn't know which one it was until the next day, when one of the cons told me he had seen Kowskoski walking down the tier in my direction and then, a few seconds later, running out of the cell house as if a ghost were chasing him. The word spread around the cell house the next day, and many of the men stopped by my cell to ask me about it. Even though my wake-up call hurt my head, we all thought the whole thing was rather funny, and the men had a good time laughing about it.

The next night it happened again, and this time Kowskoski opened a small gash on the top of my head. I jumped out of bed cursing up a storm. Kowskoski was already about halfway along the tier when he got a surprise of his own.

It was only about midnight, and although the lights in the cell house were turned off, many of the men were still lying awake. The con who

had seen Kowskoski the night before was maybe the most wide-awake. He was housed on the second tier. When I started hollering after Kowskoski, the con waited for the lieutenant to come running directly below, then dumped a jar filled with urine right on top of his head.

I heard Kowskoski holler, "What the hell?" Now he made another mistake by stopping on the tier to try to determine who had thrown the urine. Just then there was a loud crash as the empty jar shattered near his feet on the concrete floor. He almost had a heart attack right there, and it took him almost a full minute before he regained his wits, turned, and ran out of the block.

In the meantime, the other men were whooping and hollering, and the noise in the cell house was nearly deafening. Somebody hollered, "Hey, Kowskoski, why don't you open his door and do that! You fuckin' coward!"

That remark was followed by more screaming and hollering as the men directed insults at him and his mother. That was the last time that I had any trouble with Kowskoski, but I didn't sleep with my head next to the bars anymore, just in case.

I finally saw Dillon again when we were picked up by two U.S. marshals to be transported to court. We were both handcuffed and shackled before being taken to the boat. There we were joined by two guards from McNeil and taken across the water to the mainland. Dillon and I were placed in the marshals' car, and the guards from McNeil followed us in their own car as we drove to Tacoma, which was only fifteen miles away.

Dillon and I didn't speak to each other during the entire trip, and before long we pulled up to the side entrance of the federal court building in downtown Tacoma. The marshals escorted us into the building and along a short hallway until we came to their office. The room was very large, and as we entered, we faced a long counter that cut off the rest of the office. Behind the counter I could see many desks and filing cabinets, and at the rear some doors that led into smaller offices. In the far right corner a jail cell was covered with a heavy-gauge mesh screen. After the marshals signed some paperwork at the counter, we were taken to the rear of the office and placed inside the holding tank along with one marshal and one guard from McNeil.

Dillon finally spoke for the first time, but it sounded more like he was whining than talking to me. He said to the marshals, "If Mr. Harris was any kind of man, he would tell the truth and say that I didn't hurt him."

He was sitting on a bench along one wall with his head hanging down,

looking like he was expecting someone to come along any minute and shower him with sympathy. I sat on the bench across from him. We were both still handcuffed, though the shackles had been removed after we entered the cell.

The marshal said, "Listen, Dillon, Mr. Harris was injured; there's no doubt about that. Now, if you didn't do it, then who the hell did?"

Dillon's head still hung on his chest. Then he looked over at me and mumbled, "Hey, Ernie, why don't you tell them the truth?"

I sprang off the bench and swung both of my cuffed fists up alongside his head before the guard could stop me. Dillon let out a holler as he fell over on the bench, and he lay there with his eyes bulging wide-open as the marshal grabbed me and wrestled me away to the other side of the cell.

He said, "Knock it off! There ain't going to be any of that shit in here!"

A heavy silence fell over the whole office. Not another word was spoken until we were removed from the cell and escorted to the courtroom. We took our seats in the front row of the spectator section, and I was surprised to see that the courtroom was filled to capacity. There were people standing up and stretching their necks to get a look at us as we walked up the center aisle toward the front of the courtroom.

The papers had made a big deal out of the escape, mentioning that we were the first men to escape from McNeil by swimming the surrounding waters. Many of the spectators were locals who had long taken for granted that nobody could escape from the island. Curious, they wanted to get a firsthand look at the notorious escapees whom the papers had made such a big deal about.

The judge, Charles Levy, came out of his chambers, and the first thing he said was for everyone to sit down. He ordered the photographers who were snapping our pictures like crazy to leave the courtroom. As he took his seat, he emphasized every remark by pounding the top of the desk with his gavel.

He said, "This is going to be an orderly proceeding, not a carnival, and I don't want to have to remind any of you again!" From that point on, the proceedings went by quickly. After the preliminaries, we asked for a jury trial, which took all of about a half hour to impanel.

During this time I whispered to Dillon and told him to take the stand first. I said I would go along with whatever story he told because I figured they were going to find us guilty no matter what we said. He insisted that I take the stand first, and I didn't argue more about it since it made no difference to me.

While I waited for things to begin, I read the indictment against us. I saw that they had charged us with assaulting Harris with a knife, and the report said that Harris had been cut in the stomach and on the forehead. I told the defense attorney, who had been appointed by the court, that the report was a bunch of bullshit.

He said, "Well, we'll just wait and see what kind of evidence they present."

I could tell the guy didn't have his heart in it. As I sat there, I realized that all these people in the courtroom were from the same little hick town, and they all knew each other as friends and neighbors. This shyster we had as a defense lawyer was obviously in cahoots with the prosecuting attorney, the judge, and probably the jury too. Dillon and I were foreigners around here, and I really wanted to get this over with and get out of town as soon as possible.

The prosecution presented its case first, and had Harris take the stand to recall the events of the escape and the assault on him. He told so many lies that I can't remember half of them, but the most damaging lie was when he testified that I had had a small paring knife in my hand and that I must have cut him with it during the struggle. Then the prison doctor took the stand and stated that, in his professional opinion, Harris had been cut with a sharp instrument.

The prosecutor asked him if the cut could have been inflicted with a paring knife. He answered, "Definitely, yes."

That was about the extent of the case against us. In short order I took the stand and told the events just as they had actually happened. I knew that I couldn't beat the escape charge. After all, I had been caught in LA when I was supposed to be in McNeil. The evidence was pretty overwhelming on that count. But I didn't like the idea of getting stuck with a charge of assault with a deadly weapon.

I admitted hitting Harris in the stomach with my fist and on the forehead with the oven paddle when he was biting Dillon's thumb, but I denied having a knife. The prosecutor asked me where Dillon and I had split up, and I answered that we had gone our separate ways when we reached LA. After that answer, I noticed an unhappy look come over Dillon's face, but I couldn't figure out just why. I stared back at him with disgust because I had given him the opportunity to take the stand first. It didn't make any difference to me where we said we split up— he could have said whatever he wanted if he had testified first—but I didn't know what Dillon had up his sleeve until he took the stand right after me.

After being sworn in, Dillon turned to face the jury and said, "Ladies

and gentlemen of the jury, I'm going to tell the truth, regardless of the consequences." Then he began, "Ernie López lied. I don't know why he lied, but he lied. We split up on Fox Island, not in LA."

At this point he had even me confused. Why would he tell a story like that and make me out to be a liar? I found out Dillon's motivation when the prosecutor began to cross-examine him.

He asked Dillon, "So you say that you and Ernie split up at Fox Island and not in LA, as he claims. In other words, Ernie lied on the stand, is that correct?"

Dillon answered yes.

Then the prosecutor picked up a sheet of paper from his table and continued, "Now, I have a sworn statement you gave to the arresting FBI agents, which I will read to you."

Dillon's head jerked up as the prosecutor began to read the statement aloud in the courtroom. I listened as the statement recounted how, after we had made it to Fox Island, Dillon had gotten into an argument with me over the way in which I had handled Harris. So he decided to split up with me right then because he didn't like the fact that Harris had gotten hurt.

The statement went on to say that I threatened to kill Dillon over the disagreement and that we went our separate ways. When the prosecutor finished, he gave the paper to Dillon and asked him if that was his signature on the bottom. Dillon muttered, "Yeah."

The prosecutor went on, "So you say that Ernie lied on the witness stand?"

It was apparent to everyone in the courtroom that Dillon was squirming in his seat. The prosecutor saw that he was ready to break, so he continued, "Why would Ernie lie about where you both split up? Can you answer that question?"

Dillon was staring down at the floor, trying to avoid the prosecutor's eyes, but the questions continued, "Maybe Ernie didn't lie like you said. Maybe he was telling the truth. Isn't that right?"

That seemed to be all Dillon could take, and he feebly answered, "Yeah," and then hung his head again.

The prosecutor wrapped up his cross-examination, "So Ernie was telling the truth after all. It was you who were lying all along, wasn't it? Just a few minutes ago you told the jury of your own accord that you were going to tell the truth, regardless of the consequences, and now you admit that you were lying!"

That was the extent of the whole trial, really, and after Dillon left

the stand, the jury was sent out for deliberation. They returned in two hours and found us both guilty on all counts. Dillon and I were then sentenced to three years for the escape and seven years for the assault with a deadly weapon. I was twenty-three years old, and I wouldn't be a free man again until 1956.

PART TWO TRAINING

THE WELCOME WAGON

Dillon and I were taken back to McNeil to await our transfer to "the Rock," as it was nearly always called: Alcatraz Federal Penitentiary. Three days later I was awakened at one in the morning and taken out of the cell house to be handcuffed, shackled, and ferried to the mainland for our journey to San Francisco.

It was 2:00 a.m. exactly when we left, and we were driven nonstop all the way to San Francisco Bay and down to the waterfront facing Alcatraz Island. We arrived at the ferryboat dock at about six that evening when the sun had just set. As we boarded the ferry, the graceful lines of the Golden Gate Bridge were outlined black against a glowing purple sky. It was very windy and cold, and the bay waters were choppy, tossing the boat around like a cork. If I thought it was windy on shore, I soon learned what wind really was when we approached the island itself.

The ferry swung around to the far side of the island facing away from the city and then made a U-turn into the dock area. As we disembarked, I saw a prison guard wrap the anchor rope around a post and then place a chain around the looped rope and secure it with a padlock. Over the dock loomed a thirty-foot gun tower. As we walked along the dock, I saw a black panel truck parked on a narrow road that wound up to the prison compound. After securing the anchor rope, the guard walked over to the base of the gun tower. A bucket was lowered by the guard inside the tower so that the guard on the dock could place the key to the padlock inside the bucket, which would be pulled back up by the long rope to the gun tower. As we approached the truck, a short fat man in

a guard's uniform barked out the order to get in the back, where we were joined by two more guards.

The marshals helped Dillon and me climb up inside the truck since we were still chained. The two guards from Alcatraz took a seat directly across from us. The fat guard who had barked out the order was chomping on a cigar as he came over to shut the rear door of the truck, but he paused a moment and made a statement I sensed was directed at me.

"Listen up! If you try any goddamn shit around here, we'll lock you up and forget about you."

He looked directly at me as if he were fighting for the control not to take a swing at me. I stared back at him, and he finally turned his gaze away. He muttered a few more curses before slamming the door shut. I figured that he was just some miserable son of a bitch, and from his looks I could have easily mistaken him for a hobo hiding out on the island. His belly hung over the waist of his pants, his shirt was only partially buttoned, and most of it hung out untucked from his pants. Compared to him, the other guards looked like West Point cadets.

I heard him slam the front cab door of the panel truck and start the engine. We lurched forward, the force almost knocking us all off our seats. We grabbed hold of the bench as the hobo guard sped the truck up the winding road and tossed us all about. The other guards didn't utter a sound.

When we reached the highest part of the island, the truck came to an abrupt stop. The fat guard jumped out of the truck, came around to open the rear door, and ordered Dillon and me out. As I climbed down, I saw that we were at the base of the lighthouse that signaled constantly to all the ships entering San Francisco Bay. When I turned around I was facing the front entrance of Alcatraz. Above the doors was carved a large American eagle with its wings spread open in invitation. Right then the wind nearly blew Dillon and me completely off our feet. The fat guard gave us a little shove in the direction of the entrance, and he made some threats about what he would do if we caused any trouble. I took my time walking as I was still shackled with chains. More than the chains, I was shuffling slowly out of stubbornness because I had already formed a dislike of this little fat man whom I had met less than five minutes ago.

We walked through three different sets of doors before we came to stop in front of the last door. This opened into the main cell house. Here the guards removed our handcuffs along with the shackles around our legs. The door was unlocked, and we stepped inside. We were standing

inside a large shell of a building that looked like an airplane hangar. There were three separate rows of cells, each stacked three tiers high, rising from the floor.

Each row had two sides of cells, so the cells from one block faced the cells from the one across. Three aisles were formed around the rows. The center aisle was referred to as "Broadway," formed on one side by the cells of B block and on the other side by the cells of C block. Sitting off to the right of B block was A block, which was no longer used when I came to Alcatraz, because it had deteriorated to the point of crumbling.

As Dillon and I walked along Broadway, we saw that the prisoners, already locked up for the day, were watching us to see if they might know who we were. The guards escorted us to the dining room and fed us a cold dinner before showing us to our newly assigned homes, a cell on the second tier of C block, facing Broadway.

It was deathly silent in the cell house, and if I hadn't known better, I'd have thought the place was deserted. This was a far cry from McNeil, where there was usually some type of evening activity and plenty of small talk among the men in the cells. It was only seven in the evening here, and the joint was buttoned down tight for the day. I soon found that there would be no type of movement or noise until six thirty in the morning, when the wake-up bell was sounded.

I made my bunk with the sheets and blanket and then crawled in; I was very tired after the long ride from McNeil. I fell asleep immediately and didn't wake up until I heard the sound of someone pounding on my cell wall. It was the guy next door, and he told me in a very low voice that we would be going down to the dining room for breakfast in a few minutes. I had slept through the wake-up bell.

I jumped out of bed and threw on my newly issued coveralls. These had no pockets in the front and two in the seat of the pants. As I was waiting for the doors to be unlocked, I heard music coming from somewhere. I suddenly recognized the voice of Bing Crosby singing "Danny Boy." The music was coming out of a set of metal speakers that were part of the public-address system. I later found that the music was part of the standard procedure every morning. Finally the cell doors were unlocked, and I stepped out onto the tier, but I noticed that nobody was walking toward the dining room. The inmates just stood in front of their cells, so I did the same. Then a guard gave the order to "close in." The men formed a single-file line, walked along the tier to the stairwell, then proceeded on down to the dining room.

As we entered, we marched down the center aisle dividing the rows of long tables until we came to where a guard was standing at the far end of the aisle. He directed each man to one side of the dining room or the other. In silence we peeled off to the left or the right and filled in the tables on both sides. During breakfast, which usually consisted of rolled-oats cereal, prunes, and coffee, I noticed that I had a number sewn onto the upper-left part of my coveralls: 697. That meant that I was the 697th prisoner to be brought to the island since it became a federal prison in 1934. My number at McNeil had been 16541, so a three-digit number was going to be easy enough to remember.

When the government closed Alcatraz, after it had served nearly thirty years as the federal prison system's maximum-security prison, the last issued numbers for newly arrived cons barely reached beyond 1500. That was the exact count of all the men ever imprisoned on the Rock. The average daily population was 250, and only on days when a large number of men were brought to the island as transfers from other prisons did the population ever approach 300. Even that population lasted only a day or two, until the appropriate number of men were shipped out after having their cases reviewed by the director of federal prisons. To have more than 250 men on Alcatraz was very rare, occurring perhaps once a year, if that. Of course there were some rare individual transfers in cases where prisoners either had escaped or were a major disciplinary problem at other federal prisons. This was the case with Dillon and me.

After breakfast we returned to the cell house, falling in the same way we left. Each man went back to his cell to await work call. I was unassigned, so I could not leave my cell when the others went to work. We called this "laying in." So I spent the rest of the day sleeping on and off. This was my routine for the next two months until I was finally permitted to go to the yard. Saturday and Sunday were the only days that we were permitted to use the yard, and I had been restricted to my cell until the associate warden made up his mind to let me out for yard activity.

There was a saying around Alcatraz that the prison had no rules except one: don't try to escape. All decisions made by the administration were purely arbitrary and often inconsistent with decisions that had been made just a few weeks earlier. They made up the rules as they went along, and it kept us in a state of uncertainty.

When I arrived, the warden of Alcatraz was James Johnston, and the men always referred to him as "Saltwater" Johnston because of his surly

disposition. He was the epitome of the old Hollywood stereotype of a warden: an aged, nearly senile, and impotent man placed in a position of extreme power. Johnston had previously been the warden of San Quentin and Folsom prisons during the years when the cons were still forced to wear striped clothes and have their heads shaved. He ran the prison as he saw fit and never had to answer to anybody, even though Alcatraz was theoretically under the direction of James V. Bennett, director of the Federal Bureau of Prisons. Bennett had appointed Johnston warden, and he must have approved of the way Saltwater handled things because he never stuck his nose in any of Johnston's business. On the other hand, it could very well have been that Bennett didn't know what the hell was going on most of the time, because he only came to the island about twice a year. The rest of the time he was either in Washington, D.C. or visiting some of the other prisons in the system.

On my first day on the yard I was approached by Pappy Kyle, who's real name was Arnold Thomas Kyle. He introduced himself and said he had been anxious to talk to me about the escape from McNeil. He was very impressed that I was so young and yet had been able to make good on the escape after being at McNeil only a short time. He told me that since my arrival the talk around Alcatraz had been that I would very likely be the first person to escape from the Rock because I had managed to swim from McNeil to Fox Island in the near-freezing water. Then he told me that all the guards would be keeping a very close eye on my daily activities. I had not been allowed out of my cell for the first two months because the escape predictions had gotten back to the warden and angered him, so I was locked down out of spite.

Pappy was the crime partner of Joe Cretzer. The two had also been in McNeil, serving long sentences for numerous bank robberies. At the time of their arrest, J. Edgar Hoover had designated both of them as Public Enemy No. 1. In 1940, Pappy and Little Joe, as Cretzer was called, had jumped into a large dump truck inside the prison grounds and driven it right through a closed gate in an escape attempt of their own.

They drove down the road as the guards in the gun towers opened fire at them. They raised the dump bed so that it would serve as a shield, and the guards' bullets ricocheted off the thick steel. However, some of the bullets hit the rear tires and blew them out before Pappy and Little Joe could get to the water's edge, where they had hoped to commandeer a motorboat. They abandoned the trash truck and fled into the thick woods, where they were captured a few hours later after being

tracked down by bloodhounds. Taken to court in Tacoma to stand trial for escape, they were placed in the same holding cell in the marshals' office as I had been.

While they were in the cell, they noticed that the marshal had a habit of entering the cage with his revolver still in his holster. Although handcuffed to each other, they agreed to jump the marshal and take his gun away so that they could escape. The marshal was a retired state senator, an old guy who had lived around Tacoma all his life, and worked even though his doctor had advised against it because of his heart condition. There was no other person in the cell with Pappy and Cretzer when the marshal reentered the cell. They jumped up off the bench and grabbed him. Pappy tried to snatch the gun from the holster, but a guard from McNeil was sitting by the front counter and heard the scuffle. He came running into the cell and threw a body block on all three of them, sending everybody to the floor with a crash. The unconscious marshal was carried out of the cell and laid on a couch until a doctor could be summoned. He died of a heart attack. Pappy and Little Joe were charged with murder as well as escape, and after being found guilty they were sentenced to life in prison.

I couldn't help but like Pappy because he was so open and friendly with me. Later that morning he introduced me to some of his close friends. The list of names might sound like a "Ten Most Wanted" list, but I got to know them all well, and they soon became very fond of me because at that time I was the youngest prisoner on the Rock.

I couldn't meet Little Joe Cretzer that morning, because he had been in isolation since 1941 for participating in an escape attempt from Alcatraz. But I did meet Alvin Karpis; George "Machine Gun" Kelly and his crime partner Albert Bates; John Paul Chase, partner of John Dillinger; and Freddie Hunter, who was part of the Doc Barker–Alvin Karpis gang. They were all interested in hearing about the escape from McNeil, and I told them about it and about how I had been recaptured in LA after being shot up so badly. My wound was still infected, in fact, and they said that they would pull some strings to get a doctor to look at it.

I mentioned the fat guard who had picked us up in the truck when we had gotten off the ferryboat and how he had threatened me as he drove the truck up the road to the prison. The men laughed and told me that the fat man wasn't a guard but was actually Deputy Warden Miller. I knew right then that I was going to have a hard row to hoe in that prison. We were all standing in the yard against the wall in order to avoid the wind, which whipped around the island with considerable

force. Alcatraz sits aligned with the mouth of the San Francisco Bay, so the cold wind constantly jets in off the Pacific toward the island.

The yard itself was not very large and could not, unlike many other prisons, accommodate many sports activities. We did play softball, but we had to modify the rules to suit the environment. A mattress was hung on the wall near first base so that runners would not crash into the wall and injure themselves when trying to outrun the throw. Any ball hit over the right-field wall was not a homerun but an automatic out; once the ball flew over the prison wall, it rolled down a steep embankment before plopping into the frigid bay water. Center field was a precarious position to play because the fielder had to stand near the top of the steep concrete steps that led down to the yard from the cell house. Fortunately the steps were very wide—they were more like concrete bleachers—and ran almost the entire length of the yard. This permitted the fielder plenty of lateral running room, but he took a chance on killing himself when he had to run down the steps toward the infield whenever a fly ball was hit short. It was quite a trick to run down the steps and keep an eye on the ball at the same time.

Handball was more popular than softball, usually drawing a large number of spectators who sat along the wide steps, using them like bleachers. But the most popular pastime was playing bridge. Since card playing was not permitted on the Rock, the men substituted dominoes whose dots had been painted four different colors to represent the suits.

When I arrived at Alcatraz in June 1945, the "Silent System" was still in effect. This meant that the men were not allowed to talk in the prison, only on the yard or while working at the industry shops. The policy was phased out after I had been there about four months. That policy was a cause of much tension and hatred among the prisoners, and after being in McNeil, I could readily detect the bitterness in the men forced to live under the inhuman conditions on Alcatraz.

To say that Alcatraz was simply the American version of Siberia is to be much too kind to the administration responsible for its role in penology. It was designed purely to punish, and the government made no bones about it. The public at large is not to blame for Alcatraz, for they would have never approved of the conditions had they known the truth, but the Rock was always shrouded in secrecy and hidden from public scrutiny. For years its main function was to satisfy the demented tastes of those responsible for its policies.

Life at Alcatraz was generally very routine. A typical day was as follows: Wake-up bell at 6:30 a.m. A second bell is sounded to signal the

time for count. After the count at seven, the population files down to the dining room for breakfast. As you enter the dining room, you are counted again by a guard who stands at the doorway. Once you take your seat you are counted again. You are allowed twenty minutes to eat breakfast. Then you file out of the dining room; you are counted again as you pass through the doorway to return to your cell. You enter your cell, where you are locked in for five minutes, just enough time to use the toilet and wash your hands. Then you grab your work coat as the cells are unlocked again. Those who have a work assignment proceed out to the yard; they are counted as they exit the cell house. The rest of the men just lay in, napping or reading, and wait for a work assignment.

After walking across the yard, you reach an exit gate at the far wall that serves as the right-field wall for our softball games. This gate leads from the yard down to the industries area. You line up at the gate in separate lines according to the shop you are assigned to. Then your shop's foreman counts you again. As your shop is called, you file through the gate and walk down a steep flight of cement stairs to the industries area, and you enter your shop for work.

As you enter, you are counted again. Finally, each man is allowed to go about his assigned task. You could work in the laundry, where huge amounts of clothing and towels were cleaned for the U.S. Navy; the tailor shop; the glove shop, where work gloves were made for the government; the push-broom shop, which manufactured brooms for the government and for other federal prisons; or the model shop, which repaired broken furniture items for the military.

Each shop has a guard and a shop foreman. The foreman is a civilian employee hired by the prison to supervise production. The guard's main duty is to count the men as they work to ensure that nobody slips away from the industries area to the bay, which is a short climb down a little shrub-filled bluff. You are counted every fifteen minutes while you are at your workstation, and the guard checks off each prisoner's name from the count sheet. He then telephones the armory to report his total count. The process is repeated every quarter hour for the entire workday.

When it comes time for lunch, you are counted as you file out of the shops and then again when you enter the yard and pass through a metal detector. As you enter the cell house, you are counted again on your way to your cell, where you are locked in for the official noontime count. After the noontime count is cleared by the armory, you are released for lunch, when the same procedure as at breakfast is repeated.

After lunch you return to your cell for another count, go back to work, and the whole procedure is repeated until, finally, at about four thirty, after supper, you are locked into your cell for the night.

If this routine sounds boring, you can imagine what it was like for those of us who had to repeat the same process day in and day out for years and years. The monotony could be excruciating. Once you were locked in for the day, there was little to do except read. The prison had a small library from which the men could order some fiction books and an endless number of encyclopedias. Newspapers and radios were strictly prohibited because the administration claimed that the big crime bosses could get information from these sources and still be able to run their crime syndicates.

We received news in the following manner: on Saturday and Sunday while we were out in the yard, the men interested in what was happening in the outside world would wait until a guard came out of the cell house with a piece of paper in his hand. The guard would stop near the steps leading down to the yard and, with a piece of chalk, write the news events on a small blackboard hung on the wall for that purpose. The news story itself was never written out, only the headlines, such as "President Truman on Vacation," then below that perhaps another line, "Steel Strike Still On." That was the extent of the news for that week. They didn't report *where* Truman was vacationing or *which* steel company was on strike; they just selected headlines that they wanted us to see and let it go at that.

Visitors, permitted to visit once a month, were limited to blood relatives. These had to be from the prisoner's immediate family—no girl-friends or close friends of any kind, and no cousins or aunts or uncles.

The conditions under which the visits were conducted were so wretched that few visitors ever bothered to return. It was a torment for the visitors as well as the prisoner. The visitor was led through the three front doors of the prison and finally ushered into a small room that abutted the cell house. They sat until the prisoner arrived at the visiting area inside the cell house. The prisoner and visitor were separated by a thick wall and had to speak through a hole three inches in diameter and covered by a metal plate with small holes punched in it. However, to see each other, they had to stand up and peer through a thick but narrow strip of glass that ran along the length of the visiting room. If you were speaking to a visitor through the metal plate, the glass was about a foot above your head. The prison and visitor were thus unable to converse while looking at each other, unless both were able to read lips.

The visits were not private. A guard was seated at a desk inside the cell house only a few feet from the prisoner and heard every word that he spoke. The prisoner and his visitor just about had to shout to be heard. So not only did the guard hear what the prisoner was saying, but the men anywhere nearby in the cell house could also hear.

Your visitor would shout her greetings to you from the other side of the thick concrete wall. You would holler back, "Hi, Mom, how're you doing? I'm all right, Mom! Don't worry!" And just about everybody in the cellblock would be listening.

When I first got to Alcatraz, I was placed in a cell down by the visiting area. It was as quiet as could be when suddenly I heard this guy leaning against the wall and shouting, "Don't worry, Mamma. I'm all right, I'm all right!"

I went to the door of my cell and said, "What the hell's going on? This guy is sitting down against the wall, and he's shouting to no one!"

The guard at the desk said, "Oh, he's just having a visit." Well, that thought had never crossed my mind.

The guard wouldn't let the prisoner stand up while he was talking. He stood up only to say goodbye, and then he would be waving goodbye to his visitor and to the register and to the guard in the visiting room and to the guard who operated the barred double door. That's why hardly anybody ever came there: you could hear everything everybody said.

A guard terminated the visit after one hour, and the visitors were then escorted out of the prison and driven down to the boat dock, where the ferry would take them back to San Francisco. Actually there were very few visits during all the years that I was on Alcatraz. I didn't receive one until I had been there nine years. This was not uncommon. Most of the prisoners were from the East, and because the visiting conditions were so inhumane, nobody would travel two or three thousand miles just to visit for an hour and then have to return home.

The mail situation was as bad or worse, and when I first arrived I was told by the men that the manner in which the mail was handled had long been a source of bitter resentment among them. The guards opened and read all letters so that they could determine if the letter contained any hidden messages or possible escape plans. The guard in charge of mail chose a few lines from the letter, typed them on another piece of paper, and placed that in a brown envelope bearing the prisoner's name and number. This he delivered to the man's cell.

The prisoner was not permitted to see either the letter or the envelope in which it was mailed, only the typed note. It didn't matter if the

letter was two pages or ten pages; the prisoner still received no more than three or four lines. A typical letter might read: "Dear Fred, How are you? Hope you're doing well. I miss you. Johnny is in the seventh grade now. He says hello and misses you too. Your wife, Carol." The original letter was destroyed by the guard in the mailroom.

All this was bad enough, but there was a guard named Baker assigned to handle the mail who compounded the men's bitterness by destroying letters at random without typing any message at all. This was not discovered for some time until finally, out of desperation, a wife or mother would come to the island for a visit and ask the prisoner why he hadn't been answering her letters. When this happened to three or four men, they were able to compare their experiences and determine that it was more than just a coincidence.

The mail was a sensitive area to the men because they were very concerned about their families and loved ones. When men did not receive news from home, it made them feel neglected and more isolated than they already were. Once the men discovered what Baker was doing, they confronted him with their complaints the next time he came around to deliver the mail. It turned into an ugly scene because Baker steadfastly denied all the allegations. He grew angry at being accused by the prisoners, and informed the warden that the men were threatening him. In short order, a number of the complaining prisoners were taken to the hole.

Another area that was a disgrace from top to bottom was the medical care we received. A dentist came to the island about once every three months, and if a prisoner had a toothache between visits, he had no choice but to endure the pain. The prison hospital was primitive, and the doctor was a quack who hated all the prisoners with a passion. He set up sick-call procedures so stringent that if you didn't have a broken leg or some other grossly visible sign of injury, it was useless to request treatment.

If a man had a serious internal disorder, the only thing he could do was suffer until his condition deteriorated and became a matter of life and death. Then, if the man was lucky enough and sick enough, he would be transferred to the federal prison at Springfield, Missouri, whose medical facility handled the serious medical problems of federal prisoners. If the prisoner was very notorious and thought to be an escape risk, however, then the warden would deny the transfer. Instead, the ill prisoner was placed in the hospital ward at Alcatraz, where the doctor would feign some kind of treatment until the worsening condi-

tion finally caused the prisoner to die. I know of a few men who died from this kind of mistreatment.

Of all the problems everyone griped about at Alcatraz, the worst was the food. When I look back on it now, it is still a wonder to me how the men managed to work and keep up such a rigid production schedule without collapsing from malnutrition. I read years later that the government claimed that the meals had been carefully planned by a dietician. James V. Bennett, director of the Federal Bureau of Prisons, wrote in a book that the food at Alcatraz was better than at the other prisons because there was such a small population. Bullshit! Alcatraz erupted into violence more than once on account of the food.

There was seldom any meat on the menu, and what little there was had been cut into very small portions before it was served. I don't know why this was done, because the meat they served was barely edible and nobody thought of asking for seconds. Eggs or bacon were never served, and I remember constantly having a strong desire for grease because everything was steamed. Just before Alcatraz closed, the food situation improved considerably, but before that there were few changes. The few that did occur were not a result of some humanitarian effort, as Bennett would have people believe, but rather out of necessity. It was better to make some changes on the menu to keep a lid on the place. But the changes were minor and too slow in coming, as the bloody history of the Rock indicates. The prisoners finally concluded that they themselves would have to force the issue about food quality since it was quite evident that nobody in the administration was going to change anything simply out of the kindness of their hearts.

The general mood of the men when I arrived was ugly, and it was just a matter of time before they released their pent-up feelings of bitterness and hostility at the mistreatment by their keepers. The monotony of the daily routine plus the offense of the daily meals heightened tension and added to the urge for some action, no matter what form it took.

When I was finally permitted to go to the yard, I was very curious about the layout of the island. I made mental notes about the positions of the gun towers and the routines of the guards. But I also took advantage of the opportunity to get back into good physical shape after recovering from my gunshot wounds, and each weekend I engaged in some furious games of handball.

Within four months I had my first run-in with the guards, and I learned that it didn't take much to get yourself thrown in the hole. I had been allowed on the yard for weekend recreation, but I was still lay-

ing in during the week, since jobs were very scarce. The men returned from work in the afternoon for lunch. About ten minutes before they were due back in, the guys who were laying in took advantage of the open cells to step out briefly onto the tier and stretch a little, exchange a few words with someone, or trade a magazine or library book with another prisoner who celled nearby. When the men came in, we would go back into the cells before they were locked. This was common practice. I was celling at the time below a friend of mine, Thomas Robinson, convicted of a widely publicized kidnapping for ransom of a wealthy woman from Louisville, Kentucky.

On this particular day, I stepped of my cell as usual, and Robbie whispered down, "Ernie, how ya doing, buddy?"

I told him that I was doing okay, and then suddenly, one of the guards—a bull by the name of Almendares—started rushing over. He was shouting at the top of his lungs, "Get back in your cell! Get back in your cell!"

I was surprised at that reaction and hesitated a moment, looking down the tier to see whether or not he was really hollering at me. In that split second, he ran up to where I was standing.

He shouted again, "I said get back in there, you son of a bitch!"

He pulled up like a bulldog ready to kill a cat. His face was burning red, and he was panting and short of breath. His reaction angered me, but I stepped into my cell. I turned around and said, "I'm back in my cell!"

As soon as I spoke, he whipped out a small black notebook from his back pocket and wrote down my number and the number of my cell. He called me some vulgar names and left to lock the cells on my tier. A few minutes later Almendares returned with three other bulls. My cell was individually unlocked, and I was ordered to step out.

I was taken before Deputy Warden Miller, the fat hobo who had driven me up to the prison from the docks. He informed me I was being reprimanded for having cussed out Almendares.

I said to him, "You know what? If he told you I cussed him out, he's lying. He's a goddamn liar!"

The deputy warden shouted, "Put him in the hole! My officers don't lie! They don't lie! You're calling my officer a liar!"

I said, "That's what he is."

He hollered, "Put him in the hole!"

So I was escorted into D block and placed in the "dark" hole for the first—but not the last—time.

ISOLATION

In isolation, you were locked up all the time and fed in your cell. On Tuesdays we were allowed to go to a small exercise yard for about an hour. This was all the outside activity we saw during the entire week. D block, the isolation block, is made up of three tiers, each holding fifteen cells. The general policy at Alcatraz was that between forty and fifty men were to always be locked up in isolation, about a fifth of the total population. The cells in isolation are like the cells in the general population, but they face a wall of windows that look out over the recreation yard. Sometimes the guards would open those windows and let the freezing ocean air into the whole of D block.

At the end of the bottom tier were the six cells that make up the "dark" hole. In the dark hole, the cells were designed to cut off all light and sound so that it was impossible to determine whether it was day or night. In addition to the regular cell bars at the front of the cell, there was a thick wire mesh across the bars and also a four-inch-thick solid-steel door. It was this door that closed out all light, all noise, all connection with the world. The cells were made completely of steel. The ceiling and the floor as well as the walls were welded sheets of metal. This made these cells especially cold, a situation made worse because we were often dressed only in shorts and had to sit on the floor. There were no bunks or mattresses to rest on in the dark hole. At night, around eight, a guard would come by and give you two blankets, one to sleep on and one to cover yourself with. Around six in the morning he would come back and retrieve them. The guards collected and counted the blankets, and you had to go without any warmth throughout the

day. The coming and going of the guards was the only way to tell day from night.

To make things more unbearable, the cell had no sink or toilet, only an eight-inch hole in the concrete floor where the toilet would normally have been installed. At supper we were fed two slices of bread and some ground-up vegetables in a small cup, and that was our entire ration of food for the day.

The living conditions in the open cells were quite a bit better than those in the dark hole, for the cells were equipped with a toilet, a wash basin, and a bunk. The prisoners were also able to see if it was daytime or night because they faced the large, barred windows framing the San Francisco waterfront and the city skyline just beyond. The men could pass the time talking to one another all day and night, which made living in the open cells more tolerable. The men in isolation didn't have to worry about obeying the silent system, since they were already in the hole.

At night, it was beautiful to see the city's lights shining across the bay and shimmering on the water, but it also made us more keenly aware of our own miserable surroundings. Robert Stroud, the "Birdman of Alcatraz," endured the cruelty of that beautiful panorama for nearly fifteen years while he was locked up in D block. Bob Stroud was in isolation the entire time he was in Alcatraz. Counting the time he served at Leavenworth and at Alcatraz, Stroud remained in isolation for almost fifty years.

This punishment was the result of a dirty trick the authorities played on him. Stroud had been a barber in Alaska before winding up in Leavenworth for a murder conviction. At Leavenworth, one of the guards was constantly annoying and antagonizing Stroud. He would bother him and belittle him at every opportunity. In the dining room one day, this guard walked over to the table where Stroud was eating. He stood over the end of the table and then made an obscene pantomime, acting as if he were lifting his two huge balls and dropping them on the table next to Stroud's food.

By this time Stroud was fed up with the guy giving him such a bad time at every turn. Grabbing a regular butter knife, Stroud leaped up and stabbed the guard numerous times in stomach. In his rage, he killed the guard. He was tried at Leavenworth and sentenced to be hanged. The judge ruled that he should be confined in isolation until the day of his execution.

As it turned out, President Woodrow Wilson commuted Stroud's

sentence to life. But he was never placed in the general population at Leavenworth and was left in isolation. It was during this period at Leavenworth that he started treating birds. All this started because one day while walking about in the yard he came across a little hurt bird. He brought it back to his cell and took care of the bird as best he could. He had had a general interest in birds, and gradually learned more and more about them.

As time went on, he began to take care of more birds, especially canaries, and he was allowed to collect cages to house them. Stroud's reputation spread beyond the prison walls, and soon people on the outside who had a little money would send their sick canaries to him for treatment. All of this increased his expertise, and he next started studying the anatomy of the birds and learning about treatments for their ailments. He worked on this for years while he was in isolation. He found out a good deal about medicine for the treatment of birds and learned to recognize symptoms that indicated rare diseases. He went on to write a book called *Stroud's Digest on the Diseases of Birds*. He drew by hand every illustration in the book, which covered the bird's entire anatomy.

People think that because he was called the "Birdman of Alcatraz" he studied birds while imprisoned on the island. In fact, he collected and studied birds only at Leavenworth. I know this because I was often in isolation, and Stroud and I used to talk to each other from our cells. I guess the "Birdman of Leavenworth" doesn't sound as good as the "Birdman of Alcatraz."

During the time Stroud was in Leavenworth, James Bennett was director of the federal prison system. According to Stroud, he and Bennett had a falling out because Bennett wanted a percentage of the profits Stroud made from the bird business. He demanded such a large cut that he and Stroud got into a huge argument. Bennett wound up issuing an order to take away all the birds from Stroud and throw away his equipment. He did this just out of spite. To extract an even greater revenge, according to Stroud, Bennett had a knife planted under his pillow and then claimed that Stroud had plans to kill him. As a result, Stroud was sent to Alcatraz.

Stroud believed that when Wilson commuted his sentence to life, he did not mean a life sentence in isolation. This was where Bennett played Stroud a dirty trick. When the judge sent Stroud to isolation to await his execution, he meant that he should remain in isolation while his appeals worked their way through the system. When Wilson commuted

Stroud's sentence to life, Bennett interpreted this to mean that Stroud would spend his life in isolation. During all those years at Leavenworth and Alcatraz, Stroud was never returned to the general population. I remember watching him through the window when he was taken to the yard, all by himself, every week, for the one hour he was allowed outside. I would see him walking by himself, an old man pacing back and forth across the tiny yard. He was hunchbacked by then, and he would wear a green plastic visor that gamblers often wear. He was a very intelligent man who knew five or six languages well, and he got As on all the courses that he took by mail from Stanford University.

Just before they closed Alcatraz, Stroud was transferred to Springfield, Missouri. He had high hopes that President Kennedy would finally commute his sentence, but his hope was never fulfilled. He spent some fifty years in isolation before dying of old age in prison.

Stroud's case aside, the official policy was that men were not to spend longer than twenty-nine days in a row in isolation. Despite this official policy, men often served much longer, sometimes five, six, or even seven years. A friend of mine by the name of Whitey Phillips got put away in isolation for thirteen years.

Just before being placed in isolation, Whitey had been working very hard on his trial case. He was working on a writ of *habeas corpus* one day when two guards came in, tore his papers up, and threw them in the toilet. Whitey knew that that the guards would never have acted if they had not been ordered by the warden to do so.

As I've explained, the warden at the time had a habit of standing in the middle of the dining room as the prisoners walked in, directing them to sit on either the right or left side. He always held a clipboard that identified prisoners by the number on their coveralls. Walking into the dining room, Whitey made his way through the line of men waiting before the warden. Slowly he shuffled his way up to the front of the line. As the warden looked down to consult his list, Whitey sprang his revenge.

Quick as lightning, Whitey punched the warden with a left hook, a right jab, and a left uppercut. Later Whitey told me, "I knew exactly how I was gonna hit that son of a bitch."

He floored the warden, jumped on him, and continued to beat the hell out of him before being pulled off by the guards. The guards first beat him, and then they threw Whitey in isolation and left him there for thirteen years. Whitey studied during his years in isolation. He was a good mathematician and, like Bob Stroud, took courses offered by

mail from Stanford. After thirteen years, they let Whitey Phillips out and put him in a cell next to mine. That was how his story came down to me.

After seven days in the dark hole, I was escorted back to the main cell house. Deputy Warden Miller, seated at a desk, headed a small disciplinary committee that would decide the final disposition of the matter. I had learned that the prisoners always referred to Miller as "Meathead" because he was fat and nearly bald. Apparently he despised prisoners who had a thick head of hair, as I did then. Most deputy wardens dressed neatly, usually in a suit. Not Meathead. He wore a regular guard's uniform — often sloppy and unkempt — with an old beat-up fedora that had seen better days. He looked to me more like a big, fat, old wino than a deputy warden.

He read a report and then spoke to me. "Next time one of my officers talks to you, you don't cuss him out. Do you understand?"

"Look," I replied, "I didn't cuss the guy. He's a goddamn liar if he said I cussed him out. Now I wish I had!"

Miller's eyes bulged and his nose flared as he shouted to the guards, "Get him back! Get the son of a bitch back in the hole! He called my officer a liar! Get him back in the hole!"

The guards grabbed me right away and took me back to D block. I entered the block and was escorted along the bottom tier toward the dark hole. Some of the other prisoners wanted to know what had happened, and I told them that Meathead had gone crazy. That broke them up, and when the guards slammed the thick steel door behind me, even I started laughing.

Seven days later I was escorted out of D block and brought before Miller for another disciplinary hearing. He fixed his gaze on me. He asked, "Have you had enough now? Have you learned not to cuss out my officers?"

I was mad after spending two weeks in the dark and the cold for something I didn't do, and I should have kept my mouth shut. Instead, my stubbornness got the best of me, and I told Miller, "Your officer is a goddamn liar. I never cussed at him!"

I barely finished my statement before Miller sprang from his chair and shouted, "Take the son of bitch back! Take him back! I don't want to see him!"

He was still ranting and raving as we reentered D block. One of the guards escorting me said, "Goddamn, Ernie, you're gonna tucker me out."

The men in isolation hollered out as I walked by, "Hey, Ernie, what the hell happened this time? Did Meathead flip out again?" It was a hilarious situation to the prisoners, and in a way I was glad that they had a chance to laugh, since there was rarely anything about Alcatraz worth laughing about.

Seven days later, right on schedule, I was brought back in front of Miller. On the way down, the escorting guards offered some advice about what to say to Miller, but I told them that I already knew what I was going to say. Miller appeared to be calm, and I think he chose his words very carefully when he spoke. "López, don't you think you've had enough yet?"

I answered as calmly as I could. "Listen, Mr. Miller, I never cussed that son of a bitch out, and that's that."

He interrupted as I was talking. "Don't call my officer a son of a bitch! I'll put you in that goddamn hole for twenty-one more days and feed you bread and water!"

But I cut him short too and said, "I don't care if you put me *in* the hole or *under* the hole or *over* the hole, I'm still saying that I didn't cuss him out!"

Meathead shouted to the guards, "Get the bastard out of here! Give him a shower and then get him out! He's crazy—the son of a bitch is crazy!"

I was allowed to shower and to return to my regular cell in B block. It seemed like a penthouse compared to the dark hole.

After my release from D block I remained unassigned; jobs were still at a premium. My activities were limited to the same routine as before, laying in during the week and going out to the yard on the weekends. About three months went by before I found myself in hot water again.

One Saturday I had a beef with a prisoner whom I was playing handball with. I was beating him pretty badly, and he started getting steamed, so he threw a punch at me. Almost immediately the guards swarmed us to break up the fight. I could see that the bulls in the tower had their rifles and machine guns trained on us while the guards pulled us apart. Now I was really mad. The guy had thrown a punch at me, and, right or wrong, I was going to end up in the hole for being in a fight.

The guards hustled us both up the steps that led from the yard to the cell house. About five guards surrounded me, each using some type of hold to keep the two of us apart. I figured it was useless to struggle with the bulls; the guard in the gun tower might get excited and direct some rifle fire at me. So I relaxed, letting them restrain me and lead me up

the stairs. Although we were almost to the cell house, the guards continued to twist my arms behind my back and keep them in a painful armlock.

I told them to let go of me because they were causing me a lot of pain. Finally, they eased off some, since it seemed the moment of anger between the other guy and me had passed. Besides, we were at the cell house door by then, waiting to be let in. Even the guards in the tower had lowered their rifles and were scanning the rest of the yard.

When they released their grip, I sprang at the son of a bitch who had thrown a punch at me, and landed a powerful blow cleanly on his jaw. Now I was a bit satisfied, since, if I was going to the hole, it may as well be for some reason.

Just as I finished throwing the punch, a guard named Long, who was too old for this kind of thing, came running over and tried to jump on my back. Just at that moment I backed up and accidentally knocked Long over. He lost his balance and fell backward. Unable to break his fall, he tumbled down the thirty steps, picking up more and more speed as he went along until he finally landed in a heap at the bottom of the stairs.

"Uh-oh," I thought. "I'm in real trouble now."

That was the last thing I saw before I was hustled to the dark hole. I stayed there for ten days before being placed in one of the open cells. I settled into my new cell to finish out my sentence in isolation.

A few days later it became apparent that my sentence would be extended, along with everybody else's. That morning one of the prisoners on the third tier began banging his metal cup against the bars. He was feeling very ill, and had tried for hours to get the guards to call a doctor. Almost immediately the other men in the block began doing the same thing, and soon the entire D block was hollering and banging like raving maniacs in an attempt to help the sick prisoner get some attention. Instead of a doctor, the guards called for reinforcements, and soon about twenty guards were milling around the block and trying to quell the noise. When their attempts failed, they decided to take some men at random and lock them in the dark hole.

This caused all hell to break loose, and suddenly what had been an extremely loud demonstration erupted into a deafening riot of noise. In a matter of seconds, the men began breaking up the toilets and sinks and even tearing the steel bunks off the cell walls. The light fixtures were smashed, and glass went flying everywhere.

Naturally I joined in the melee, and soon the entire cellblock was lit-

tered with strewn debris. We set fire to all our blankets and mattresses, and within minutes the block was black with smoke. The deafening noise never ceased. The guards ran out of the block looking for some air and further orders from the captain about what to do next.

When they returned, they were dragging large fire hoses. These were connected to hoses fed in from outside D block through the windows. The other ends of the hoses were connected to fire hydrants pumping in water from the bay. When the hoses were in place, the guards ordered the water turned on. After the fires were extinguished, the guards turned the water on the men in their cells. Because the bars were so close together, much of the water—along with the small rocks and pieces of coral and shell from the bottom of the bay—bounced back and hit the guards. That got them to turn the water off. Rather than spraying all the men at once, they moved along the tiers, placing the hose just inside the bars of the prisoner they wanted to spray. They then signaled for the water to be turned on again, and in this way they could direct the full force of the water on the prisoner without having any of it splash back on them.

When it came my turn, it seemed as if nothing but sharp rocks and small razor-sharp pieces of shell came gushing out of the hose. When they finally shut it off, I had thousands of small cuts all over my body, and these cuts stung even more because of the saltwater. The ocean water was extremely cold, and it left us nearly freezing; we had burned our blankets, and all the windows were open.

When the guards left, the entire block looked a shambles. On the first tier, the water stood a foot deep. The block had suffered extensive damage. After about five days the warden ordered many of the men moved from isolation to the main cell house so that repair work on the block could begin. Among those released to the general population were Floyd Hamilton—of the Bonnie Parker and Clyde Barrow gang—and Little Joe Cretzer, the friend of Pappy Kyle, who had been so friendly to me on my first day on the yard. Both of these men had been kept locked up in D block for years, Hamilton for three and Cretzer for five. They had every right to be bitter after the long years of brutality and inhuman treatment they had received while in the hole.

Though I had seen Cretzer when I was in the hole, we never had the opportunity to speak to each other until after his release from isolation. Pappy Kyle introduced us while we were out on the yard the first weekend after Little Joe was back in the general population. The three of us cut up about our escapes from McNeil Island and had a good time

laughing and joking. I was impressed that Cretzer had not lost his sense of humor, even after five years of solitary confinement.

Later we were joined on the steps by Bernard Coy, in for bank robbery; Joe Carnes, serving a ninety-nine-year sentence for kidnapping; and Blackie Thompson, another bank robber. This group regularly congregated out on the yard every weekend, playing handball or just walking around the yard and shooting the breeze. This was our routine for the several months that D block was being repaired. About this time I got assigned a job in the cell house as a painter.

In April 1946, Marvin Franklin Hubbard arrived on the island to serve a long sentence for bank robbery. As it turned out, he was a close friend of Bernard Coy, and he was introduced into our clique right after his arrival. By then the group was looking rather notorious, even by Alcatraz standards. It was about this time that the steadily mounting tensions within the prison began coming to a head.

It was no surprise, then, when I heard some of the men in the group begin discussing the idea of breaking out. After Hubbard joined the group, the plans for escape took on a very serious tone. We always walked around the yard when the topic of escape came up because we were concerned that the wind would carry our conversation up to the guard on the gunwalk if we sat at our regular spot on the steps.

By the end of April, we had kicked around several plans and agreed on the method thought to have the best chance of success. However, as was proven a number of times, the Rock was a hard case to crack. The agreed-upon escape plan went afoul, and that resulted in the famous Battle of Alcatraz on May 2, 1946.

To my knowledge the details of the escape plan and the actual intentions of the men involved have never been disclosed to anyone, and that includes the FBI and the prison authorities who investigated the "riot" immediately after they managed to regain control of the prison. I have since read many accounts, but I have yet to find one that recounts the events as they actually happened.

One of the more popularly known versions was told by James V. Bennett in his book *I Chose Prison*. He recounts the events as they were relayed to him over the teletype and telephone while he was in his office in Washington, D.C. Naturally, he could not have known the intentions of the men or the details of the incident—he was not anywhere near Alcatraz when the riot occurred. Still, he did endeavor to relate his own

peculiar version the incident. His account provides only the sketchiest of details. In general, he twisted the events so as to place himself and the prison authorities in the most favorable light. He completely ignored the cruel and sadistic practices employed against the men of Alcatraz, the real cause for the outbreak of violence.

He presents a picture that is highly unrealistic, and in his typical bureaucratic fashion, he refers to my friends Coy and Cretzer as, respectively, a "degenerate" and a "psychopath." I knew them both very well, and they were far from being what Bennett claims. Though they had doubtless broken the law, in truth both men were extremely articulate and well read. They would not have shot it out with the authorities had they not been desperate to escape the cruel treatment we all endured at the hands of Bennett and his henchmen.

In his book, Bennett presents himself as an honest-to-goodness humanitarian, explaining how he recommended prisons without fences and other progressive reform projects. He did not, however, bother to mention the inhumanities that the men were forced to endure under his capricious policies. Nor did he mention that he was personally responsible for keeping Sam Shockley in the hole for seven years for simply being *accused* by a guard of stealing some meat from the prison kitchen. Nor that he personally placed a man named Regan in isolation for three years because the guards found a stick of gum in his shirt pocket. Nor that he himself placed Louie Fleisch in the hole for several years after he was caught with three candy bars smuggled into the prison by a guard. Fleisch was placed in isolation because he refused to reveal who the guilty guard was.

This was the type of "humanitarian" Bennett was at the time of the riot in 1946. He polished up the official version for the press by covering up the truth. From his book, he would have you believe that a "riot" was led by a group of bloodthirsty animals driven by madness to lash out violently at authority. The guards involved were brave and daring men willing to risk their lives at all costs in order to protect the public.

In the end, it was the prisoners who willingly gave up their lives rather than live another day in wretched debasement and under inhuman conditions. They gave up their lives in order to remain men.

I will trace, I believe for the first time, the tragedy from its inception to the final moments, when I saw the bodies of all the dead laid out on the cell house floor. I lived through an experience in which the island was so wracked by machine-gun fire and so torn apart by hand grenades that I thought nobody would be left alive to tell the story.

ESCAPE FROM ALCATRAZ

As I mentioned, Joe Cretzer was finally released from the hole around April 1946, and soon he brought up the subject of escape. From that point on, the idea took hold with Bernard Coy, Blackie Thompson, Clarence Carnes, Marvin Hubbard, me, and a few others.

From the beginning, the key aspect of the plan centered on the possibility of climbing out of the main cell house through one of the skylights in the ceiling. These were constructed of large panels of glass fitted together and positioned to form a slight arch over the opening in the roof. The prison designers must have foreseen that the skylights offered a possible means of escape, because a steel grille was welded to the ceiling, preventing access to the skylight. The grille created a space beneath the skylight similar to a small attic. Supposedly a source of light in the cell house, the skylights' effectiveness was limited to only those cells high up on the third tier of each cellblock.

Getting up to the grille, some sixty feet above the floor, would be relatively easy using the tall rolling scaffold that was used to change burned-out ceiling lights. When not in use, the scaffold was chained to a screen fence of heavy-gauge steel that separated the library from the cell house. The screen could be cut with a hacksaw in just a matter of seconds, and it would then be simple to pull the chain free.

The initial problem we faced was getting to the steel grille and being able to work on it without being spotted. There were two guards in the cell house who kept watch during the day, when most men were out working in the shops. One was Dean Burch, the armed guard patrolling the gun gallery that ran along one side of the cell house. The other was

William Miller, the guard stationed at a desk on the first floor between the entrance to the dining room and the doorway leading to the yard.

Miller could see the scaffold from where he was stationed, so there was no choice but to divert his attention to another part of the cell house or to grab him and lock him in a cell. We were not likely to able to divert his attention long enough to give us time to cut the steel grille, so the plan was to grab Miller and lock him up. Before this could be considered, Burch, the armed guard on the gunwalk, would have to be taken out of the picture, at least temporarily, until Miller could be subdued.

The guard in the gun gallery left the main cell house only when he was summoned to D block to provide gun coverage for the guard in isolation who was about to open a prisoner's cell. On these occasions, the guard in D block would signal with a buzzer that the guard on the gunwalk could hear in the main cell house.

Since D block was completely separated from the main cell house by a thick wall, the guard in the gun gallery had to push open a swinging door to enter the block. Once he was inside D block, the door swung shut behind him, preventing him from hearing anything in the main cell house. This would give us the opportunity to jump Miller. We had no way of knowing, however, exactly how long the gunwalk guard would stay in D block. If he were to come back before we could position the scaffold under the skylight, cut through the steel grille, slide out one of the glass panels, and climb through to the roof, he would spot us and cut us down with automatic rifle fire.

Clearly the guard in the gun gallery also had to be subdued. This seemed impossible: he was caged in the gunwalk behind bars that ran vertically from the steel floor of the gunwalk to high above a second gunwalk that was almost never used. Just above the second gunwalk, the bars curved in toward the wall, where they were secured. There seemed to be no way to get into the caged walk in order to subdue the guard.

After considering this problem for a few days, Coy figured out a way to breach the gun gallery. He told us his plan when we next met out on the yard. He explained that the gunwalk guard could be subdued only after he was summoned to D block. Then, by standing on top of a table, a man could be boosted high enough to grab hold of the bars covering the gun gallery. From there he could climb up the vertical bars by using the horizontal bracing bars as rungs. Climbing up, he could reach the very top, where the bars turned in toward the wall. Coy reasoned that the bars would be weakest at the point where they curved. With the aid

of some kind of "spreader," the bars could be opened just wide enough to enable a thin person like him to crawl through. Then he could remove the spreader, drop into the top gunwalk, then walk down a small stairway leading to the gunwalk that Burch used.

Standing on the bottom gun gallery, he could wait for Burch to return from D block and then knock him unconscious with the spreader. Although it was risky, the plan seemed feasible, and everyone agreed to it. Plans to assemble a bar spreader began immediately. If we could subdue the armed guard in the gun gallery, we would be in control of the entire cell house since he was the only armed guard inside during the prisoners' working hours.

Normally, there would have been another armed guard posted in an identical gun gallery on the opposite side of the cell house, but he had been pulled from that position and assigned to a gun post overlooking the industries area. It was unnecessary to have both gunmen in the cell house when there were hardly any prisoners to watch except the few laying in. The gun-gallery guard was armed with an automatic rifle, a .45 automatic handgun in a holster, and a belt of cartridges.

Once we obtained these weapons from Burch, it would be possible to tackle our next objective: the armed guard stationed on the cell house roof, overlooking the yard. We reasoned that he could be approached from behind and taken by complete surprise. Since he sat facing away from the skylights and looking out on the yard, he would never expect anyone to approach him from the roof. He stood watch in a small hut, and that would help mask our approach. Armed with weapons, we could easily overtake him and tie him up.

After adding his weapons to our arsenal, we could climb down from the roof and enter the front entrance of the prison under the carved American eagle. There we would face the next and most important obstacle in our path. Entering the front door, we would find ourselves walking in the direction of the armory, which was the main control center of the island. It was enclosed by thick concrete walls and bulletproof glass. The armory contained the communications system for the island, and, behind a locked door, a guard who coordinated the ongoing activities throughout the prison by pushing buttons or issuing keys to unlock doors in various sections of the prison. In case of an emergency, he could issue weapons to guards summoned from their living quarters.

There was a hole cut into a section of the thick glass for the purpose of handing out weapons, and it looked much like a ticket seller's

window at a movie house. The plan was to wear the captured guards' uniforms and approach this area undetected. Once directly in front of the window, we would shove the automatic rifle through the hole and order the guard to unlock the armory door. If he refused, the plan was to keep the rifle pointed at him so that he could not move from his desk, sound the alarm, or send an SOS to the mainland. The guard would be neutralized, but our hope was that he would simply unlock the armory. Then the entire prison would be under our control, and there would be no way to radio for help, should anybody else detect us. Since we planned a daytime escape, we felt our chances of going undetected were good; everyone else would be occupied in supervising the large number of prisoners working in the shops at the far end of the island.

At every point, the plan was to avoid situations that could cause gunfire, and we all agreed to fire no shots unless absolutely necessary. Firing shots would be the same as sounding an alarm and would force us into a shootout with the guards. So we tried to make provisions for every critical area where a guard might challenge us, and one spot was the armory.

In the unlikely event that the guard inside the armory should try to signal the alarm, then rifle fire would be necessary. We would not shoot the guard unless he reached for a weapon. Instead, our plan was to fire at the communications equipment until it was shot to hell, accomplishing our main goal of knocking out communications. At that point, it wouldn't matter to us what the guard did, because he would be helpless to stop us. It also wouldn't matter how many guns and grenades he had in the armory, because we would have him trapped.

I remember that when this part of the plan was discussed, Coy assured everyone that he knew how the guard in the armory would respond. Coy's job in the prison was to distribute magazines to all the prisoners, and during the course of things he had been asked by the guard for some reading material. Coy used to bring this particular guard magazines to read almost every day. He was sure the guard would not hesitate to open the door if someone thrust an automatic rifle at him, so this part of the plan seemed set.

We figured on meeting no more resistance until reaching the ferryboat dock overlooked by the thirty-foot gun tower. The guard in the gun tower was our last obstacle. This was the stickiest problem, and we discussed at length how best to overtake his position. After much thought, Cretzer came up with what we thought was the best solution.

Once the armory was under our control, the plan was to cross the

walkway bridge to the guards' apartments, a three-story building that faced the dock and the gun tower. From within one of the apartments, Cretzer would telephone the tower guard and inform him that the prison was now under the control of our group. The guard would be allowed one minute to phone the armory if he had any doubts. He would also be directed to look at the porch of the apartment building, which was at the same level as the top of the tower. There he would see Coy dressed as a uniformed guard, aiming a rifle straight at him.

This was the only part of the plan in which there was a real possibility that a guard might have to be killed. If Coy opened fire from the porch with a .30-06 rifle, it would be impossible for him to miss the guard. We talked about it, and felt that a man who had anything to live for was unlikely to foolishly choose to give up his life when he was obviously outnumbered and outgunned.

We felt that the call to the armory would be the clincher. The phone would be answered by one of us or not answered at all, since the guard inside would be covered and not allowed to move an inch. Once persuaded that he was outnumbered, the guard was to come down from the tower and discard his weapons. With the tower guard removed from his station and disarmed, it would be a simple matter to escape the island by boat without anybody on the mainland knowing. At the same time, we would be leaving the guards on the Rock stranded until they could get help. And the only way to do that would be by using smoke signals or by manipulating the lighthouse signal.

So this was the escape plan all of us agreed upon. Of course, we went into much more meticulous detail, such as precisely who would put on the captured guards' uniforms and who would take what weapon from which guard. Through it all, we planned not to fire a shot unless absolutely necessary.

We scheduled the escape for Thursday, May 2, 1946, because the prisoners in D block always took showers on Thursdays, and the guard in the gun gallery would frequently be summoned to provide coverage while the prisoners were let out of their cells.

After we laid out our plans, one of us assembled the bar spreader in one of the industry shops, using parts that had been hidden in the area for many years for just this type of occasion. The spreader was two pipes, each threaded so that one would screw into the other. The inside pipe had a hole bored in it, through which you could pass a metal bar that would serve as a handle. Turning the inside pipe clockwise caused it to

retract into the outside pipe; turning it counterclockwise caused it to extend. The two pipes were measured to just about fit the space between the bars surrounding the gun gallery.

From the industries area, the spreader was hidden in one of the laundry hampers and delivered to the dock area. We had a man waiting to remove it from the hamper before it could be scanned by a metal detector prior to the laundry being sent to the basement of the cell house. After the laundry passed through the metal detector, our man placed the spreader back in the hamper. This was then delivered to the basement, where the laundry was distributed among the prisoners in the main cell house.

In the basement the spreader was given to Coy, and the escape was underway. On the appointed day, Coy walked over to where Carnes and I were locked in our cells and gave us the signal that the escape was on. He returned to his workstation, where magazines were stacked on a large table, and waited for the bell to signal the work call.

At 12:50 p.m., the bell rang for the men to file out of their cells and report back to work. Carnes and I were laying in along with several other men who were also part of the break. By one o'clock the main cell house was nearly deserted. At one fifteen the guard in D block rang the buzzer to summon Burch for gun coverage. After he passed through the swinging door to the isolation block, Coy came over to where Carnes and I were locked in and quietly told us to stand by. Then he walked toward Broadway, where the guard William Miller was seated at his desk.

Cretzer, who had a job as the main cell house orderly, was mopping the floor in the vicinity of Miller's desk. At a prearranged signal, he edged over to where the guard was sitting at the same time that Coy approached. Together they jumped Miller and easily overwhelmed him.

Applying a choke hold to him, Cretzer and Coy walked the guard over to an empty cell nearby on the Broadway side of B block. They ordered Miller to remove his shirt and pants, and took away the key to the lockbox that controlled all the cell doors. Coy took off his prison coveralls, put on Miller's uniform, and locked the guard inside the cell.

Cretzer and Coy set about unlocking the cells of the men involved, being very careful not to tip off the other prisoners about the escape. The men in our group stayed in their cells until a signal was given. This way, if a guard entered the cell house unexpectedly, it would appear as if everyone was still locked up.

All but Hubbard stayed in their cells. He quietly slid his cell door open, stepped out, and slid the door back to an almost locked position.

Carnes and I were the last to be unlocked, waiting for a signal from Coy before we took up our positions.

I saw Coy and Hubbard push the large magazine table under the bottom gun gallery. Using the table as a platform, Hubbard hoisted Coy up until he could grab hold of the bars enclosing the gunwalk. From there Coy climbed up above the second gun gallery to where the bars curved. He positioned the spreader right at the curve and forcefully turned the handle, slowly spreading the two bars open. Within a minute he was able to crawl through into the gallery. He removed the spreader and made his way down to the bottom gun gallery. Cretzer pushed the button inside the cell house, summoning Burch back into the main cell house, while Coy positioned himself next to the swinging door. When Burch pushed the door open, Coy clubbed him on the head with the pipe from the bar spreader.

Burch was knocked out cold. Coy took his rifle and the holster containing the .45 and the cartridges and threw them down to Cretzer and Hubbard. He removed Burch's uniform and put it on, took the ring of keys, and climbed up until he could crawl back through the gap in the bars. He made his way down to the first gun gallery and dropped himself onto the magazine table. He gave Carnes and me the signal, and we stationed ourselves near the corner of B block to keep an eye out for anybody who might enter the cell house.

Coy joined Cretzer and Hubbard and put on the gun belt. He stuck the .45 in his holster; Cretzer took the rifle. Now they both were armed and wearing guard uniforms. From where I stood they could have passed for Miller and Burch. After conferring a few seconds, they headed for D block, where they intended to free Whitey Franklin. Using a key from Burch's key ring, Coy unlocked the door to the isolation block, and the three of them entered.

A guard by the name of Corwin was at his desk. Sam Shockley, one of the prisoners in isolation who served as the porter in the block, was out of his cell mopping the floor. Coy, Cretzer, and Hubbard took Corwin by surprise. They told him to freeze and asked Shockley which cell Franklin was in.

Up to this point, the escape was going exactly as planned, but they ran into their first problem after entering D block. Franklin was supposed to be in one of the open cells on the third tier, where he had been celling for quite some time. Shockley told them that Franklin had just recently been locked in the dark hole. This didn't seem to be much of a problem, because it seemed simple enough to unlock the lockbox

on the first tier. This would open the inside door of the two-door cell. They had only to walk over and key open the thick steel outer door of Franklin's cell. However, it was exactly this maneuver that brought disaster to the escape plan and eventually cost these men their lives.

The cells on the first floor of D block were electronically operated, whereas the other cells in the prison were manually operated by mechanical levers. When Cretzer activated the inside door of Franklin's cell, a red light lit up on the gun gallery where Burch was lying unconscious. We were all aware of that signal beforehand. What we didn't know was that any time a cell on the bottom floor of D block was opened, a similar red light went on in the armory. Unless the guard in D block had notified the armory before opening the cell, it was automatically assumed that there was trouble in the isolation block.

This is precisely what happened. Immediately after Cretzer opened the first door to let out Franklin, Corwin told the three that an alarm had just been set off in the armory. Cretzer became furious when he realized that, if the guard was telling the truth, he had waited until *after* the alarm had been activated before saying anything. Cretzer jammed the barrel end of the rifle against Corwin's head and told him, "You better hope no goddamn alarm went off, you rotten son of a bitch!"

They marched Corwin over to where Miller was locked in on B block and ordered him to remove his uniform. They locked him in with the other guard. Hubbard, who had not been on the island long, pointed up at the red light on the gunwalk and told Cretzer and Coy that maybe the guard was telling the truth about the alarm. The other two told Hubbard not to worry, that the plan was still on. They either didn't believe the guard or didn't want to believe him. We all wanted our freedom badly, but not nearly as passionately as Cretzer, who had spent years locked up in solitary confinement. He gave the signal to the other men involved to get the scaffold ready for cutting the grille. He came over to where Carnes and I were standing and said to me, "Well, Ernie, looks like you won't have to swim away from here after all." He gave me a slight grin.

The whole chain of events to this point had not taken more than ten minutes. Had it not been for the red light in the gun gallery, I would have felt that the plan was going along perfectly. But I wasn't as sure as Cretzer and Coy about the guard from D block having lied, so I held my ground at the rear of the cellblock and waited to see what developed. Just then we heard the sound of a door at the front of the cell house being unlocked.

A second later a loud voice hollered, "What the hell's going on in the hole, Miller?"

It was Captain Weinhold, and he had mistaken Coy for Miller. Since Coy was wearing the gun belt, he nonchalantly walked behind the far end of C block, just out of Weinhold's view. The captain was striding down Broadway, and Cretzer was still standing by Carnes and me behind the far end of B block.

Cretzer whispered to us, "Goddamn it, the light must have gone off in the front."

I saw the anger in his face. He blinked his eyes rapidly, and I could see his mind was racing. He said to me, "Ernie, go back. Go back to your cell because the jig is up. It's all fucked up now." He readied the rifle at waist level and turned his back to Carnes and me to wait for Weinhold.

When the captain reached the end of the cellblock, he turned left to go toward D block and was confronted by Coy, who had the .45 aimed directly at him. Cretzer closed in behind.

The Captain could only utter, "What the hell . . ."

Coy told him, "Shut up and start walking!"

They took Weinhold to where the other two guards were locked in on B block. They opened the door and shoved him in as well. A few moments later the front door again opened, and this time Lieutenant Simmons came hustling down Broadway. As he turned left, Coy and Cretzer met him too, and he was quickly locked in with the rest.

By this time the other men had freed the scaffold from the steel screen, but they returned to their cells when they realized that the alarm had been activated. Only Joe Cretzer, Bernard Coy, Marvin Hubbard, Blackie Thompson, Joe Carnes, and I were still out of our cells in the main cell house, and Sam Shockley was still in D block, waiting to see what would happen next. Since he was not part of the escape, he was wondering what the hell was going on. Carnes told me that he was going to ask Coy what he was planning now that the alarm had been sounded. I watched him walk over to C block.

I hadn't gone back to my cell yet, and remained in the same spot at the far end of B block. I was still clinging to some hope that the other guards around the prison were as yet unaware of the events. I figured there was still enough time to place the scaffold under the grille and cut through. My heart sank when I heard the door at the front of the cell house open again. I saw Sundstrum, the records clerk, and Baker, the highly despised mailroom guard, hurrying down Broadway like the other guards before them.

I knew then that there was no use in continuing with the escape plan, and I regretfully returned to my cell. I stayed out long enough to see Sundstrum and Baker captured. I thought for a moment that Coy was going to shoot Baker right on the spot; that's how much he was hated around the Rock for tampering with the men's mail. Coy had personal reasons for hating Baker, and the guard was fully aware of it.

Sometime before, Coy had been appealing his conviction, and was excited because he had some very strong points in his brief. The court of appeals refused even to consider the merits of the brief because it had been filed *one* day late. Everyone in Alcatraz knew that Coy had mailed his brief weeks before the deadline. So when they learned that Coy's appeal had been denied for being late, they were stunned. Coy was crushed; his hopes had been high for winning a reversal and a new trial, and it was hard for him to accept the denial. Later we all learned that Baker had kept the appeal in the mailroom until just before the deadline; he then sent it off, knowing it would not reach the appeals court clerk in time.

Now with Coy pointing a .45 at him, I thought it would be all over for Baker. Luckily for Baker, one of the other men, I think it was Blackie Thompson, shouted at him, "Get in that cell, you fuckin' mail thief!"

Right then Carnes came running back and told me, "Ernie, let's go back to our cells quick. Cretzer told me they're going to sell out. There's nothing we can do now."

So Carnes and I went back to our cells, which were on the far side of B block, facing away from Broadway and toward the unused A block. We tried to slide our doors shut so they would lock. The doors wouldn't engage, no matter how hard we slammed them, because the lockbox still had our cells on the open position. Carnes stepped back out to get one of the others to manually operate the lockbox once we were both inside our cells. He returned and told me that Coy would be coming as soon as he locked in the others. Carnes said that Coy, Cretzer, and Hubbard were still on various tiers, locking in the rest of the men.

Just then we heard the sound of shots being fired into the cell house from the outside. Cretzer was shouting and cursing as the bullets crashed through the windows. Carnes said to me, "Well, it's started now, Ernie. I don't think we're gonna get locked in."

I heard someone shout, "Those bastards are trying to kill us all!" Later I learned that it was Sam Shockley, who had come running scared out of D block. Guards stationed outside the windows were firing wildly and blindly into the isolation block. The gunfire in D block increased and then suddenly stopped long enough for one of the captured guards

to shout, "It's useless for you guys to shoot it out! There'll be reinforce-ments here soon!"

Suddenly the volley of shots started up again with renewed fury. I remember hearing the men in D block hollering their heads off, trying to get the barrage of gunfire to stop. They had had absolutely noth-ing to do with the escape, but they were the most convenient targets for the guards to shoot at without endangering themselves. The cells were completely exposed to the windows, so the men had to take cover by huddling together under mattresses that they piled on top of them-selves as a makeshift shield. Glass and bullets were flying everywhere, with chunks of concrete spraying the cells, and bullets ricocheted off the metal bars and concrete walls.

At that point I heard Shockley yell, "Kill all those motherfuckers!" referring to the guards locked up in the cell. Shockley was a bit loopy at the best of times, and I know he meant nothing by his comment except to express his own rage and fear. A few of the guards began pleading with Coy and Cretzer not to shoot them. I strained to hear what was being said, but right then bullets came crashing through the windows of the main cell house. That seemed to set off the armed prisoners.

The sound of gunfire increased as bullets sprayed into D block and the main cell house simultaneously. The gunfire grew even louder and sounded closer, and I knew it was coming from inside the cell house on the other side of B block. There was no doubt in my mind now that Cretzer and Coy were determined to go down with the ship. At first I thought they were returning the fire of the guards outside, but after the shooting stopped I couldn't hear the slightest noise coming from the Broadway side of B block, when just a moment before the guards had been pleading with Coy and Cretzer to spare their lives.

Carnes spoke to me again in a hushed voice, "Ernie, I think they just blasted the screws."

"Well," I said, "we better brace ourselves, 'cause all hell's gonna break loose."

For the next two and a half days there must have been five thou-sand rounds fired into the cell house. All into the night bullets crashed through the windows and ricocheted off the walls and the steel bars, and it seemed a sure thing that all of us would be killed before it was over.

THE "RIOT" OF '46

Not long after the shooting started, Cretzer unlocked the door leading into the dining room. From there he shot a few rifle rounds at a guard named Levinson, who occupied the gun tower overlooking the yard. Levinson dropped to the floor inside the tower and did not attempt to return fire. Later we learned that he never moved a muscle for almost five hours until other guards took his position in order to shoot into the cell house. Before they climbed Levinson's tower, the guards thought he might have somehow been captured because he never answered the phone, despite their frantic calls. They were surprised and relieved to find him cowering on the tower floor. Levinson himself admitted later that he had been scared to death, and said he wasn't paid enough money to serve as a target for armed prisoners.

The sound of gunfire continued sporadically until early evening. When the shooting tapered off, I could hear the hushed voice of a guard who had managed to enter the cell house undetected. He was saying something to another guard crouched down beside him, and I watched the hunched figures inch their way toward my cell. When they got nearer, I noticed that there were more than two. The first pair wore a type of uniform not familiar to me. As it turned out, they were some of the many guards who had been sent over from San Quentin as reinforcements to help regain control of the prison.

The two guards from Quentin cautiously inched their way toward me. As they neared my cell, I saw that they were both carrying submachine guns. They seemed to pay no attention to me lying on top of my bunk with my head next to the bars. Since my cell door was still

unlocked, I had to press the door closed with my thumb so that it appeared to be securely locked. If the guards found my door unlocked, they would know that I had been involved in the breakout.

The Quentin guards passed in front of my cell just inches from my face, followed by three guards from Alcatraz. As the Alcatraz guards neared my cell, I could see the fear etched on their faces. Their eyes apprehensively scanned the upper tiers in case a prisoner was lying in ambush. I heard a familiar voice whisper hoarsely, "Close in, close in."

It was Deputy Warden Miller—Meathead—giving orders to the guards as he brought up the rear. He kept pushing the guard in front of him forward. None of the guards seemed to pay him any mind, and they continued to inch along in a stooped crouch. They ignored him again when he ordered a couple to run across the corridor and station themselves under the second-tier walkway of A block. He wanted them to provide gun coverage for the rest of the assault team as they approached the far end of B block. Instead, they clung to the edge of B block rather than expose themselves to gunfire. Miller wisely didn't press the issue.

When his head was less than a foot away from mine, Meathead suddenly saw me. He whirled around to face me, then shoved a shotgun into my cell, smashing my face with the cold barrel. He must have thought I would pull my head back or cower. He didn't know that I couldn't budge for fear of letting the door come open. I just took the brunt of the shotgun barrel on my left cheek below the eye and kept my thumb pressed tightly against the door.

He snarled at me, "You bastard, I'll kill you for this! You son of a bitch, I'll kill you!"

Had he discovered my door unlocked, I have no doubt that he would have shot me dead right there and then. He pulled the shotgun out of my cell, muttering, "I'll take care of you later."

I saw the guards reach the far end of B block and then turn the corner in the direction of C block. The question going through my mind was why Miller thought that I was involved. I wracked my brain to retrace my steps, and I remained sure that no guard had seen me out of my cell. Later I learned that Burch had regained consciousness in the gun gallery just as Carnes went searching for Coy to lock us into our cells. When the shooting started, Burch managed to escape through a door in the gun gallery that led to the outside. Miller asked him who was involved, and Burch named all the prisoners he could re-

member. He wasn't sure if he had seen Carnes or me leave our cells, so he told Miller that he had seen me running back to B block just before the shooting started. All of this I would learn in the aftermath of the "riot."

A few minutes after they had turned the corner toward C block, the assault team came back, retracing their route by my cell. They were carrying the guards wounded by gunfire. I saw them bring Captain Weinhold first, then Lieutenant Simmons. They both looked shot up pretty bad, but they were still breathing. Next came Baker, and he was moaning from the pain as they carried him. Finally they brought Sundstrum and the guard from D block, Corwin. All of them had been shot more than once and had lost a lot of blood. As yet I did not see them bring back Miller, the first guard taken hostage.

After the wounded men were removed from C block, one of the guards from the assault team finally thought to check the lockbox for the first tier of B block. He saw it had been tampered with, and he activated the lock-bar into the "deadlock" position, locking Carnes and me in our cells. My thumb was numb from applying constant pressure, and when the door was finally locked, I turned over on my back to rest from the strain.

Later that night I saw many more guards from other prisons: McNeil Island, San Quentin, and Folsom. Apparently Coy, Cretzer, and Hubbard had been driven to take cover somewhere in the cell house, because the guards were running around all over the place. Nobody knew where Cretzer and the others were hiding. Meanwhile, the guards standing on the gunwalks outside the isolation block continued shooting indiscriminately.

The guards had fired first on D block because, as they claimed later, they had received rumors of armed prisoners in the isolation block trying to liberate all the prisoners. For this reason, those of us locked up in the main cell house and hearing the shooting over in D block thought that the guards had gone completely berserk. This was very close to the truth anyway. They would discharge dozens of tear gas bombs into the isolation section, and then, when the smoke was thick and the prisoners were choking and gagging, the guards outside would run up to the windows and fire long bursts of machine-gun fire in every direction. In the end, D block suffered the most damage, though Cretzer and Coy had only gone there briefly to release Whitey Franklin.

All into the night the shooting went on, and it was almost impossible to breathe without inhaling the tear gas that was as thick as the

ocean fog. I lay down on the floor of my cell and covered my face with a wet towel, trying to keep the tear gas from further irritating my already badly burning eyes.

It was now early Friday morning, and the cell house was extremely dark because the guards had not turned on the inside lights. The shooting had stopped for a considerable length of time. I could not hear any noise whatsoever, and it became apparent that all the guards who had sneaked in earlier had left the cell house.

It later came to light that the guards had entered the main cell house thinking that Cretzer and the others were still in D block. This was also the reason why the guards outside were pouring all the lead they could into the isolation section. However, the trio had already made their way in among the pipes and air vents located in the plumbing corridors that ran behind the cells of each block. They had chosen to make their stand in the service corridor of B block near the main entrance. B block was cut in half by an aisle that intersected Broadway. The first section, where the men were hiding in the plumbing corridor, was closest to the main door. I was in the second section of B block, in the first cell next to the cut-off aisle.

The sun still hadn't come up yet. I hadn't been able to sleep a wink because of the gas and the shooting, but neither had any of the other men still in the cell house. The rest of the prisoners were huddled in the yard. They had been given blankets to sleep on until the cell house could be recaptured. During the cold, windy night, the men built fires with whatever pieces of wood they could find in the yard, mostly torn from the long wooden railing that ran along the steps from the cell house to the yard.

When the sun came up, I was able to see the bullet holes in the windows and the spent tear gas shells scattered all over the floor. Then I heard the sound of activity outside the cell house and the murmur of many guards' voices. I couldn't make out their conversations, but I could tell there were an awful lot of them. It was still very quiet in the cell house, and I was beginning to wonder if the trio had been killed or perhaps had managed to escape during the night. Friday was rather quiet the whole day because the guards had no idea where the men were hiding. They were reluctant to come back into the cell house for fear of being ambushed.

Friday night passed. By then I was getting very hungry, and so were the other prisoners in the cell house. Some of them began hollering

to be let out of their cells so they could eat with the prisoners outside. Little did they know that those outside were not being fed either.

When the sun came up Saturday, May 4th, I woke up with a start, trying to get my bearings straight and wondering what the situation had become. Soon I heard the sound of people scurrying around the outside gunwalks, which were at the level of the bottom row of windows. It looked as if they were preparing to provide gun coverage so that some of the other guards could charge into the cell house.

Shortly after, I saw Meathead again with about ten guards from various prisons carefully making their way down the B block corridor where I was celled. I heard a guard tell another that the marines would soon have a grenade launcher available and would be sending it into the cell house. That was the first I learned of the marines being called in to help regain control of the cell house. I watched the guards file past my cell and cautiously advance toward the front of the cell house. I stuck a mirror through the bars so that I could see them when they passed the cut-off aisle.

Some of the guards turned the corner in the direction of C block. After a few minutes I heard a shot, followed by the shout of one of the guards, warning, "They're in there!"

A guard had opened the door to the utility corridor of B block, and one of the prisoners had shot at him. Now that the men had given away their position, the guards swarmed to the area of the plumbing-corridor door, which faced the front entrance of the cell house. The men inside the corridor were hopelessly trapped. It was a stalemate, though, since there was only one entrance to the service corridor. Because the corridor was only four feet wide, it would be impossible for the guards to swarm the men successfully. Only a line of men could go in, and they would be mowed down by gunfire.

The door was opened again, and a guard dashed across the entrance, blasting away with a machine gun. The many pipes along the narrow corridor deflected the bullets before they could hit their targets. The next strategy was to saturate the corridor with tear gas. This had no effect, and it seemed that nothing could drive them out. At this point I saw Meathead come around to a small barred window in the cut-off aisle that looked into the service corridor. Meathead was armed with a shotgun, and I could tell he was going to shoot through the window.

I heard him holler at the men, "You guys better come out of there!"

A few seconds later he fired the shotgun through the opening. At the same time, machine-gun fire was directed down the corridor from the

utility-door entrance. The men were being shot at from both ends of the corridor.

There was a long silence. I figured that they were either dead or too badly wounded to continue fighting. By using a mirror, I could see a guard warily approach the door to the corridor. Suddenly, he jumped for cover as a bullet exploded against the doorjamb next to where he was crouched. It seemed incredible that there could still be anyone alive inside the service corridor after so many rounds of ammunition had been directed at the three men. Later we learned that the men had crawled into a pipe tunnel that burrowed slightly below the cell house floor. This gave them a bit of cover and kept them below the line of fire.

Soon I heard a tremendous explosion that rocked even the second section of B block, where I celled. The explosion was from an anti-tank cannon the marines had brought with them. This was followed by a steady stream of gunfire from every type of handheld weapon the guards had at their disposal.

Another long silence ensued. This surely indicated that the men were now dead.

Finally a guard stuck his head around the corner to peer down the corridor and have a look at the damage. Just then another shot rang out and hit the entrance wall just a few inches from his head. Some of the guards grabbed him to keep him from falling faint to the floor. Things had been so bleak that I actually found this little performance quite comical. The expression on his face showed that the narrow miss nearly scared him to death, and it seemed that he was even having trouble breathing. As the guards helped him to the side of the block, I saw him clutching his hand over his heart, apparently trying to stave off a heart attack. They helped him sit down on the floor with his back against A block, away from the action.

This must have put me in a humorous mood because the next thing that happened I found hysterically funny. Meathead was running around nearly out of his wits. It seemed impossible to get the men out. I saw him finally dash to the cut-off aisle next to my cell, extremely excited because he was armed with a tear-gas-grenade launcher. Careful not to get too close to the barred opening at the rear of the corridor for fear of having the escapees shoot his head off, he approached it at an angle and then let loose with the launcher.

The grenade hit a metal pillar a few feet in front of him and—just as in the cartoons—the projectile bounced back, hitting him on the side of his face. He came running by me holding his hand over his face and

cussing like mad since the very hot projectile had burned his skin. I didn't see him again until the shooting was all over.

It wasn't quite noon when I heard the sound of jackhammers up on top of the cellblock. Above the utility corridor, the marines were drilling holes about fifteen feet apart. When the jackhammers stopped about an hour later, the leathernecks began throwing hand grenades through the holes into the deep recesses of the corridor. Sometime after the explosions ceased, I heard the guards talking among themselves. The men inside had finally been killed. Their bodies were being brought out. Later I learned that the marines had used concussion grenades; shrapnel-type grenades would have been ineffective because of the pipe tunnel angling beneath the corridor floor. It was the force of the explosions, not the shrapnel, that killed the men.

A few hours later, I saw Meathead, his face bandaged, return with numerous guards. He unlocked Carnes's cell and ordered him to step out. As soon as Carnes stepped into the corridor, Meathead and a few others began kicking and hitting him until they knocked him to the floor nearly unconscious. I figured I would be next. But Meathead had found out that Dean Burch had seen Carnes, not me, looking for Coy during the escape attempt. Now the Alcatraz guards were getting their revenge. Carnes was in no shape to put up much of a fight, since he hadn't eaten in almost three days and had gotten at most a few hours sleep. After being soundly beaten, he was taken to D block and put in the dark hole. He told me later that they didn't feed him for another two days.

There was a high stack of stretchers by the entrance of D block because the guards had originally believed that the trio was holed up in the isolation block. After shooting up the section, they assumed that they had killed nearly everybody in there, including the prisoners who had not participated. It was a miracle that only three or four men were slightly wounded; they were quickly treated and locked back up. The prisoners who had been huddled in the yard were returned to their cells, and clean-up crews were put together to remove the spent shells and the shrapnel strewn everywhere about the main cell house and D block.

I expected Meathead to return for me, but after a few hours passed without incident, I felt reassured that I had not been seen outside my cell by any of the guards. Numerous other men involved also were not seen and were never implicated. Some of the guards had recognized Blackie Thompson standing near the cell where the captured guards

had been locked in, so he was implicated. But to illustrate how badly the administration wanted revenge, it charged Sam Shockley with inciting a riot and murder. When the guards outside had gone berserk, blindly shooting up D block, Shockely had run out and shouted, "Kill all the motherfuckers!" after Coy and Cretzer had captured the guards.

The murder charge stemmed from the death of the cell house guard first taken hostage, William Miller, who had been killed when the guards were shot in the cell. As it turned out, a second guard had also been killed, but he had been shot by his fellow guards, who had mistaken him for one of the armed prisoners. His name was Harold Stites, and he had been shot while he was crawling along the upper gunwalk inside the cell house.

Stites had attempted to be a hero when the shooting first began. He had entered the cell house through the outside door that led into the upper gun gallery, the same door Burch had used earlier to escape. Stites was acting on his own and had not told anybody of his intentions. Though he was wearing his uniform, the guards outside had already learned that Cretzer and Coy were wearing guard uniforms. So when they saw a man slithering along the gunwalk, which was visible to the guards outside looking through the windows, they opened fire.

When it was all over, the casualty list was five dead and eight more wounded. Among the prisoners, Coy, Cretzer, and Hubbard had been killed, four others wounded. The guards suffered two men dead—Stites and Miller—and Captain Weinhold, Lieutenant Simmons, Sundstrum, and the much-despised Baker all received severe wounds. Baker suffered especially serious injuries because he had been shot numerous times. Permanently disabled as a result of his injuries, he never did return to work. From then on, the mail service did get better.

The authorities called this incident a riot. During the following weeks and months, many news stories portrayed the events as a large-scale insurrection led by Cretzer and Coy. The prison administration easily manipulated the public and the press into thinking that the guards and the military had put down a riot of bloodthirsty killers after nearly three days of bitter fighting. As the story I have just recounted should illustrate, nothing could have been further from the truth. If anybody rioted, it was the guards who shot indiscriminately at unarmed and defenseless prisoners.

It should also be mentioned that just before the marines started drilling holes through the roof, the navy or coast guard had placed a couple

of destroyers in position with their guns ready to bombard the south side of the island where D block faces the San Francisco wharf. Had they not discovered Cretzer and the others in the utility corridor in B block, they might very well have blown D block—and all the men inside—completely apart.

As it was, many guards thought that everyone in the isolation block was dead when the shooting was over. This is why they had stacked such a large pile of stretchers beside the door. In the weeks that followed, the FBI interviewed all the men who had been inside the cell house when the escape began. Though the agency tried to implicate as many prisoners as possible, it failed to come up with even a single name beyond those of the men the guards had already implicated.

About three months later, Shockley, Thompson, and Carnes were brought to trial at the federal courthouse across the bay. I was Carnes's star witness because I testified that he had withdrawn from the conspiracy before the guards were shot. The prosecution claimed that Carnes, Thompson, and Shockley all witnessed the shooting and that they were active participants or coconspirators. The guards who had been shot lied on the witness stand about Carnes being present. And Corwin could have exonerated Shockley had he told the truth. He knew full well both that Shockley was not in on the escape and that he was just as surprised as the guard when Cretzer and Coy entered D block with weapons drawn. It was also clear to the guard that Cretzer had been trying to liberate only one man, Whitey Franklin, and not the entire block, as the prosecution claimed.

It was just bad luck that Shockley had been mopping the floor when the events took place. The only reason that the poor guy had taken the job in the first place was to get out of his cell for a short while during the day. He had, after all, been locked in isolation for almost five years.

When Coy had thought it possible that the alarm had been set off, he and Cretzer withdrew from the block, taking Corwin with them. Shockley did not go with them, for the simple reason that he had no connection to the escape plan. Only after the isolation block was being shot up did Shockley come running out. He had every reason to believe that if he stayed inside he would be gunned down. The defense explained that in his excitement Shockley had shouted to kill everybody the way a baseball fan would holler "Kill the umpire" during the heat of the moment.

Director Bennett and the others were bent on revenge for the killing of the guards, and they tried their best to implicate as many men as

they could. I was unable to testify for Shockley without incriminating myself. If, as I claimed, I had been in my cell at the time of the events, then I could not have known Shockley's actions. Unfortunately, none of the other men could offer much in his defense, for the same reason.

We had to sit in the courtroom and listen to the guards lie about Shockley's involvement, and then sit helplessly as the jury found him guilty as charged. I at least succeeded in convincing the jury of Carnes's withdrawal, and they gave him the benefit of the doubt when they handed down the sentences. Thompson and Shockley were found guilty of conspiracy and murder, and both were sentenced to death. They were taken to San Quentin, where they were executed in the gas chamber in December 1947. Carnes was sentenced to life imprisonment.

Since the courtroom was jam-packed, U.S. District Judge Louis Goodman made the most of the limelight and the publicity surrounding the trial. He wanted to put on a good show for the public. Besides me, other men testified for the defense. One of them was Thomas Robinson. It was Robinson I had been talking to when the guard Almendares came down on me for supposedly cussing him out. The prosecution claimed that Robbie and I were somehow coaching the witnesses for the defense. Though the charge was completely untrue, and they failed to show any evidence supporting the accusation, I was later made to pay a heavy price for my testimony.

Director Bennett saw to it that I never got transferred to another prison, and made me serve out my entire sentence on Alcatraz. To my knowledge, no other prisoner was set free directly from the Rock. The policy was to transfer the prisoner to a less-restricted prison in an effort to prepare him for eventual release on parole or discharge. The warden made sure that I was frequently harassed and locked up in the hole for trivial rule infractions. On one occasion I was sent to isolation simply on suspicion of inciting a disturbance.

For the rest of the time I was on Alcatraz, I waged my own private war against Bennett and the prison administration by sabotaging the operations of the prison whenever I had the chance. I was determined to make them spend a ton of money just to keep the joint operable. More than any other thing, this single purpose kept me going from day to day and helped me break the deadly monotony that extinguished the spirit of many men. I saw more than one man leave Alcatraz little more than a body without a soul. I would not give up.

"WHAT ABOUT THE PLUM JUICE?"

It became a routine: after the authorities had confined me to isolation for a few weeks, I would retaliate once back in the general population, when the opportunity presented itself. I derived a great deal of pleasure from never being directly linked to the many "accidental" catastrophes that occurred on Alcatraz. To me, that is the true essence of sabotage. Even my fellow prisoners were not aware of the things I was doing, and it amused me to hear them discuss the possible culprits whenever they suspected that one of the deeds was not an accident.

I found myself striking out against anything—or anyone—I disliked. Had I not been such a willing and able worker, I'm sure that I would have spent my entire sentence in the hole. But the authorities had seen that I was capable of working productively whenever I was assigned to any of the industries shops, so they would give me a break on my time in isolation if I would return to work in one of the shops. Usually I ended up assigned to the tailor shop.

On one occasion another prisoner and I had been assigned to paint the inside of the cell house a bright pink, the color it is to this day. On the third day of the assignment, we were standing on a couple of ladders placed on the third tier. The paint was in a large water pail that hung by a thick wire from the rungs of my ladder. We were trying to reach the very top bars of the cell house. By now, Saltwater Johnston had been replaced as warden by a man named Edwin Swope, who had a very high-pitched voice and sounded just like a woman. The men had a good time making fun of his voice and the way he would come around, slap us on our backs, and ask, "And how are you doing, my boy?" He

wanted us to paint the cell house the bright pink color, which I thought was a silly choice.

While I was standing on the ladder, George Dillon rounded the corner of the third tier, carrying a pile of library books stacked on a large piece of plywood. Since he had ratted on me about the McNeil escape and had tried to blame me for hurting the guard Harris, I considered him a rat. I had already warned Dillon to stay away from me, not even to speak to me.

As he neared the ladders, he said in a loud voice, "Ha, ha, ha, I wonder what would happen if I bumped this ladder?"

He tried to act as if he were talking to the other guy, but I knew goddamn well he was talking to me. When he walked directly below me, I unhooked the paint pail and turned it upside down, dumping the whole can of paint on his bald head. Just for good measure, I let the pail drop on him.

With his outstretched arms holding the books, Dillon was unable to do anything. He stumbled along the tier for a couple of steps and finally placed the books down. When he took the pail off his head, I saw the pink paint running down his face and dripping to the floor. He looked like a pink candle that had melted at the top, but I was too angry to laugh.

Dillon said, "Goddamn it, Ernie, if I knew you did that on purpose, I'd kick the shit out of you."

I jumped from the ladder onto the tier and started banging away at Dillon with both fists. Then I pushed him to the railing of the tier, picked him up, and rolled him over. He just barely managed to grab hold of the railing and avoid falling three stories to the concrete floor below. I continued hitting him in order to break his hold.

Finally, some guards came running to his rescue. From the second tier they were hollering at him, "Hold on, Dillon, hold on!"

When they were directly below us, they grabbed his dangling legs and pulled him onto the second tier. When I stopped to think about it afterward, my biggest surprise was that the guard in the rear gun gallery had not shot me during the fight. Evidently he couldn't find an open shot that would have avoided hitting Dillon.

On the other hand, he might not have viewed the situation as very serious until Dillon was hanging over the third-tier railing. By then the other guards were already running to his aid. When it was all over, nobody was hurt, though Dillon did receive a few lumps. Of course I was taken directly to the hole, where I stayed for twenty-nine days. When I

came out, the fight was still the talk of the joint because of how Dillon had looked with all the pink paint covering his head.

Not too long after this, I was again sent back to the hole. This time I was sentenced to twenty-nine days in the dark hole and three months more in an open D block cell. If there was one thing that Alcatraz could accomplish with ease, it was to create a sense of tension that seemed always to ripple like an undercurrent, just below the surface. Many times fistfights broke out among the men because of seemingly trivial matters. The springs of violence were always wound tight, and it didn't take a whole lot to cause them to uncoil.

This was the case when I had a falling-out with a man named Benjamin Williams, a bank robber from Sacramento who had also tried to escape from McNeil. Before our trouble began, I had taken an interest in his case because the committing judge had handed down an illegal sentence totaling twenty-four years. As I mentioned, after my experience with the lawyer who defended me on the gas stamp charges, I had taken to learning as much as possible about the law on my own. Williams had been charged on two separate indictments with identical charges for two separate bank robberies. Each indictment specified two violations of the law. However, I noticed that one of the sentences on each charge was illegal, and I advised him to file a writ of *habeas corpus*. He told me that he didn't know how, so I prepared the writ for him and filed it with the court.

A few months later, he received word that ten years had been knocked off his sentence. Because I helped him, it is strange that a beef developed between us. This just demonstrates how Alcatraz could so distort reality for most prisoners that common sense and reason failed to guide their actions. A trivial matter sparked the incident, but I recall the fierce rage that quickly boiled to the surface when the falling-out took place.

We were eating breakfast one weekday morning; soon we would return to our cells to pick up our work jackets. Every morning before breakfast the kitchen staff would set a large pot of hot coffee and a large thermos of coffee at the end of several tables; these were for refilling the coffeepots as they emptied. Each table held ten men, five to a bench on each side. That morning I was seated in the middle, opposite a good friend of mine, Mike Strignano. I asked Mike to pass me the coffeepot, but when he reached for it, he realized it was empty. It was common practice for the man seated at the end of the table by the thermos to refill the coffeepot and then pass it down to whoever wanted more

coffee. This was a courtesy—really, more of a rule—that we had established because it was very difficult for someone sandwiched between two other men to get the coffee without disturbing everybody else on the bench.

Benjamin Williams was seated at the end of the table, close to the thermos. Mike turned to him to see if he would fill up the pot, but Williams just stared down into his plate.

Mike turned to me and said, "This guy acts like he's afraid to get up to fill the coffeepot."

After a bit he added, "He never wants to get up. He does this all the time."

That remark brought a quick response from Williams, who just seconds before had appeared to be in a deep daydream.

"Fuck you, Mike!"

Mike told Williams to fuck himself as well.

I decided to intervene, since I was the one who had asked for the coffee in the first place. I told Williams not to get excited and just pass the coffee down before we were all ordered to leave the dining room. Then he said, "Fuck you, too!" and whipped off his glasses, indicating he wanted to fight. As I sat there, rage and frustration welled up in me. That expression "seeing red" is a pretty apt description of how I felt.

I had enough control to tell him, "Look, you son of a bitch, you act pretty brave in here where there's bulls all over the place. Let's see how tough you are when we get back to the cell house."

Breakfast was over a few moments later, and I had still not gotten my coffee. I wouldn't have taken it at that point even if he had suddenly decided to pass the pot down. As we filed back into the cell house, I could feel the hair on the back of my neck standing up. I knew nothing was going to stop me from trying to use Williams to wipe the cell house floor.

He was up ahead of me, and arrived at his cell before I had finished climbing the stairs to the third tier. As I approached his cell, he stood by his opened doorway and rolled a cigarette. When I got to him, I suddenly reached out and gathered up the front of his shirt tight around his neck, pushing him into his cell. I let loose with a straight right that knocked him against the rear wall of his cell. I followed up with three more quick punches, then turned to leave before I got locked in his cell. Just as I was about to step out, Williams managed to lunge at me and pull me back inside by my shirt. At that moment the cell door slammed shut.

Being found in another man's cell was akin to high treason. There were few worse infractions one could commit.

Even angrier now, I spun around, ducking a punch Williams threw. I fired him up with every punch I knew how to throw. Blood flew from his nose and mouth with each blow I landed, and the walls of his cell were getting splattered with flecks of his blood. Finally he collapsed in a heap on the floor. I had to stay in his cell for about another minute before the door opened to permit the prisoners to go work. As I walked toward my cell, Mike was waiting for me with my work jacket in his hand. I put it on and went to the industries.

About three hours later, while I was still at work, two guards came into the shop and told me to go with them. I was escorted back into the cell house and led directly to D block. I was again placed in the dark hole. After about an hour, the outside door of the hole opened, and a lieutenant stepped toward the bars of my cell.

"That was a rotten thing you did." He stared at me for a response.

I told him that I didn't know what he was talking about or why I was in the hole. He said, "You know what I'm talking about—jumping on that guy while he was taking a shit."

Now I *really* didn't know what he was talking about, but I still had to be careful how I answered. I told him that if he thought I had jumped on somebody, he should have a doctor examine my knuckles and fingers and the rest of my body, which is the first thing they usually do when they suspect a person of being in a fight. When they didn't examine me before locking me in the hole, I knew that they had very little evidence except Williams's word. Nevertheless, a few days later I was brought before a disciplinary committee and found guilty of assaulting an inmate. In addition to sentencing me to four months in the isolation block, they took away 120 days of good-time credit that I had earned over the years.

At the hearing they again made reference to the fight as a low-down thing, and I couldn't for the life of me figure out what they were talking about. It was after I had been in isolation for about two months that I finally learned what the guards had meant. Williams had evidently lost control of his sphincter after I had knocked him nearly unconscious to the floor. Embarrassed, he had spread the story that I had jumped him while he was sitting on the toilet. But the cons nearby had seen the incident from beginning to end, and they knew full well that I had pushed him into his cell after he had been standing outside.

Harry Knight, who celled next to Williams, was unassigned, so he

had stayed in his cell after we went to work. Moments after the fight, Harry heard moaning coming out of Williams's cell. Harry knew we had been fighting next door, and he thought that perhaps Williams was hurt pretty bad. He used a small mirror to look into Williams's cell.

He asked Williams if he was all right, and watched him for a response. Williams picked himself up in a daze and sat down on his bunk. When he sat, he realized that he had defecated, so he stood up and removed his coveralls, and that was when Harry noticed that Williams's legs were covered with shit. Word of what Knight had seen got around to me while I was still in the hole.

Some of my more loyal friends were putting pressure on Williams to tell the warden that I was not the guy who had assaulted him. They were angry because Williams had ratted on me—although he vehemently denied it to everyone—and because of the story he had made up about being jumped while taking a crap. At any rate, Williams would not make a statement, so the men took a more drastic approach to cell house justice. They made plans to kill him.

Williams knew the score, and he somehow convinced the warden that his life was in danger. Shortly after, he was transferred to another prison on the mainland. When a person fears for his life, he can become very crafty. Labeled a rat, Williams knew that his life was in danger even in a new prison. He managed to avoid being killed by not leaving his cell except for meals. When he did come out, he made sure he was in full view of an armed guard on the gunwalk.

When I returned to the general population, I was informed of all the intrigue. Harry Knight couldn't wait to tell me himself what he had seen.

He said, "Ernie, have you ever heard of a guy getting the shit kicked out of him?"

I could see that he was enjoying himself, and I just smiled back at him.

"Well, I'll tell you. I put that mirror on Williams when you went to work, and that guy had blood and shit all over the place."

Then he shook with laughter. "Hey, Ernie, you really knocked the shit out of him!"

Harry had told that story to everyone, and for a long time the men used to kid me about it to no end. "Hey, there goes Ernie," they would say. "You better watch him, 'cause he'll really knock the shit out of you." They would howl with laughter.

As for Williams, the damage had already been done. Even though he

had avoided death on the Rock, he was still pegged as a rat, and such a reputation follows a convict wherever he goes. Shortly after his release on parole, he was found dead in a cave outside Reno, Nevada, with a bullet in his head. No suspects were ever arrested.

Not long after I came out of the hole, the tension that had already led to sudden eruptions of furious violence among the men steadily increased. After being away four months, I could feel the tension even more strongly. The joint was a ticking time bomb, though to an untrained eye it might have looked perfectly peaceful.

Meathead Miller had been replaced by a deputy warden named Paul J. Madigan. He tried to make friends with the men by promising them everything. He quickly earned the nickname "Promising Paul" because no matter what the complaint, he always "promised" to look into the matter. Of course, he never did. The men were running out of patience, and soon tired of all of his false promises about improvements. The tension felt like electricity in the air before a lightning storm. The guards were aware of it too, and began to feel uneasy. A number of them were outwardly fearful, perhaps remembering similar tension before the "riot" of '46. When such an atmosphere pervades a confined and rigid structure like Alcatraz, it leads to paranoia. All of us, prisoners and guards, were wondering what was going to happen next.

At times like these, the men seemed to exercise greater caution. They became more polite and considerate to one another. There was no problem getting someone to pass the thermos of coffee or perform some similar courtesy. To refuse was to light a match to a gas tank or set off a spark in a dry forest. Sometimes, certain small acts of defiance served to relieve the pent-up emotions, almost as if the men were trying to stave off an explosion of their own. That seemed to be the case when the prisoners selected the food as a target of their frustrations.

During each meal, a team of guards positioned themselves in the wide center aisle that separated the long rows of tables. It was their duty to supervise the dining area and the steam tables and to ensure that no extra rations were taken. Among the guards, there was usually a lieutenant who stood in the most prominent spot, looking very stern with his hands folded formally behind his back. Often this lieutenant was joined by the captain of the guards, the deputy warden, and—whenever the urge struck him—the warden.

These occasions were a sight to behold: the three top brass trying to outdo each other in standing the straightest and looking the stern-

est. They stood as if they were gods overlooking their divine empire, defying anyone to disrupt the order of things as they stared across the dining hall at the 270 men seated at the tables. We used to call them the Big Three.

I recall how the sight of them standing so pompously would cause a feeling of deep resentment to swell within me. But I was aware of the all-too-present armed guards patrolling the gunwalks just outside the dining room windows. I would control my anger and resentment before they might cause me to do something dangerous. I knew the other men felt the same way, and that created a common bond during times of stress or tension. We showed our disgust for the guards, the food, and the institution in many ways without bringing about any violent retribution. The most impressive and successful actions, I thought, were those that occurred without any planning whatsoever.

One such occasion occurred when the kitchen served something the menu called "hamburger." Whatever it was, it crumbled apart at the slightest touch, revealing an inside that looked like very fine and dry sawdust. It tasted even worse than it looked, so the men would not eat it. Then an old diversionary trick was used. A man on one side of the dining room suddenly made a loud noise by slamming his metal cup on top of the table. This caused the already paranoid guards to jerk their heads in the direction of the sound.

Just as the guards turned their heads, the men on the other side of the dining room quickly threw the sawdust patties on the floor near the feet of the guards. These landed without a sound. When the guards looked back to the other side of the room, they were confronted by an aisle full of sawdust hamburger. When they tried to see who was responsible for throwing the food, the men on the other side threw their portions of sawdust at the same spot.

Now the center aisle was covered with hamburger, and the guards quickly huddled together to decide what to do. Finally, the lieutenant announced that the meal was over and that all the men were to return to the cell house. Everyone complied without a sound, quickly filing back into the cell house for lock-up.

For what it's worth, the incident allowed the men to let off a little steam rather harmlessly. It provided some much-needed laughter for the prisoners, but it left the guards spooked. Promising Paul continued to make promises, but no changes in the food ever came about, and the other deplorable conditions remained the same.

The prisoners became more determined to show their dissatisfac-

tion, but there was no organized effort to stage a protest or make a stand. The men just had a common feeling that something had to be done. This set the stage for the next dining-room incident.

I recall that we had just returned from the industries shops and were filing into the dining room for lunch. Everyone seemed to be rather weary, and most definitely hungry, as we grabbed our trays and received our portions. We watched in disgust as the food was slopped onto our trays. Our lunch consisted of only two items: dry white noodles and plum juice. The noodles looked as if they had been dipped in a vat of Elmer's glue and left to dry in the sun.

As I left the steam table to sit down, I noticed that those who had been served before me had not started eating. They were looking at their trays in disbelief. I sat down and waited to see if anyone was going to eat. Meanwhile, the dining room filled up. All the prisoners were obviously as disgusted as I was. I sat at my table and contemplated the idea of dumping the entire tray onto the floor, and others must have had the same idea. As I sat there, I was startled by a loud crash. This was immediately followed by another, and then another, and the crashes continued. I looked across the dining room to see where the noise was coming from.

The rear tables had been overturned, and the tables in front of them were in the process of being tipped over also. One by one the tables were sent crashing to the floor like a row of dominoes. When the entire left side of the dining room had finished dumping their tables, the right side started doing the same. The men overturned the remaining tables one by one, making a deafening clatter, until every table in the dining room had been tipped over. The floor was covered with trays, and the noodles and plum juice were spattered everywhere. The men, all standing, looked around at the upended tables and the mess on the floor.

At the first crash the guards had all run to the rear of the dining hall by the steam tables, expecting a riot. But the men just stood by their tables before slowly walking over to the side walls. The outside gunwalk guards were having fits, and it was difficult to tell what exactly they were doing. From where I stood, it looked as if at least one of them was frantically looking for a way to jump off his gunwalk and flee. After a few moments, it was evident that there was not going to be any violence, and the guards settled down some.

We were finally ordered to return to our cells, and the men cooperated without any hesitation. Later that afternoon, one by one the men were interviewed by teams of the prison brass. The warden wanted to

know what had caused such an outbreak. Late that afternoon I was finally escorted down to an area where the warden and the captain were seated behind a desk, conducting their investigation.

I sat down in a chair across from Warden Swope and listened to his high-pitched feminine voice asking me what had happened. I told him that I didn't know exactly, except that all of a sudden the tables went over.

Swope asked, "Well, why would the men want to overturn the tables?"

That was a rather stupid question, I thought, but I decided to give him an answer and get it over with so that I could return to my cell. I said, "Look, Mr. Swope. You know the food's pretty bad, and the men have been complaining about it for a long time now."

Swope stared back at me as if I had insulted him personally. "What's wrong with the food?"

I thought for a second and said, "Well, the noodles were in pretty bad shape. You can see that for yourself."

He leaned forward for emphasis and, with his voice climbing, shrieked, "And what about the plum juice?!" As if the plum juice had been a delicious treat.

I honestly had to fight myself for control in order not to break out laughing. I managed to answer, "Well, I don't know . . . it seems that the plum juice went over with the noodles."

That was the end of the interview. Swope turned away and motioned for the guards to take me away. The prison had returned to normal by that evening, and by the weekend we were enjoying cracking jokes about the incident while out in the yard.

One of the warden's more memorable lines turned out to be one that I told the men he had said during the investigation: "What about the plum juice?" And the men roared whenever someone mimicked Swope asking the question.

The food remained one of the major problems the men faced daily, and I figured if it didn't improve soon, there would be trouble. The prison grew increasingly tense, and by this time there were prisoners actively involved in organizing the convict population to force the issue.

By this time, the kitchen workers had grown very dissatisfied with their work on account of a guard by the name of Mitchell, who had come to Alcatraz in 1955. He weighed about 300 pounds and was a World War II hero who had seen a lot of action. Because of this, they

gave him a job in the cell house, which was a big promotion, be-cause usually the guards started out in the tower and worked their way through the system until they were finally assigned the cell house. Right away he got a big notebook and started writing down changes he wanted to make in the way the place was run. He wanted to whip the whole cell house into shape.

When he got to the kitchen, he started making new rules that really upset the crew. Workers now couldn't smoke in the kitchen area, not even in the storage room. The men were no longer allowed to use the showers located in the kitchen basement. One of the benefits of work-ing in the kitchen had long been that the workers could take their showers apart from the general population. Mitchell did away with this privilege, forcing the kitchen crew to shower with the rest of the men. Once one man finished his assigned job, he was now required to go help another worker rather than knock off for the day. Men were no longer allowed to eat in the kitchen with the rest of the crew. They had to take their meal out to the dining room and eat with the general population. All the little privileges that had made working in the kitchen desirable were now against the new rules Mitchell imposed.

Mitchell wrote out his rules on a large notice that he posted promi-nently in the kitchen area. The notice also said that if any man did not want to work under those conditions, he could request another job or just lay in. This was the last straw. All the kitchen workers decided that they would refuse to serve any more food until the working conditions changed and the food improved. This happened on a Friday morning, and when we went to the dining room for breakfast, we all filed past the empty steam tables and took our seats.

Within minutes Madigan arrived on the scene to appraise the situa-tion. Because it appeared that only the kitchen workers were involved in this little uprising, Madigan took the soft approach and tried to act like an understanding father. He promised the kitchen workers that there would be no reprisals if any of them wanted to quit working in the kitchen, but that first he wanted them to put in a request slip. He would see to it that the next day they would be unassigned. In the meantime, they would have to serve the men their breakfast, lunch, and supper. This was met with approval by the kitchen crew, and the prison routine proceeded as usual for the rest of the day.

By noontime several unassigned prisoners who were laying in had been approached by the guards and offered a job in the kitchen. It be-came apparent that Madigan was planning to break the strike. Under

normal circumstances, the men would have jumped at the chance to have a job, but because of the organized effort to strike, the men turned down the offers. Madigan had figured that he would simply replace the dissatisfied workers with unassigned prisoners and that things would get back to normal. His plan was foiled when the men who were laying in refused to work.

After the evening meal, the kitchen workers washed the pots and pans, silverware and trays, and swept and mopped the floor before returning to the cell house to lock up. The prison had a standard form for requesting an interview to lodge a complaint. The form had space for the prisoner to state the nature of his request: an interview with the warden, job change, cell change, etc. After the prisoner completed the slip of paper, he placed it on the bars in front of his cell. A guard would pick up the forms and take them to the appropriate authority for the specific request. That evening the entire kitchen crew requested to be unassigned, and the prison was left without anyone to cook or serve the food.

At six on Saturday morning, the deputy warden and his henchmen came into the cell house and walked down Broadway to the area called "Kitchen Row," where the kitchen workers were housed. Normally, by 5:30 a.m. all of kitchen row was busy preparing breakfast and performing other chores around the cooking area. This morning was another matter. The warden had come in early to try to arrange for some temporary workers until he could reassign the positions to other men who might want to work. But this was a very well-organized strike, and the warden was unsuccessful in recruiting even one man.

Breakfast was an hour late, and had to be cooked by the stewards who, along with a few guards, supervised the prisoners in the kitchen. Breakfast was served by the guards. When the meal was over, it was the guards who swept and mopped the dining room after the men had gone back to the cell house. Lunch and supper were handled in the same fashion, and by that evening the guards were grumbling among themselves, saying that they had not been hired to perform kitchen duties.

Come Sunday morning, Madigan changed his tactics and revoked his previous promise that there would be no reprisals against kitchen workers who requested a transfer. This really came as no surprise to the men, since Madigan had never made good on any of his promises. Attempts were made to force the men to go to work. The guards would bodily pick up the prisoners assigned to the kitchen and carry them to the dining hall.

"Go ahead, guy," the bulls would say, "Go to work." The men would just lie on the floor and not move a muscle.

When it became apparent that they were not going to work, the warden ordered them locked in the hole. This continued throughout the day and into the evening, when the last of the kitchen workers had been removed from the main cell house and taken to D block. Word passed among the prisoners in the main cell house that because of the reprisals taken against the kitchen crew, the rest of the population would not return to their jobs on Monday. By Sunday evening, all the prisoners on Alcatraz Island were officially on strike.

Monday morning the population went to breakfast, which was again prepared by the prison employees, and returned to their cells as usual to pick up their work jackets. Except this morning all the prisoners lay down on their bunks and got comfortable when the bell rang to signal work call. Every man in the cell house ignored it. When the guards saw that the men were not coming out for work call, they locked the cells back up and notified the deputy warden. Madigan was on the spot in minutes, and when sufficient reinforcements arrived, he instructed the guards to carry the prisoners out to the yard where they normally lined up for work.

They began carrying men out one by one from the first section of C block. The entire section was out on the yard, lying down where the guards had dropped them. The men refused to move when ordered to go to work, and they continued to lie on the ground. So the warden ordered them all taken to D block. When the men reached the isolation block, they found the door already open and waiting for them. D block, including the six dark holes, was built to hold forty-five men, and it wasn't long before the block filled up. That didn't stop the warden. He continued with his plan of having the men carried out, ordering them to work, and then dumping them in the hole. Soon enough I heard my cell door click open.

One of the prisoners asked, "Whose cell are they at?"

Another one answered, "They've got Ernie's open."

The first guy said, "Oh no, not again. The poor son of a bitch is always going to the hole."

I pulled my cell door open so that I could look down the tier and see what was going on. When I stuck my head out, a guard motioned for me to step out. He said, "Come this way. We want to see you for a minute."

I walked to the end of the tier, where there were several guards wait-

ing. As soon as I approached, I was told to walk to isolation. Entering D block, I was ordered to strip off my coveralls, undershirt, and socks. I was placed in the dark hole in just my shorts for three days, and then locked up in an open cell.

I was followed by other prisoners whom the warden deemed trouble-makers or key organizers of the strike. I saw them bring in Alvin Karpis —he was Public Enemy Number One back with the notorious Barker-Karpis gang—and he was placed in one of the dark holes. It was apparent that there wasn't going to be enough room in the isolation block to handle all the men involved in the disturbance.

About this time I heard all hell break loose in the main cell house. The men were banging the bars of their cells and hollering at the top of their lungs. After a few seconds, the men in D block joined in. Soon the entire prison population was participating in the most memorable jamboree that the Rock ever experienced. Mattresses were set on fire, covers were thrown onto the tier, and the whole population joined in the strike. The guards continued to bring in prisoners, and by the end of the day D block had anywhere from five to six men in each of the cells. Over half the prison population was crammed into the isolation block.

The deafening noise did not cease for even a moment. The clamor continued all night and into the next day, when more prisoners were brought into isolation. We were packed in like sardines because almost all of the population was now in D block. Although we were all locked in, it was still pure bedlam inside the prison. The noise actually became louder when many of the men managed to break the steel bunks away from the angle irons they were welded to. By stomping on the loose steel slabs against the iron fixtures, the men were able to create an enormous racket that seemed to shake the foundation of the prison.

There were now eight men in the cell I occupied. By then, the guards had turned off the steam radiators and opened all the windows and vents, which are no more than forty or fifty feet from the cells. The blowing wind and frigid salt air permeated the block. The cells did not have a mattress or a single blanket, and by evening it was miserably cold. It felt like an icebox. All of us in D block had been stripped down to our shorts so that we would feel the effects of the cold more intensely. We were growing colder and colder as the San Francisco sea air blew in. We took to huddling together and hugging each other in an attempt to keep each other warm with our body heat. We even unhooked the linoleum flooring and rolled it up, wrapping it around ourselves to try to keep warm. Two or three men at a time would take turns wrapped in the linoleum flooring.

In the meantime, the noise never abated, not even for an instant. When some of the men grew hoarse or tired or managed to doze off, others took their place. Working in shifts like that, we managed to keep the din going twenty-four hours a day.

For the first four days, nobody ate any food. Our single daily meal consisted of three slices of bread and a cold mush of ground spinach, carrots, beets, and potatoes served in a small paper cup. We used to call this "shit in a cup." When we were served this revolting meal, the men would eat the bread and, on the count of three, throw their cups against the far wall of the block and resume the noisemaking. Eventually the guards got a little bit smarter, and they started giving us the cup of mush first. If we didn't want the cup, we had to return it in order to get the three slices of bread. Well, they pretty much had us then, since the bread was the only edible part of the meal. Nevertheless, we continued making noise day after day after day.

Most of the guards lived on the island with their families, and word got back to us that the children couldn't sleep at night because of all the racket. Many of the children caught the ferryboat half-asleep in the morning when they had to go to school.

Since the administration would not permit newsmen on the island, we found it difficult to get word out to the public about the general situation on the Rock. There was a ferryboat specifically chartered to tour people around the perimeter of the island. Normally in D block we could hear the tour conductor talking through a loudspeaker. On our way to work in the industries area, we could often hear the tour conductor describing us as the most dangerous men in America. We used to call this boat the *Rubberneck* because we imagined the passengers, who were usually tourists to the San Francisco area, stretching their necks to get a good look at the prison and the "most dangerous men in America" as we made our way down the steps from the yard to the shops.

It was our plan to make such a terribly loud noise when the boat neared the island that the passengers couldn't help but know that the prison was experiencing some kind of serious disorder. It was our hope that word of the disturbance would then spread and, hopefully, cause an investigation into the conditions at the prison. So during the jamboree, when a voice would holler out, "Here comes the *Rubberneck!*" the volume of noise would become deafening.

I still don't know if they were ever able to hear us, but it would be a small wonder if they couldn't. The noise continued for forty days and nights without stop. Finally, a lieutenant came into the block to inform

us that the prison had received word from Washington. They were to "make some concessions," and soon after we were released from isolation in small groups and allowed to shower and return to our old cells in the main cell house.

Approximately a week later, either by coincidence or design, Congress passed a bill to issue all federal prisons some of the surplus food that had been stockpiled to the rafters in warehouses across the country. From that time on, we were fed such unheard-of luxuries as eggs, cheese, butter, milk, assorted cold cuts, and — for some absurd reason — an endless amount of strawberry and apricot preserves. This sure beat the three slices of bread and the cup of ground carrots and spinach we had had to eat as our daily meal. Now we had real food!

When the prison resumed normal operations, we were greatly delighted with the change of menu. All the men had lost a considerable amount of weight after years of enduring the same monotonous and awful food. But the food strike paid off. The Rock finally gave in and fed its specially selected prisoners a decent meal and, in the process, found a very simple solution to most of the prison's problems. Tension and hostility disappeared. From that point in 1955 until Alcatraz closed its doors for good in 1963, there was never another serious incident that involved the whole prison population.

At the Preston School of Industry, Ione, California, 1936. Dressed for parade marching, Ernie is the cadet without a jacket, *right.*

In Los Angeles after Ernie's release from Preston, 1937. *Left to right:* Ernie, his brothers Sal and Bob, and their father, seated.

Ernie dressed up for a night out in Los Angeles, 1940s.

Ernie and Freddy González (?) on their junior high football team, c. 1937.

Ernie, 1960s.

Ernie with a friend, 1980s.

Ernie, 1982.

Ernie visited by friends Frank Telles, *left,* and Charlie Johnson, Vacaville state prison, 1989.

MY LIFE AS A FREE MAN

As I stated before, I never got a transfer from Alcatraz, because I served as a witness for Clarence Carnes. As a result, James Bennett, director of federal prisons, hated me and took my testimony as a personal affront. But I never went to talk to that bastard about seeking a transfer, as all the other men received, and I waited for my release from Alcatraz.

Bennett had been the director of all federal prisons since 1937, and I soon learned he had a vendetta against me. The first time that I knew he had it in for me personally was when he visited the prison with Warden Swope. Swope was from New Mexico, and he spoke Spanish pretty well, a fact I learned because he sometimes spoke with me a little in Spanish.

On this particular day, Swope brought Bennett down to the tailor shop where I worked; he wanted to show off the most productive industries to impress the bigwigs. I was working the double-needle sewing machine at the time, and Swope recognized me and brought Bennett over. Swope was always trying to make it seem that he was real chummy with the prisoners, I think to prove that he had the prison under control. He came over, patted my back, and in his thin, reedy voice offered his customary greeting: "How're you doing, my boy?" Then to Swope he said, "This is Ernie López. He's been working here in the shop quite a while. He's a very good worker."

He was talking up my skills, talking about this and that, when Bennett took off like a jackrabbit. He didn't want to be anywhere near me. The funny thing was that Swope didn't even notice that Bennett was

gone. He was still talking away, unaware that Bennett had hightailed it out of there. But because of Bennett, I never did get parole.

I was finally released from Alcatraz in 1956, on conditional release. By law, if a prisoner managed to stay out of trouble while he was doing time, he earned credits of ten days for every month served. If he got in trouble for any reason, they could take some of that credit away. But I had earned enough credits to get out. Now thirty-four years old, I had spent eleven years in Alcatraz. Little did I know then about the trouble I would soon find myself in, but even less did I suspect how much those years in Alcatraz would keep coming back and making my life difficult.

The first time that I was haunted by Alcatraz came very soon after my release. My wife had divorced me while I was in Alcatraz, so I took a room alone in a duplex that sat on a narrow block where two streets came together in North Hollywood. At the very point of the block was a gas station where I made phone calls, since I didn't have a phone of my own.

As luck would have it, a pretty spectacular bank robbery took place in West Covina soon after I moved in. Two masked men had gone into a bank, waving a machine gun around. They robbed the tellers and took money from the vault before escaping. Nobody got hurt, but the robbery was a daring daylight job, so the newspapers splashed the story, including a rough sketch of the masked robbers, all over the front page. At the time, some joker was going around saying that one of the bandits in the drawing looked like my friend Joe Morgan and that the other one looked like me.

It didn't take too long at all before the authorities heard these rumors, which became innuendo and finally—in their minds—fact. I became a possible suspect. The local FBI and the LAPD knew that I had just been released from Alcatraz, and they were itching to catch me doing something that would send me back behind bars. They were hoping to clear the books on the bank robbery, but they had no leads. So the easiest thing for them to do was to pin the blame on me.

When they finally did get around to arresting me, they made a huge production out of it in order to make themselves look good. On the day I was arrested, I was walking to the gas station to make a phone call. A swarm of officers descended on me. The operation had been set up because a fellow by the name of Robert Castillo Luna had told the cops where I lived. I found out too late that Luna already had a long

history as a police informant, one that would end up getting me into even deeper trouble down the line.

I first met Robert Luna at his sister's apartment in Los Angeles, near Washington and Normandy. Luna was living there at the time. Joe Morgan and I had gone over because Joe had agreed to meet a business partner at the apartment. We walked up to the second-story apartment and were let in. A group that included Luna and his brother was sitting in the kitchen and talking about some deal that had to do with cocaine. We were introduced to everyone, and Luna's brother wanted to continue their conversation in another room so that we could be left alone in the kitchen. Considering the topic of conversation, I didn't think there was anything particularly wrong with this. I didn't know these guys from Adam, and they certainly didn't know me. But Robert Luna told his brother that if they were going to talk, they were going to talk in front of me, or he wasn't going to listen. Luna apparently had heard about me, and he told his brother that I could be trusted. The two brothers finally settled down to discuss business in the kitchen, Joe spoke with the guy he had come to see, and I thought nothing more about it.

Sometime later, I ran across Luna again when I happened into a cocktail lounge called The Airliner. I had walked in late at night to make a call and use the restroom, and as I was leaving, he and his girlfriend called me over. She was a very good-looking girl who said she was from Colorado. I told her that I had just been to Denver, and she asked me where I had stayed.

"The Ritz," I told her.

She said, "Oh, big spender" and smiled. I don't know what Ritz she was thinking about, but the only classy thing about the dump I stayed in was its name. We chatted like that for a while, but I had no interest in remaining there. When I left, they followed me out and asked if I could give them a ride home. I had heard by then that the authorities were looking for me in connection with the West Covina bank robbery, so I didn't really want Luna to know the kind of car I was driving—which was a nice little brand-new Plymouth. There was nothing I could do without looking suspicious, so I had no choice but to drive the two home.

They asked me first to drop off Luna's girlfriend, who lived on North Broadway. I parked right in front of the house. Luna opened the car door and took her by the arm, telling me he would be right back. He

guided her into the dark house while I sat in the car. I waited and waited, and finally got fed up and tooted the horn. Sometime after that Luna finally came out. He told me some story about how they had had a fight, and that was why he had taken so long.

It was getting late, and I wanted to get home, so I headed down the Harbor Freeway to take him home. As we were driving along, Luna all of a sudden asked me to drop him off at the corner of Normandy and Washington rather than take him all the way to the apartment. I figured he wanted a hamburger because there was a little stand there at the corner.

I dropped him off and he walked away. As I was turning into the parking lot to turn around and get back on the freeway, I decided to get a cup of coffee for the long drive back to North Hollywood. When I walked to the front of the stand, I found, to my surprise, that Luna wasn't there. I then went around the corner to a side street where I saw Luna in a telephone booth. He was talking on the phone, looking nervously over his shoulder every now and then. When he saw me, he slammed down the receiver. I didn't know whom he was talking to or why he seemed so nervous (and didn't really think that much about it at the time), but I soon found out who was on the other end of the line.

On a warm June morning in 1956 I went to make a phone call at the gas station. Immediately I could sense that I was being followed. As I was walking toward the gas station, which was on the narrow edge of the knife-wedge block, I could hear a car rolling slowly across the gravel and the ping of pebbles hitting the fenders. I didn't want to turn around and appear suspicious, so I kept walking, looking for possible escape routes. At the gas station ahead of me, I spotted a car. Four men with hats sat in it, two in front and two in back. It was so obvious that they were agents that I found it funny. When they saw me looking at them, they all turned away or slumped down in their seats. Now I actually laughed.

Just as I got to the gas station driveway, the car that had been following me rolled up onto the sidewalk. The head FBI agent in LA, a man by the name of John Malone, opened the car door, jumped out, and put a Thompson submachine gun right up against my chest, stopping me dead in my tracks.

I said to him, "What the hell is going on? Are you guys gangsters?!"

He didn't appear amused.

"What's your name?" he barked.

I gave him a false name. Malone reached around to my back pocket to

pull out my wallet, where he found an ID that matched the phony name. Now he looked more confused than fierce. He thought he had somehow stopped the wrong guy! Just then another agent, by the name of Jones, shouted out to Malone, "That's him! That's him! I recognize him."

It seems Jones had been out to my duplex not long before, trying to find my friend from Alcatraz, Mike Strignano, who was suspected of shooting a cop. So Jones knew my face, and he started shouting into his radio, "Close in! Close in! We've got Ernie López!"

He kept shouting to Malone, "That's him!"

At that, all these cops came running over. They were swarming in from everywhere. They came running out of houses, out of cars, from around alleyways. There must have been fifty cops with rifles drawn and guns unholstered, and they all came running over to surround me. There were so many cops to arrest me that I got to feeling just a little special.

Jones confirmed my identity, so my best efforts at throwing the cops off my track failed. I finally had to admit who I was. They wanted to know where I lived, but I wanted them as far from my apartment as possible, so I told them that I lived in Long Beach. They, of course, didn't believe me, and sent someone to the gas station to question the attendant about me.

He pointed out where he thought I lived, and the FBI went over, but knocked on the wrong door. They barged into an apartment occupied by a young woman who at that moment had just stepped completely naked out of the shower. When this band of agents came storming into her room with their guns drawn, she started screaming bloody murder. I would have loved to see the faces of the cops then.

It was only a matter of time before they found my actual apartment, and they dragged me over while they searched my rooms. There was a large group of them searching everywhere and turning everything over. They were like a bunch of horses clomping clumsily around my little apartment. I was cuffed and seated on the sofa; two cops close by were assigned to keep an eye on me. I was getting a little nervous as the search went on because the night before I had hidden a huge wad of money in one of the sofa pillows. Most of the cops were in the kitchen and the bedroom at that time, but I knew that sooner or later they were going to find the money.

I leaned back and crossed my legs, trying to make myself comfortable, when one of the police watching me barked, "Put your leg down!"

I put my leg down. Just then one of the cops came from the kitchen to the living room and absentmindedly picked up the very pillow in

which I had stashed the money. Suddenly I made a big show of crossing my legs again.

The same cop yelled, "Put your leg down!"

I leaped up in a rage. "Goddamn you, you motherfucker! Who in the fuck are you to tell me not to cross my legs?!?"

All the cops came rushing out to see what the commotion was about. The one who was holding the pillow set it back down, ready to jump me in case I started to get rough.

I was yelling at the guy, "You goddamn yellow son of a bitch, you got all these goddamn cops with you. You're scared to death because I got my knee over my fucking leg? Fuck you!" I was making as much racket as I could.

Malone came rushing in. "Take it easy, Ernie. C'mon, I know you. Take it easy. Everything's gonna be all right."

Slowly I sat down and made as if I was trying to control myself. The cops got back to searching the place, and pretty soon one of the agents started shouting, "I got it! I got it here! Look at what I found!"

He had found a clip to a grease gun, which is a type of machine gun whose handle looks like those grease guns used in garages. He got very excited with this discovery because the bank robbers had used a machine gun in the heist. However, the robbers had used a tommy gun, not a grease gun, which was much more cheaply made.

They all went rushing over, wanting to see what he had found. Now they started looking for the actual grease gun, which I didn't have in the apartment. So it didn't matter to me if they searched for that gun all day; at least they were no longer interested in the pillow. Eventually they finished their search and took me to the old County Jail.

As the agents led me in to be booked, one of them commented, "Boy, Ernie, we almost had you the other night. Yeah, it was right around two o'clock in the morning over on the Harbor Freeway by Normandy. We were driving around and around looking for you, but we musta just missed you!"

So Luna had phoned the police that night by the hamburger stand! Now I was certain that he was the one who had led the cops to my car and my apartment. The police found me only because they had used Luna's description to identify my car. As I said, this was not the last time I got into trouble because of Robert Luna.

With all the commotion over the grease clip, they never did find the money in the pillow. As soon as I could, I sent a trusted friend of mine back to the apartment. I told him where I hid the key, and he let him-

self into the apartment and got the money. Instead of just grabbing the money, though, he took the whole pillow with him. So later on my landlord gave me a hell of a time about the missing pillow, refusing to release my things to me.

He kept insisting, "You owe me for the missing pillow."

I told him, "I don't have it. Maybe a goddamn agent took your pillow."

"If I don't get my pillow, you don't get your stuff."

I ended up paying something like twenty dollars to the landlord so that I could get my clothes and other possessions out of the apartment.

To prepare my defense, I got this rather famous lawyer by the name of Alan Ross to represent me. As soon as he could, Ross came over to the jail to talk. He told me that the bank had asked all its employees not to speak to anybody about the case, so he was having a hell of a time getting information. He told me that he knew of a good, reliable investigator who would surely get information. I told this to Joe Morgan, who also had been picked up by then, and we agreed that it would be a good idea to get the investigator. He was this little guy whose fee seemed pretty reasonable—I think about seventy-five dollars a day—so Joe and I hired him. This investigator turned out to be pretty slick. He normally worked for insurance companies, which is how I guess he got to be so slick.

He first went to the bank in West Covina, but nobody would talk to him. Apparently, the FBI as well as the bank had instructed the witnesses not to say a word to anyone. So he got nowhere fast trying to talk to the bank employees. As he was driving away from the bank, he got pulled over by a couple of cops. When he asked why they had stopped him, they said it was for speeding.

"I was going about five miles an hour! How can you say I was speeding?"

He refused to tell the cops who he was, so they took him in. They kept him detained for about three or four hours, suspicious of anyone who would come around asking questions about the robbery. He kept telling them, "I'm an investigator. I'm investigating the case."

In the end, they probably figured that since he was an investigator, he would turn out to be more trouble than he was worth, so eventually they turned him loose. This whole incident really got him mad, and it stoked his desire to investigate the case. For him, this wasn't just a job anymore. It had become something a little personal.

His next scheme was to read all the newspaper stories about the bank

robbery. He gathered the names of several of the people mentioned as witnesses and used a phone book to find their numbers and addresses. After work hours, he went to their houses one by one. He would knock on the door and tell the employee that he was an insurance investigator investigating the bank robbery. This was the truth, though he failed to mention that he was investigating the robbery for us, not the bank's insurance company.

He would tell the employee, "I just want to know the truth about what happened: who saw what, who can identify whom." Then he would run down a list of questions about the robbery: could the employee identify any of the suspects; what happened when the suspects entered the bank; did they hurt anybody—a whole range of questions to find out what the witness might know.

The investigator learned that both the robbers wore masks, so none of the employees were able to describe them adequately to the police. They had come in very quickly. One held a tommy gun, and the other jumped over the counter to collect the money from the vault. A number of witnesses noted that he was very agile and leaped the counter with little effort. They also emphasized how polite the robbers were and that nobody got hurt.

He wrote down every bit of information the witness offered. He then had the witness read over the statement he had just written and sign the paper at the bottom, affirming its truth. He went through the whole list of witnesses this way. It was the only means we had of getting the depositions necessary to form our case.

In the meantime, I was laying over in jail. Alan Ross would come around every now and then and tell me that the district attorney either had a really strong case against us or had absolutely nothing. Either way, he couldn't learn anything about the case without access to the witnesses.

Finally Ross decided, "You know, I don't have to fool around with those goddamn bank people. You know what I'm gonna do? I'm gonna hit 'em with subpoenas."

We found a law on the books under a section titled "Perpetual Testimony." It seems that if there is any possibility that testimony may disappear or be destroyed, or if someone's recollections may be lost, an attorney can get a court order to preserve that testimony. So Ross went to federal court and had the judge issue an order to a state judge to subpoena all the witnesses to the bank robbery. Using this end run, we finally managed to get sworn depositions for the case.

Rather than meet the witnesses in court, Ross had them come to his office in groups of three or four. Each group that came to the office was accompanied by an attorney provided by the bank.

Ross told each group that he wanted to make the process very easy. He was not going to ask any embarrassing or irrelevant questions. All he wanted was to ascertain the truth. He was trying to ease their concerns, letting them know that they weren't in trouble and weren't going to get into any. He then led them through a series of very specific questions about the case.

He asked them about the lineup procedure. It turned out that they had all been interviewed by the FBI before they went into the lineup. The FBI had told the witnesses that I was the prime suspect in the robbery and would be in the lineup. All they had to do was to point me out in order to make the case conclusive. The agents also told them that I had just come out of the penitentiary and that, though I had never been convicted of it, I was a murderer as well as a thief.

There had been four of us in the lineup: me and three barefoot kids who must have been no older than twelve. Of course the witnesses knew that the young kids hadn't robbed the bank. And since they had been told that the prime suspect was in the lineup, they had no choice but to identify me as the culprit.

It became pretty obvious that the DA had no indictment against either Joe or me. But we were taken before the U.S. commissioner anyway. Ross asked that the case against us be dismissed for lack of evidence, since there was no *prima facie* case.

The district attorney said that if the commissioner would wait a day, he would be able to get a grand jury indictment against the two of us. Sure enough, the next day he got an indictment. The grand jury is composed of prosecutors anyway, so they suspect everyone. They are more than happy to indict almost any suspect.

After several more weeks passed, we went to court to submit a plea. The day when pleas are submitted can be pretty chaotic. During a trial everything proceeds in a dignified and orderly fashion, but on plea days people walk in and out of court with their attorneys, marshals hustle along the aisles, lawyers consult with their clients and run around making deals with the prosecution. No jury is seated; instead, the jury box is occupied by the group of prisoners waiting to make their pleas.

On this day I was sitting in the bottom row of the jury box, and Joe was behind me in the top row. There was a probation officer running

from here to there and questioning people. He would ask each prisoner a series of questions and write down the answers on a little tablet. Soon he came over to where I was seated.

He called out, "Ernest López! Ernest López!" I was there, sitting directly in front of him, but I didn't answer.

The probation officer went over to the marshal and asked him if he had a guy by the name of Ernest López. The marshal looked at him, "Yeah, he's sitting right in front of you."

The probation officer looked at me and came back. "Are you Ernest López?"

I still didn't answer, but he carried on anyway. "Okay, Ernie López, what's your mother's name?" He asked me a whole series of questions that I refused to answer.

Finally I said, "Get the fuck out of my face, you punk! Get the fuck away from me!"

He was startled, but said, "Now, Ernie, you shouldn't have a chip on your shoulder. The federal court will give you a fair trial."

"Fair my ass. Just get the fuck out of my face."

He had no right trying to get information about me for probation before I had even been tried. He was just trying to cut corners and save himself more work later when probation was granted. The probation officer gave up and looked back to his list. He started calling Joe's name, "Joseph Morgan! Joseph Morgan!"

Joe had already seen what I did, and he didn't answer the officer. Again the guy went to the marshal to ask if he had anybody by the name of Joseph Morgan.

"Yeah," the marshal smirked, "he's right there above Ernie."

When he came back to talk to Joe, Joe started from his chair as if were going to grab him, shouting, "You motherfucker! Get the hell out of here, you goddamn son of a bitch!"

That got rid of the probation officer.

We had all our motions to make at the arraignment, and we pleaded not guilty. Finally we were ready to set a date for trial. The judge tried to find a trial date agreeable to the defense and the prosecution. There were many dates unacceptable to the government because, as it turned out, the federal prosecutor, Lon Waters, was going to try this case. Waters was a tall guy, maybe six seven or six eight, and a rising star on the federal circuit. Because he was such a big shot, scheduling was very difficult.

The judge would say, "How about the 23rd of July?"

Ross would say, "That's permissible by me."

One of the prosecutors would say, "Nope, the 23rd of July is not permissible, because Attorney Waters will be in Washington, D.C. Attorney Waters very specifically said that he wants to try this case personally."

Alan Ross was a great trial lawyer, but he had one flaw. He talked too loud. So when he heard the prosecutor say that Waters would be trying the case, everyone in the courtroom heard Ross laugh and say, "Well, that's good for us. He's never tried a case in his life."

The prosecutor got mad at the disrespect and snapped back, "He'll of course get help!"

Ross turned to me and said even louder, "Well, he's gonna need *a lot* of help!"

While we were sitting there trying to set a court date, Joe Morgan hit me on the elbow and leaned over. He said, "Mira los calcetines del abogado." So I looked at Ross's socks, and the tops were unraveling. It looked as if you could pull a string and the whole sock would come completely undone.

Joe said to me in Spanish, "You know what? I'm going to give him the clothes I had in that motel when they arrested me. I'm gonna give him a lot of socks. Maybe while I'm at it, I'll give him some nice-looking suits, too."

I don't know if Ross ever took Joe up on his offer, but he sure could have used it. Anyway, they finally set a date for the trial.

On the Monday that the trial began, I sat in the holding tank. On trial days, you are allowed to have a dress shirt, a tie, and your shoes. The rest of your clothes—your coat and your pants—you have to put on in the bathroom just before your appearance. So that morning I had my tie and my shirt on, and I was just waiting to get called out.

The officer come down and called out the names of the guys going to court first. He called about six or seven names, but I wasn't among them. I didn't know if they had called Joe to trial because we were being held in separate tanks. Something seemed wrong to me, since I knew that we were supposed to stand trial first thing in the morning.

I informed the sheriff, and he told me that my name was not on the list. "Maybe you're scheduled for the afternoon."

I waited until one o'clock, when the same thing happened and my name was not called. I thought that maybe I would be called at two.

Even if they were going to postpone the court date, they would have to take me to appear in court so that all the parties could agree to a postponement. I knew that something was definitely wrong.

Finally Ross came around to see me. His face was red, and he looked steaming mad.

He shouted, even louder than he usually did, "You know what those sons of bitches did? They dismissed your case without notifying me! They didn't even have the courtesy to call me. I knew they didn't have a fucking thing on you."

After going through all the contortions of settling on a court date, they threw in the towel. Neither Joe nor I went to court. Ross was so mad that he was practically smoking from the ears. I told him, "Well, Ross, you may be mad, but this is goddamn good news to me!"

It wasn't until much later that we learned how the feds had got the indictment against me. An FBI agent had gone before the grand jury and testified that a John Doe had told another John Doe that another John Doe had said that he believed Ernie López and Joe Morgan had robbed the bank in West Covina. All of this information was third-person hearsay, but the grand jury accepted it and issued the indictment. As I've said, grand juries are composed of prosecutors, and most of them would happily indict a wall.

The hearsay was admissible because in 1956 the feds had brought a case against a big-time gambler from New York by the name of Frank Costello. The feds relied on hearsay evidence to indict him, then arrested him on charges of income-tax evasion. He went to the Supreme Court to prove that the government had no grounds for the indictment. The court ruled that any kind of evidence, even hearsay, is admissible when securing a federal indictment. Only during a trial is hearsay or illegal evidence not admissible. So Joe and I were indicted on the strength of *Costello v. United States.*

I was awaiting my release when my parole officer—a man by the name, ironically enough, of Freeman—came to see me. This was not, of course, the same Harry Freeman of the LAPD, who had tormented me years before. To my surprise, he told me that I wasn't going to be released, then ran down a list of supposed parole infractions I had committed before being arrested for the bank robbery. This was all news to me, and I insisted to him that I had done none of the things I was accused of. I reminded him that I had reported to him as ordered every

Monday, and that I had told him where I lived, where I worked, and every other kind of information he wanted from me. He said that if this were the case, there would be no grounds for parole violation.

"Listen, Ernie," he said, "if what you say is true, then I promise that I'll turn you loose. I ain't got nothing against you. If you come out all right on these violations, you'll be out on the street."

A few days later, Freeman came back to see me. He looked long in the face.

"I'm sorry, Ernie. I have to violate you. I can't let them turn you loose."

"What are you violating me for?" I demanded.

He said, "Well, it's not my fault, you know. But I've got a boss, and I've gotta do what he tells me to do."

My problem was the result of Freeman's carelessness. Though I was reporting regularly, my report wasn't getting to him. All along he knew where I was, where I lived, and where I was working, but the reports weren't going in, and he never followed through. So the violation was actually his fault, and he admitted as much. This was the reason he was willing to turn me loose. But the chief parole officer, a man by the name of Van Meter, had ordered Freeman to charge me with violating parole.

In part, the violation was because of a priest named Father Clark, whom I had met in Alcatraz. He was very close to Van Meter, and had become pretty well known because of his acquaintance with Howard Hughes and other celebrities. Also, he would often go to Alcatraz and offer counsel to the big names there — Machine Gun Kelly, Freddie Horner, and Alvin Karpis among them. Every now and again you would see him walking up and down the yard, talking with one of the better-known convicts.

I got to know Father Clark in Alcatraz because I was to appear before a committee he sat on. This committee reviewed your case if you happened to lose a recommendation for transfer or if you lost your time off for good behavior. The escape from McNeil had cost me 500 days of good time, and I was appealing to get some of it back; it had been almost ten years since the escape. Even Alvin Karpis put in a good word for me with Father Clark.

I went before the committee, and a number of people talked about how well I was working and how I got along with everybody. When Father Clark saw me, he expressed surprise at my behavior. "I didn't know you were behaving and getting along so well. They really said some great things about you before the committee." As a result, they

gave me my good time back, which was the reason for my conditional release from Alcatraz and my return to LA.

After the bank robbery charge against me was dropped, I was remanded to County Jail, where I was detained until the whole issue of my parole violation could be worked out. Father Clark came to see one day, walking into the attorney room and looking me over. It struck me how much he acted like a cop reading me my rights.

"How're you doing, Ernie?" He said, "I talked to Van Meter. Van Meter is a very religious man, you know."

This was an odd way to begin. I told him that I didn't care how religious Van Meter was; he should not have violated my parole. If the priest put in a good word for me, he might change his mind.

He said, "Well, he says that you robbed the bank."

I confronted Father Clark about this. "The district attorney went before the court and admitted that there was no evidence against me. What evidence did Van Meter have that I robbed the bank? He couldn't know any more than the district attorney who had dismissed the case."

Father Clark finally admitted that Van Meter was going by what the FBI had told him, and the FBI believed that I was guilty, even though they had no evidence. When I refuted the allegation, all he could do was to keep repeating that Van Meter was a very religious man.

Father Clark never did put in a good word for me with Van Meter, so the board charged me with violating parole. I was sent back to Alcatraz for two and a half more years.

This was when James Bennett, director of federal prisons, stepped back into my life. Alan Ross had written a letter to Bennett, arguing that I should serve my time in Terminal Island prison, just off the coast of Long Beach. This would allow my elderly mother and young son to visit me during the two years of my sentence. Bennett wrote back a short, terse letter: "We cannot consider Ernest López for incarceration on Terminal Island. He is to be remanded immediately to Alcatraz."

PART THREE SURVIVAL

HAUNTED BY ALCATRAZ

I was sent back to Alcatraz for thirty months. I rode back on the very same ferry that had taken me away. Then, I had been happy to be leaving the Rock, and now, as you can imagine, my spirits were pretty low. The boat made a regular run from San Francisco to the island several times a day. It would take provisions out to Alcatraz, sometimes dropping off the mountains of laundry that the inmates washed for the armed services. Its last run was about ten at night.

I used to watch the boat from the hospital ward, where Bob Stroud and I would often talk. I would time how long it took the boat to make the trip each way. The boat took exactly ten minutes to get from San Francisco to Alcatraz and ten minutes from the island back. I timed it often.

I often thought that the surest way to get off Alcatraz was not by swimming, which so many other men had thought of trying. The tides were too strong, the seas too rough and cold, and the waters were infested with sharks — or at least that's what we were told. Instead, I decided the easiest thing to do would be to hitch a ride on the boat. All you had to do was to sneak out of the hospital ward on a very dark or foggy night, make it down the shrub-covered hill to the docks, and slip quietly into the water to await your ride to freedom.

The hospital ward was generally off-limits to prisoners unless they were very ill and unlikely to be thinking about making a major effort to escape. One door that led from the hospital's second floor to an outdoor walkway looked particularly weak to me, and I thought it would give way with one good strong kick. It would be easy enough one night

to make your way down the three flights of stairs outside the hospital ward and into the thick bushes between the prison and the thirty-foot guard tower above the island's dock. If you could sneak out of the ward, your absence wouldn't be detected for a while. You would have enough time to get down the pier in the dark, slip into the water, and grab onto the boat, which docked only long enough to unload supplies or (on very rare occasions) board prisoners leaving the penitentiary.

A number of round holes lined the wooden prow just above water level. I thought of fashioning a rope and tying it to a thick wooden dowel that you could jam into one of the holes. If you could hold onto the rope for ten minutes and keep your head just above water, you could be dragged by the boat all the way into San Francisco. The boat docked at Pier 21, but before it pulled up next to the pier, you could let go of the rope and swim quietly away. Eventually you could come out somewhere off where there were few people, search for some dry clothes, and blend into the city. I thought about this plan a lot, but my time left was pretty short, and I didn't feel the need to take such a risk for the couple years I had yet to serve.

I was thinking about this plan as I rocked back and forth in the boat carrying me back to my island "home." Shackled, I was led off the boat and onto a rickety old truck. It bumped its way up the steep cobbled switchbacks leading to the prison. Once more I passed under the talons of the stone eagle that hovered over the entrance to the Rock.

The first night back they put me in a cell by myself on Broadway. In the morning, the guard came along and told me to collect my things. I asked him where I was going.

"You're going to Kitchen Row," he told me. "You're assigned to work in the kitchen."

I realized right away they were trying to get back at me because of the food strike. I told him I refused. Obviously they thought that they were going break me by having me work in the place that I had worked so hard against. They would finally have the satisfaction of putting me where they wanted me. But I had long before sworn that they were not going to break me.

The guard said, "Hey, *I'm* not trying to put you in the kitchen, son. I just got orders to put you in there. So you tell the warden what they can do."

Soon the deputy warden called me up. He was a southern guy with a harelip by the name of Latimer. He had an attitude a mile long.

"Sit down!" he said, when I went to talk to him. "Who in the hell do you think you are? You think you can come in here from right off the street and run the joint?"

I told him that I didn't want to get in an argument with him. But I did have an argument a long time before over the kitchen, and I told him I didn't want another one.

He said, "What in the hell? Who in the hell do you think you are?"

"Well, let me tell you something," I said. "I'm not going to work in the kitchen, so let's make it short. You do whatever you want, but I'm not working in the kitchen."

Latimer screamed at me, "You're going to the hole!"

I told him, "Well, put me in the goddamn hole."

So the guards took me away and threw me in the hole, where it was as cold and miserable as usual. At least I didn't have to work in the kitchen.

The guards at Alcatraz were a special breed. All of them thought that they were the toughest and baddest of all the guards in the system. It was partly this attitude that got them to Alcatraz. As far as I was concerned, almost all of them were assholes, including this one Chicano guard by the name of Pasilla, who was a dirty son of a bitch.

Pasilla was always dogging me for no reason. After working down in the industries area, we had to climb a long flight of stairs to get to the yard. When they opened the gate to let us back into the yard, there would be about six or eight guards watching. As you came through the door, they would randomly pick prisoners for a search down.

Whenever he saw me pass through, Pasilla would get me. I had had no run-in with that son of a bitch, and I had never said anything to get him mad at me. But he would search me each time he saw me come up from the shops. He would very carefully pat me down, feeling the seams of my pants cuffs and inseams, the sleeves and cuffs of my jacket, the collar and shoulders of my shirt, and take his own sweet time about it.

When he was done with all that, he would say, "Now, take off your shoes."

So then I had to take off my shoes. None of the other guys had to go through this procedure. But Pasilla and I went through this same routine every time he manned the gate.

Even the other guards would get mad at him because they had already finished searching every one else, but they were forced to wait for

that bastard to finish searching me before they could go home. It was quitting time, and there he was messing with me when they wanted to get the hell out of there.

Finally one day I told him, "You motherfucker. Go ahead and search me, you son of a bitch asshole. I don't give a fuck what you do."

Well, that got me put in the hole.

Pasilla would sometimes man the gunwalk in the general cellblock by day and go to isolation in the evening. So once when I was in isolation, the other guys hollered over to me, "Hey, Ernie, what's the dirtiest word you know in Spanish?"

"Oh," I told them, "I don't know, there's a lot of them." Then I looked up directly at Pasilla. "But I don't know if I can really come up with the one word that would best describe that asshole on the gunwalk."

The men all broke out laughing. Then someone else shouted, "Let's look in the encyclopedia!"

That caused us to laugh all the more.

As I recall, there were very few Chicano guards at Alcatraz. Pasilla was one, but there was another guard who was different. He was from New Mexico, but I can't recall his name. He would mind his own business, not hassle the prisoners, and not really talk to the other guards either. He just did his work and went home.

Sometimes he was assigned to come around to the hole, give out blankets at night, and collect them first thing in the morning. As I've explained, this was the routine in the dark hole. At night you got two thin blankets that you could use to try to keep warm on the metal floor, and they were taken away from you in the morning.

I was in the hole one day when it was so cold that the walls were sweating from the moisture of my breath. I kept wondering why this was happening, then realized that the guards had opened all the windows to the bay. Every once in a while I could hear the guys upstairs in isolation hollering, "Hey, guards, give me some more blankets!" They had their own blankets already and were hollering for more. Meanwhile I was in the hole, and I didn't have *any* blankets.

This guard from New Mexico came by in the morning and said, "Listen, López, it's so cold that I'm not going to take those blankets away from you. You can keep them all day, but I have to take them away when I go off my shift at eight o'clock."

He was the only guard at Alcatraz who ever treated me in any humane way. As far as I can remember, he was the only decent guard I ever came

across there, and he didn't last too long. The other guards were constantly giving him a bad time, and he ended up quitting.

So here on my first day back at Alcatraz I was already in the hole. When my time was finally up, they took me before a disciplinary committee. They had everybody there: the warden, the captain, and Deputy Warden Latimer. He greeted me by saying, "Ah, this is Ernie. He just came back from the street. He thinks he's running the place."

I said, "I'm not running the place. You can do whatever you want to do. I got two years to do, maybe two and a half. If you want me to do the entire time in the hole, it's all right with me. You're not going to keep me over the two and a half years."

As I was walking out, the captain came running after me. "Hey, Ernie, come here. Don't be stubborn. You've done all right. Listen, I know how you think. If you want a job, I'll give you a job down in the basement. You can give towels to the guys taking showers and hand them back their clothes. You don't have to work in the kitchen."

I thought this would be all right, so I took the job in the clothing room of the shower and worked there the rest of my time on the island.

I was released from Alcatraz for the last time in August 1959. I was now thirty-seven, divorced, and starting my life on the streets over. Less than four years later, the prison on Alcatraz was closed for good. The last man to leave the island as a federal prisoner was Frank Weatherman. The one thing he had to say about the place: "Alcatraz was never good for nobody."

When I got out, I made my way to Los Angeles and got a job driving a truck, making occasional runs from Los Angeles to Bakersfield and back. At that time I was making monthly reports because I was still on conditional release, based on the good time I had earned on Alcatraz. I regularly let the parole board know my job and my address. But I was glad to be out and back in civilian life. As it turned out, things got pretty sticky pretty quickly, and once again Alcatraz affected my life in ways I could never have expected.

Not long after getting settled in my new apartment, I went to see a girl on Whittier Boulevard. She caught me at the door, told me she was busy, and asked me to come back an hour later. I walked over to a little outdoor burger joint, where I saw three guys arguing off in the corner. For some reason, I really don't know why, one of them bumped into me intentionally. I pushed him back and slugged him in the belly. He

yelled, and stumbled over to his table. The other guys saw what had happened and came at me. I ended up fighting all three. Suddenly, a fourth guy grabbed me by the coat and pulled it back over my arms, pinning them. As I was flailing around, trying to get my arms free, another one of them hit me in the mouth with a chain, loosening my tooth and breaking my nose. Luckily, my girl happened to be coming down to her car at that moment, and the guys ran off. She took me to the hospital, where I was admitted with a serious concussion.

I was recuperating in the hospital when, to my surprise, Red Winhoven, an old friend from Alcatraz, came to visit. His actual name was Willard Arthur Winhoven, but everyone called him "Red" because of his hair. I had last seen him on Alcatraz, and I had no idea that he would ever be paroled. As it happened, he had been transferred to McNeil not long after I left the Rock, and he was finally granted parole from McNeil. It was great to see him again.

He and I had often talked in Alcatraz because he used to live in East LA. We would talk about the old hometown, and I would tell him about my mother and my brother and the nursery that they ran. He knew the exact location because he was well acquainted with that area. As soon as he was released, he had come down to LA to visit his family. He took the time one day to drive out to my mother's nursery and ask for me, and he learned about my being hospitalized.

He came to visit on a Sunday, so the desk nurse wouldn't let him come up to my room. When he pulled five dollars out and placed it on her desk, the nurse reconsidered her decision.

I was glad to have Red as a visitor. I was bored up in the hospital, and we got to talking, as old friends do. He said that he had just landed a job and had to report to it on Monday. I told him that I would be getting out of the hospital Monday and that I could drive him down to his job and help him in whatever way I could.

I was released from the hospital in the morning, and we drove to his job that afternoon. He had rented a nice little apartment close to work, and I helped him out by bringing some sheets and blankets and pillowcases over from my apartment. I even brought him some shirts. He was earning pretty good money, and things were looking up for old Red.

It so happened that just before finding me in the hospital, he had met a friend of his who lived in Bakersfield. They began to talk by phone regularly, and he ended up driving over to Bakersfield fairly often. In fact, sometimes right after work he would take off for Bakersfield, then return to LA early the following morning for work. That same evening

he would head back to Bakersfield and do it all over again. Sometimes he would come back and stay a few days, then head on out again. I had no idea what he was doing all this time, but he made many trips to Bakersfield.

One day I was walking into my girlfriend's dress shop on Third and Broadway when Winhoven pulled his car over to the curb and hollered over to me. He had called my house, and my sister had told him where I was going. He asked if I wanted to go with him to Bakersfield that evening. I told him that I didn't really have any other plans, so sure. I should have known better.

On the drive to Bakersfield, he told me that he was going to see a friend of his by the name of Ed Bishop. I knew about Bishop, and I told him that I didn't really want to meet with him. It seems that Bishop had ratted on some guys while serving time in Oregon. Bishop knew some prisoners who were trying to smuggle guns into the prison for an escape, but Bishop squealed and the guns were found. I didn't relish spending any time with someone like that.

I told Red to go ahead and see him. He could drop me off in town and pick me up later, when he was finished visiting. I gave him the name of a street where I knew a girl. We agreed to meet around three thirty or four in the morning at a particular restaurant the truck drivers used. So around 4:00 a.m. I went to the restaurant and waited for him. He finally arrived around five o'clock, and we began to head back to LA.

We had just pulled through an intersection, not too long into the drive, when we saw flashing red lights behind us and a cop waving us over. A lone policeman came over to Red's window and said that we had run a stop sign. We had stopped, but apparently it had been too much of a rolling stop for his liking. Pretty soon a backup cruiser arrived, and two more cops came over to the car.

All of a sudden they drew their pistols and, pointing them through our windows, yelled at us to get out of the car, which we did. As we stood on the curb, they started rifling through the car. They got pretty agitated when they found a .357 magnum underneath my seat. Next they searched the trunk, where they found some masks and more guns. I think there were about thirteen guns in all.

Now they were pretty worked up because of all the guns, and they figured that we had been up to something. They searched Winhoven and found a key for a motel room; the address was on the key tag. After locking us up, they searched the room, where they found more guns and another mask.

While we were jailed, the police supposedly obtained information that we were planning to rob the Lamont Bank. The bank cashed paychecks for grape pickers in the area. It was just about payday, so the bank had vaulted over $250,000 in order to have enough cash on hand. The cops spun out an elaborate theory that we had robbed a hardware store, stolen some cars to use for our getaway, and then hidden the cars in a vineyard. It was pretty clear that they were trying to clear their books of every unsolved crime by pinning them all on us. We were finally charged with conspiracy to rob the bank and burglary. The day before we drove to Bakersfield, someone had broken into a hardware store and stolen some shotguns, rifles, and other guns.

With these charges in place, they booked us and ran us through the usual questioning. I told them that I didn't know anything about the burglary and that I didn't know anything about the guns under the seat or in the trunk. I was just riding along with Winhoven. Red told them the same thing: he never told me about the guns; I knew nothing of them; and he and some other guys he knew in Bakersfield had put the guns in the trunk.

I spent several weeks in the Kern County Jail waiting for the preliminary hearing date. Sitting in the tank one day, I saw, to my great surprise, Robert Luna hobble into the cell. Luna was on crutches because of a misadventure he had had the last time I saw him in LA, a few weeks before. He had just escaped from a prison camp in Tehachapi and had come to see me one Saturday night. He claimed that some friends of his were waiting for us and that they had a message for me from Joe Morgan. I agreed to go along.

As we were getting into his car, he showed me a gun and told me the whole story of his escape from the prison camp. At the time I lived on Eastman Street, so I told him not to be flashing any guns around, because Eastman is a regular route for cops driving downtown from East LA. I thought he was being extremely reckless. We drove over to a restaurant called Las Carnitas, on Olympic near Indiana. Though greatly changed, the restaurant is still there.

I walked in and saw two close friends: Bill Stabler, whom everyone called Big Zeke, and Fat Boy Davenport. We hadn't seen each other in quite a while, so after they gave me Joe's message, we got to eating and talking and catching up. Zeke is a big guy, and he eats like a horse, so we were there for a good long time. I had had a nice time, but I told them that I had to leave. They said that they had to leave pretty soon, too. Luna offered to drive me home, then to come back

and pick up Big Zeke and Fat Boy. I took him up on the offer, and he drove me home.

The next morning, I went over to my sister's house, and she showed me a front-page story in the Sunday paper about Big Zeke, Fat Boy Davenport, and Robert Luna getting arrested the night before. It seems that after Luna took me home, he went back to Las Carnitas and picked up the other guys. They had driven over to Manchester and Hoover before realizing they had left a satchel containing about $5,000 and some guns underneath the booth.

They turned around and went back to the restaurant. Luna and Fat Boy waited in the car while Big Zeke went in to get the satchel. Big Zeke was about six four and had pretty big fists, so he was picked to go back in.

Sitting in the booth were four detectives, the satchel on the table between them. Well, Zeke had run into a shit storm. The only thing he could do was to pull a gun and hope to get the drop on the detectives. One of the men was named Buckley, and he had been a World War II hero. Like Zeke, he was also a great big guy.

Because he was a vet, Buckley knew a lot about guns. When Zeke pulled his automatic pistol on him, Buckley grabbed the muzzle and jammed it back so that Zeke couldn't get a shot off. The two men got into a huge struggle, wrestling and rolling around the restaurant, trying to control the pistol. They broke the restaurant apart. Zeke knocked Buckley over, then Buckley threw Zeke back, and tables and chairs and plates went flying everywhere. The four detectives together finally managed to pin Zeke down and hold a gun to his head.

Panting, Buckley looked down at Zeke and yelled, "So where do we go now, huh? C'mon, where do we go now?"

Zeke looked up at him and at the gun pointed at his head. He said, "Let's go to jail."

In the meantime, Luna and Fat Boy had taken off on foot. Luna had run up an embankment behind a house by the freeway. He planned to go up the embankment, drop on the freeway, and run over to the other side. He was about halfway up, and the detectives were hot on his trail.

One of the cops yelled, "If you go over that fence, I'll shoot you."

Luna didn't care, and he tried to go over. The detective fired off a shot that hit him in the foot. Luna was taken to General Hospital, and he eventually ended up back in Bakersfield because the prison camp he had escaped from was in Kern County. Charges for robbery and rape,

crimes Luna had committed while on the lam, were added to the charge of escape from the prison camp.

When he came into the tank in Bakersfield, Luna was still on crutches from the gunshot wound. There were about six other men in the cell with us, each with a top or bottom bunk. I gave Luna my bottom bunk and took the top, since he had trouble getting around. I tried to help him out in other ways, too, on account of his wrecked foot. I would get him the food and soup that the jailers brought to the door—little things like that, just to make it a bit easier on him.

While we were in the tank together, he got to telling me stories about his friends and families. I knew some of the people whom he mentioned in his stories. One story was about his going to Mexico to visit his father, a movie actor by the name of Margarito Luna. Luna said that Big Zeke and Fat Boy had gone along with him. He went on and on about what a great time they had had with his father, fishing, drinking beer, and generally carrying on. When I later mentioned this story to Big Zeke and Fat Boy they told me that they had never gone to Mexico with Luna and hadn't ever met his dad. I found out that a lot of the stories Luna told me were pure lies.

In any case, he and I told stories back and forth to pass the time. The days were interrupted only when Luna was taken out of the cell every now and again to have the bandages on his foot changed. He seemed to need them changed pretty often, but at least he got some time out of the tank, away from me and the other six guys there.

All eight of us were sitting in the tank one day, when I heard the jailer holler out my name. When I was called like that, it usually meant that my attorney was coming for a visit. We had been preparing for the preliminary hearing on the weapons-possession charge, but he had also been telling me about some trouble brewing for me in LA. He didn't know the specifics—just rumor—but he said he would let me know more about it as soon as he could get some solid information. So as the jailer called my name, I prepared myself for a visit from my attorney.

When the cell door was opened, the jailer led me away from the visiting room and straight to the isolation cell. It seems that the authorities had decided to put me up in the hole in the hope that I would break down and make some kind of incriminating statement. I remained in isolation from that day up until the hearing.

When the preliminary hearing finally started, it lasted eighteen days, thirteen of which were taken up with testimony about crimes com-

pletely unrelated to the charges against me. Winhoven or others allegedly committed all these crimes, but they had nothing to do with the robbery or the weapons possession. During those thirteen days, the line of witnesses parading through the courtroom testified about a long list of crimes such as burglarizing a hardware store, stealing cars, and smuggling guns. However, none of the witnesses could link these events with me.

When the authorities finally got to the case against me, they brought in the officers who had arrested us. They were supposed to testify that they had found guns in the car, but we made a motion to suppress this testimony because they had conducted the search illegally. We made the point that since they had only made a traffic stop, the cops had had no due cause to search Winhoven's car. The officer even admitted that he wasn't sure if we had actually run the stop sign or not.

The two officers who had arrived later on the scene testified that they had grown suspicious about us when they saw a crowbar on the floor between my feet. They said that a red crowbar had been used in the burglary of a hardware store the day before, and because of this they had ordered us out of the car. Of course, none of this actually happened. Though it was clear that they had conducted an illegal search and seizure, the judge denied our motion to suppress the testimony. The only thing we could do was to prove that the officers were lying.

The first officer testified that it was dark when he stopped us, and he couldn't see inside the car. This testimony contradicted that of another office, a policeman by the name of Frank Mobrice.

The district attorney asked Mobrice if he had had his flashlight with him when he approached the car to look in. Mobrice told him that he wasn't carrying it, because the stop had happened during the morning, and it was already light out.

When my attorney cross-examined him, Mobrice testified that he had grown suspicious of us when he saw the red crowbar peeking out from under the seat of the car. He emphasized that this was the same color as the crowbar that had been used to break into the hardware store just before our arrest. My attorney asked him if he had been the officer at the scene of the burglary where the red crowbar was used, and he said no.

My attorney then asked, "Were you actually on the scene, and did you inspect the site in order to determine how the burglars had come in through the door?

Again he said no; he had just been a standby on the scene, not an

investigating officer. I could tell that Mobrice was getting awfully nervous because at the beginning of his testimony he had made it seem as if he had been the investigating officer. That was supposedly how he knew about the red crowbar.

My attorney asked him, "As a standby, did you know that the crowbar had been used in the burglary? Was that your opinion?"

He said no.

"Then how did you know that the crowbar was used? Did they find a crowbar later on?"

He said no. "But," he said, "I did see red paint on the jamb of the door."

My attorney closed in. "Now, could the paint have been left by a screwdriver with red paint on it? Or maybe by a pair of red pliers? Or, for that matter, any other instrument that had red paint on it? It didn't have to be a crowbar, did it?"

Mobrice could see that he was being closed in on, so finally he had to say that, yes, the instrument must have been a crowbar. He didn't want to concede anything to us.

He finally testified that because he *knew* it was a crowbar, he had had reason to search Winhoven's car. So we introduced the testimony of an expert from Griffith Park Observatory, who noted that at 5:20 a.m. on the day of our arrest, it was still dark out. The sun didn't rise until 6:10; even then, there would have been only the dim half-light of early morning, not enough light to see clearly into a dark car. As the trial wore on, it became clearer and clearer that Mobrice was lying.

The day the actual trial was set to start in Superior Court, the district attorney asked all charges against me to be dismissed because of insufficient evidence. The motion was granted, and I was almost a free man again. I was remanded to the Bakersfield jail until I could be released. A couple of days later, some members of the LAPD came to see me. It was then that I learned what kind of trouble had been brewing for me back in LA. The detectives had come to arrest me for robbery and murder. I headed back to LA not as a free man, but once again in handcuffs. Little did I know then just how deep my trouble would soon become.

JUDGMENT ONCE MORE

I later learned the details of the events that led the LAPD to me. A robbery had occurred at a store called the MORE Discount House on Sepulveda and Santa Monica Boulevards in West Los Angeles. It seems that a messenger had picked up some money and was driving off the store lot when a man wearing a mask jumped in front of the car, forcing the messenger to slam on the brakes. In the messenger's confusion, the man rushed over to the passenger door, flung it open, and hopped in. He pulled out a gun, and the messenger tried to reach for it, leading to a struggle. The robber obviously did not want to shoot the messenger, and he tucked the gun away. During the scuffle, the robber kept slugging the messenger until he managed to pull him from the car and beat the messenger until he fell to the sidewalk. He grabbed the briefcase from the car and began to run.

An off-duty cop happening by saw the scuffle and ran over to help the messenger, just as the robber jumped from the car. He grabbed him and pinned his arms in a bear hug, trying to hold the robber until the police arrived.

As he was holding him, the off-duty cop saw the robber's partner come running around the corner of the building with a gun drawn, shooting wildly. The cop was hit by one of the bullets, and he let go of the suspect to clutch his wound. Luckily, he survived. Having heard shots, the manager of the store came running out to the parking lot. One of the bullets hit the manager in the head, and he later died of his wounds.

With two men shot and the messenger pretty badly beaten up, the

two bandits made a break and ran off to the getaway car. The car, which the partner had hot-wired, wouldn't start. Still holding onto the briefcase with the money, the first robber ran into the middle of Sepulveda Boulevard. He pulled his gun on a driver who was slowing for a stop, pointed the gun at the driver's head, and told him to get out of the station wagon. The bandit hopped behind the wheel, hit the brakes, and picked up his partner, who was running after him. The two drove off.

The men didn't get away cleanly yet. A Good Samaritan driving behind the commandeered car started to follow them. They kept trying to shake the man by making lefts and rights, turning down alleyways, pulling into driveways, and turning back the way they had come. No matter how many turns they took, they couldn't seem to lose the car behind them. Finally the partner leaned out the window and fired a couple of shots. One of the shots ricocheted and hit the Samaritan in the head. Only then did he pull over and give up the chase.

The LAPD had learned about the charges against me and Winhoven in Bakersfield, and they came to suspect us of being the robbers in the MORE Discount case. Given my past record and my reputation with the cops, they were only too happy to charge me with murder and robbery. In addition to these charges, they tacked on four counts of attempted murder because the off-duty cop, the Good Samaritan, and two other bystanders had been wounded by ricocheting bullets.

The cops filed charges and escorted me from the Bakersfield jail to the Glass House in Los Angeles. The Glass House was what everyone called Parker Center, the central jail in LA. It was a very modern building with huge windows, very much like you would see on any skyscraper today. Back then, it was a new and unique design.

When I got to Parker Center, my attorney in LA — Barbara Warner — was waiting for me. She had heard of the charges against me, and she had asked about representing me in court. This was a high-profile case, and she was eager to take the case on.

Having arrived on a Friday, I spent the weekend in the Glass House, and on Monday they took me straight to court. I was arraigned there, then taken to the old LA County Jail. When I was getting booked, and while nobody was watching, I took a look at some of the messages that had been left on the booking desk. I saw a little slip of paper that read "López and Winhoven—LAPD at 5 p.m."

I knew right away that they wanted us to be ready for a lineup that

evening, which was definitely bad news. I called Barbara Warner, but she wasn't in her office. I left word with her secretary that I needed to see her *right away* because they were taking me to a lineup and I wanted her present. I also telephoned my sister and my brother and told them to get hold of my attorney, no matter what it took. I needed her there to be sure that the policemen did not coach any of the witnesses.

After being booked into Country Jail, I was about to be taken to the tank when one of the cops told me not to undress. "You're going to court, López."

"Well, I'm not going no place," I told him. "I know you're going to take me to the lineup, and I'm not going without my counsel present."

He called some deputy sheriffs over to me. "What's wrong now?"

"I want my counsel to be present at this lineup," I told them. "I know you people are going to take me to the lineup, and I demand counsel to protect me."

One of the sheriffs said, "You know what, López? Your attorney may be well-versed in the law and all that, but she don't tell us what to do."

All of a sudden they jumped me, knocked me down, and handcuffed my hands behind my back. They had to literally drag me down the hall and throw me in the elevator. The officers took me all the way down to the basement, where they tossed me bodily into the backseat of a patrol car and drove me back to the Glass House. No matter what I said, they were determined to hold the lineup.

I was taken to the tank and prepared for the lineup. They gave me a number—number 19—as they did everyone being held in the tank. When they wanted you to appear, they would holler out your number. You had to get up on a little, brightly lit stage in a darkened auditorium, and they had you stand on a little square marked on the stage to answer a series of questions.

Eventually my number was called and I was taken out onto the stage. My attorney still had not shown up. The stage was lit up very brightly, and bright white lights were in my eyes. The auditorium where the police and witnesses sat was completely dark. From out of that blackness I started hearing questions: "What's your name? What are you in for?"

They want you to talk so that the people can hear your voice, but I refused to answer. I wouldn't answer even the simplest, most innocent-seeming question without my attorney present. They kept asking questions, telling me that I was a wise guy and asking what did I think I was doing.

Now, even though it is dark, if you keep looking up at the auditorium where the people are seated, you can start to focus your eyes beyond the lights to the point that the first few rows become visible. It took some time, but I focused my eyes and started to make out some of the witnesses, or, more precisely, prospective witnesses. Sitting all around the witnesses were a number of policemen and detectives. I could tell that the left side of the auditorium was almost completely empty. All the people were concentrated in the middle of the auditorium, just like at a theater.

On the nearly empty left-hand side I could make out a few figures: an FBI agent named Crow, an LAPD detective named Max Herman — the head of the robbery squad — and another detective named Rafferty. These three officers weren't looking at me but at the people, to see if any would make an identification.

The cops at the back of the auditorium hollered down to the witnesses, "Any identification? Can anyone identify anybody?" Nobody said anything, because of course nobody could identify me.

All of a sudden Crow and Rafferty got up on the left side of the aisle and started hollering, "Number 19!" They raised their hands up in the air and hollered out, "Number 19!" as if they had been witnesses to the crime and could positively identify me. They were hoping that by doing this they could induce some of the other people also to make an identification.

I could see clearly who was making the racket. I was all set to holler at them and make a big scene so that later on I could complain about it. But for some reason I held back and didn't do it. In any case, as far as I knew at the time, nobody identified me.

After the lineup, my attorney caught up with me.

She said, "Ernie, they wouldn't allow me to go in."

She told me that my sister had finally gotten through to her, and right away she had sent telegrams to the district attorney, to the captain of the robbery squad, and to the captain of the homicide squad, demanding that she be present when the lineup took place. She reminded them that the denial of counsel at my lineup was a violation of my constitutional rights.

When she didn't get a reply, she went on her own to Parker Center. She was detained at the entrance to the auditorium where the lineup was held, though she demanded to be admitted. A policeman blocked her way and told her that the officials at the lineup were not going to allow her to be present, that it was not the practice to allow an attor-

ney at a lineup. She made her demands as best as she could, but in the end she was denied. Barbara made a record of all the officials she had tried to contact, in the hope that we could present this as evidence of misconduct at the preliminary hearing.

During the preliminary hearing, we presented the names of all the officials at the lineup: the district attorney, the head of the homicide squad, the head of the robbery squad, and also the officer who was running the lineup. We did this to establish for the court that I had demanded the right to have counsel present and that these particular officials had denied that demand. The officials took the stand, admitting that my attorney had sent telegrams and that she was at the auditorium entrance before the lineup took place. They admitted as well that the officer present had advised her that she would not be allowed to attend the lineup. But, they argued, this was policy, so they had done nothing wrong.

We took this issue all the way to the California Supreme Court, but our case was finally sent back down. In 1967, the attorney Luke McKissack, working for a man named Skinny Gilbert, took this same issue to the U.S. Supreme Court. That court upheld the motion and declared that it was unconstitutional to prevent counsel from attending a lineup. Unfortunately, they ruled that the decision could not be applied retroactively, so it had no bearing on my case.

Barbara made so many objections at the preliminary hearing that the court let us have what they call running objections. It was assumed that, for the record, we were making objections all along without having to stand up and interrupt the proceedings. The point of all these objections to the witnesses' testimony was to preserve a record for appeal, in case I was convicted. This, in fact, turned out to be the case, despite a number of discrepancies in the testimony. They got the conviction because of a dirty trick that the detectives pulled at the trial. After the preliminary hearing, a trial date was set. My attorney and I prepared, and we felt that we had an unimpeachable case to show that I was not guilty.

In the old County Jail, they put me in the High Power tank, which meant I was isolated from most other prisoners. To make things just a bit harder, they put me way in the back, behind a door where hardly anybody passed. This made it even more isolated, since no one even passed by that particular cell. Because I was in High Power, I was not allowed to go anywhere unless accompanied by some jailer. They kept me

locked up in that isolation for about six months. Their idea was to harass me to the point that I would finally offer a statement or confession.

Throughout the course of the preliminary hearing, the assistant special prosecutor—Joseph Busch, Jr.—repeatedly approached my lawyer.

He would tell her, "Look, Barbara, get Ernie to plead guilty to one count. We'll drop all the other counts, and it won't be so hard on him. I'll recommend parole, and we'll forget about the whole thing."

She presented Busch's offer to me, but I told her that I would never do anything of the sort. Almost every week Busch came back to her with the same offer. Over and over I told her that I refused. This happened I don't know how many times, but I told her the same thing each time: I would never cop a plea.

When the actual trial began, they would regularly call me upstairs to the attorney room. Each time Barbara would present the same deal that the DA had offered her: one count, a recommendation for parole, and everything else would be dropped. One time I went upstairs and even found my brother sitting next to my attorney.

He said, "Ernie, don't get mad at me. I'm here to tell you what they are telling me. They tell me they are still willing to cut a deal for you. There's nothing they're offering Winhoven, but for you they're willing to drop all the charges but one, and they'll forget about it."

Later on I told Barbara, "Listen, you don't have to bring my brother to try to convince me what to say. I know what to say. I know what I did and what I didn't do, and I didn't commit that crime. If I'd committed the crime, what they're offering would be a good deal. But not for me. I didn't commit the crime, and I would rather die in the gas chamber than plead guilty."

And that's where the matter stayed.

It was February 1961 when my trial started. First my attorney asked for my trial to be severed from Winhoven's. The authorities had evidence that he had been in possession of the deadly weapons, and we figured that I could get a fairer trial if I were to go up by myself. The prosecutor in my case, Joseph Busch, Jr., would gain some fame because of his role, and he later ran for—and was elected—district attorney of Los Angeles County.

He, of course, opposed the motion for severance, claiming that it was a waste of money and that the state could guarantee us both a fair trial. He knew that all the evidence against Winhoven would be heard by the same jury that was deciding my fate, and whatever evidence was

brought out against Winhoven would harm my chances of being found not guilty. The DA loudly opposed our motion, and indeed the motion was denied. We had to stand trial together.

At first I thought that my attorney seemed to be doing a pretty good job because she made many motions and objections. When we had first met, she told me that she had been practicing law for the past five years and that she had been involved in some pretty important murder cases, like that of Caryl Chessman. She kept insisting that she was well learned in law, and at first she had me convinced. I later found out that she had been lying to me all along, and that she had actually been practicing law for only about a year. I think she wanted the publicity from the trial, so she told me a bunch of lies that would convince me to let her represent me. While I was dealing with my attorney, Winhoven decided that he didn't want an attorney at all, but would represent himself.

After the motion to separate the trials was denied, we picked a jury. Because this was a capital case, they sent fifty prospective jurors into the trial, but we quickly exhausted all fifty. One reason they were dismissed so quickly was because the judge, Herbert V. Walker, asked them as a group, "Listen very attentively because I am going to ask you questions, and I want to be sure that you are paying attention. The first thing I want to know is how many of you are against capital punishment?"

About thirty of them raised their hands and automatically were excluded from serving on my jury. Then they sent another fifty, and Judge Walker asked them the same questions. I watched this process very carefully. I was studying the jury pool when something occurred to me.

I leaned over and told my attorney, "Listen, Barbara, I've been watching, and there are no people of Mexican descent coming into the courtroom as prospective jurors. Something's wrong here."

Los Angeles had more Mexicans than any other city outside of Mexico, and it was odd that there were no Mexicans in the jury pool. Barbara said that she couldn't do anything about this exclusion at the moment, but she said that she might be able to use this fact later on. After they sent in the second fifty, and there were still no Mexicans in the pool, I demanded that she investigate.

She made a motion and we went into the judge's chamber. We discussed that because many Mexicans lived in East LA and all around Los Angeles, it seemed wrong that not one person on the panel was of Mexican descent. You would have expected at least one or two in the hundred that had come through.

Judge Walker said he would call the jury commissioner to take the

stand so that we could question him. The jury commissioner testified that they selected jurors from the voter rolls, that the names are put into the computer, and that the computer selects every sixth person. They ran about 60,000 names through the computer, the commissioner said, and the whole process was random, so he knew nothing of any discrimination in the process.

Of course, what he described was how things *were supposed to be,* not how they actually were. And how things *actually were* seemed to exclude people of Mexican descent from hearing my case. Following the commissioner's testimony, to nobody's surprise, the motion to dismiss the panel of prospective jurors was denied. Twelve jurors, with three alternates, were finally chosen, and so we went to trial with a jury of my supposed peers.

Most of the witnesses testifying for the defense were of Mexican descent, which was why I wanted to have Mexican people on the jury. Someone who shared my background could probably understand the demeanor of the witnesses who were testifying. They could maybe understand little things that other jurors might not, because of the culture and customs that could appear foreign to an outsider.

In any case, the trial proceeded. The district attorney introduced witness after witness to the MORE Discount House robbery. He would have me stand up, then ask each witness if I was the man who had committed the robbery. Every single one denied having ever seen me before. Some of the prosecution witnesses testified that the man who struggled with the messenger was a small man, and that they had seen him jump easily over some cars as he was running through the parking lot. The partner must have been about nineteen or twenty years old, they thought. I was in my late thirties at the time, and didn't resemble the description provided by the witnesses.

They brought in the victim whose car had been stopped and commandeered on Sepulveda. His name was Leroy Caldwell, and he was a big black guy, about six eight. He testified how the bandit had put a gun to his head and told him to get out of the car.

The prosecutor asked, "Is this the man who took your car away from you?" He pointed over to where I was seated.

He looked at me very carefully.

"No."

By this point Judge Walker seemed to be getting mad that the witnesses were unable to identify me. He told Caldwell to get down and stand next to me, which he did.

Busch asked him again, "Is this the man who took your car?"
Again he said, "No. This guy is too big."
The prosecutor asked him how close the bandit had come to him.
He said that he was maybe a foot away, holding the gun to his head.
"And you don't recognize this man?"
"No, sir, I don't."
They dismissed that witness.

Even the witnesses who were supposed to be most damaging to my
case proved to be helpful. A witness by the name of Howard Theodore
Jensen was called. He testified that I had solicited him to help me pull
off the MORE robbery and that, even though he didn't want to do it, I
had convinced him. He testified that we had cased the MORE Discount
House before the robbery and that we had followed the messenger —
the one we were planning to rob — on his regular route.

He said that he remembered very well the day we had followed the
messenger because the day before he had applied for a job with the tele-
phone company.

"It was a Friday," he said, "when I submitted the job application. The
following day Ernie and I followed the messenger to learn his route."

This would have been Saturday the 18th. He kept saying that he re-
membered the day very well because he was hoping to land the tele-
phone company job and that had been on his mind.

We recalled the messenger to the witness stand after Jensen's tes-
timony. The messenger testified that he never worked on Saturday.
Saturday and Sunday were his days off because the banks were closed,
and there was no point in making a pickup if he couldn't deposit the
money.

As it turns out, the authorities had convinced Jensen to testify be-
cause he had committed a parole violation and was trying to cut a deal.
His wife and he had gotten into a nasty fight, and he had pulled out a
gun and threatened to kill her. The neighbors called the police, though
Jensen was gone by the time they arrived. The next day the cops picked
him up at work and searched him and his car, looking for the gun, but
they couldn't find it. His wife had filed a formal complaint against him,
so he was taken down to the station. Because he was out on parole, he
was sure to be sent back to prison on account of the assault.

This is why he agreed to testify against me, and why he wound up
manufacturing a story about us casing the joint and following the mes-
senger. I found out later that even while Jensen was testifying in my

case, he was robbing banks around the city. He was finally caught, and ended up back in county jail.

I knew someone who was in the High Power tank with him, and that guy asked him, "Hey, aren't you the one that testified in the López case? It seems like I read that there was a guy named Jensen who testified against López."

He said, "Yeah, I was just jiving, you know. I didn't know nothing about Ernie."

He could laugh about it because while he was testifying against me, he was free to commit those bank robberies. He wound up getting twenty years in the federal penitentiary.

Nothing seemed to be going the DA's way. About halfway through the trial, the prosecution said they had a new, secret witness who, they claimed, would prove my guilt. This witness would testify that I had solicited him to commit the MORE robbery and, though he declined, had told him all about it afterward. We asked for his name but were not given it. My attorney made several motions to learn his name, arguing that she had the right to investigate the witness and prepare relevant questions. The district attorney said that if we were given the name of the witness, his life could be put in jeopardy. The district attorney brought an officer named Ed Benson to the witness stand to prove his point.

Benson testified that he had talked to the witness and that this person was deathly afraid of me. The judge asked him, "What do you mean by deathly afraid of him?"

Benson said, "He's afraid of Mr. López because of his past record." He went on to say that this person had told him that he did not want his name to be revealed ahead of time because he was sure that I would have him hurt or killed.

Based on this testimony, Busch was able to call my parole officer from Alcatraz as a witness. He took the stand to testify that I had been in serious trouble in Alcatraz and had been put in the hole numerous times. I had always been considered very dangerous, he said, and I had had many fights because I enjoyed beating men up. I liked to raise hell with the prison system and to organize strikes. I could certainly be the type of man who would try to intimidate a witness or exact revenge if he did testify.

We advised the court that if I had solicited this witness to commit the crime, then I knew who the witness was and there was no need for

secrecy. The judge replied that if I had solicited anybody, then I already knew the witness, and the prosecution did not need to supply me with his name. The motion to have his name revealed was denied.

It was only while sitting in court on the appointed day that I finally got to see the prosecution's so-called secret weapon. Limping up the courtroom aisle was none other than Robert Castillo Luna. Six detectives surrounded him: three in front, two at his sides, and one in back. They were certainly putting on a big show for the jury.

The last time I had seen Luna was in the Bakersfield jail, when he was hobbling around on his lame foot and I was helping get him soup from the jailer. It seems that after my arrest in Bakersfield, the Los Angeles district attorney suspected Winhoven and me of participating in the MORE robbery. He had just shipped Luna back to Kern County, and he arranged with the Bakersfield police to put Luna in a cell with me. The DA made a deal with Luna to reduce his sentence on the charges stemming from the rapes, robberies, and the prison escape: he was to report anything I might tell him about murdering the MORE manager.

As I said, while Luna was in my tank, we never talked about crime. He just kept bulling about how well he knew Fat Boy and Big Zeke, about his trips to Mexico, and about his movie star father. We never talked about anything to do with the case or any type of violation of the law in all those days leading up to my preliminary hearing on the weapons-possession charge.

Now here was Luna testifying that I had tried to get him to commit the MORE job with me when I saw him in Los Angeles. He claimed that we had talked about the robbery while we were held over in the Bakersfield jail, and that I had told him all about the murder of the manager, the commandeering of the car, the escape, and the rest of it. From start to finish he was lying. He even had some of the facts from the case mixed up. But he insisted that we had talked in the tank and that I had told him about the crime.

When it came time for my attorney to cross-examine him, he admitted that he had been in the prison camp up in Tehachapi for robbery and that he had escaped. She asked him if he had any charges pending against him, and he said he did not. We found out only later that the district attorney had dismissed all the rape and robbery charges against Luna so that he would testify against me.

Up to the time that Luna testified, the DA had not been able to present an ounce of credible evidence against me. We were even on the

verge of filing a motion to dismiss the case for lack of evidence, since not one person could connect me with the crime. But when Luna came along with his bogus testimony, things started to look pretty bad for me. He convinced the jury that he had heard my jailhouse confession and that his information was accurate because he had kept dated notes of our conversations. Up to the day of my preliminary hearing, he had passed these notes on to the jailer every time he was taken out of the cell to have his bandages changed.

As Luna was on the witness stand testifying, Winhoven got so mad that he leaped up and shouted, "That man is a goddamn liar!"

After being reproached by the judge, Winhoven asked if he could approach the bench. He, my lawyer, and the district attorney huddled around the judge's desk. What happened next was about the most amazing thing I have ever witnessed in a court of law.

Winhoven told the judge, "This man is lying! For some reason, he wants Ernie convicted of this crime he didn't commit. I don't know what's behind it, but I know this man is lying!"

He said he wanted to take the witness stand and make a statement. The only condition was that he didn't want to be interrupted. He was prepared to tell the whole story of the robbery, and he didn't want the district attorney interrupting him with objections or cross-examination while he was testifying. Judge Walker asked him if he intended to make a confession. He said he intended to tell the truth about what happened.

The judge said, "All right. This is what we'll do: you take the stand and make the statement. Nobody will interrupt you. At the conclusion of your statement, the district attorney can ask you questions, and the attorney for the defense can ask you questions as well. Is that agreeable to you?"

It was, and Winhoven took the stand. He ran down the whole story about how he had robbed the MORE Discount House with his partner, a young guy about twenty years old. I think that he knew him from McNeil, but the partner was originally from Texas. This young man—whom he refused to identify—had told Winhoven of his plan to hold up a liquor store. Winhoven talked him out of it by telling him that he knew of a place that could be robbed very easily and would provide a bigger payoff than any liquor store.

He testified that he had felt responsible for this young guy becoming involved in the crime, and so when he saw him struggling with the

off-duty cop during the robbery, he was worried that the partner was going to get caught. He went over to free his partner, and that's when he started firing. He recounted all the events of the crime: how the robbery was planned, how it was committed, how he got away, and how he took different routes in order to escape.

He went on to say that for some reason Luna was lying and that I had had nothing to do with planning or committing the robbery. In fact, I hadn't even known about the crime until we were arrested and accused. Winhoven went through the string of facts that Luna had presented, and showed how wrong his testimony was about many of the details of the crime.

After he finished, the district attorney questioned him about some details of the robbery, and my attorney did the same. The questioning went on like that for a while.

We've all seen some Perry Mason show where the guilty party finally confesses in a dramatic last-minute courtroom scene. In reality, this never happens. What Winhoven did was the most surprising and dramatic thing I have ever witnessed in court. But I was sure glad I saw it!

The district attorney, of course, knew all along that Luna was lying. He had put him up to it. In fact, he was trying to put on two more witnesses to testify against me. During the trial we had these two witnesses called, and they told of being approached by Busch. He had said that they would get the same deal as Luna if they testified against me. Even though they could have avoided going back to prison, they told him that they were not interested in manufacturing testimony.

When these two witnesses were presented in court, Busch got mad, and denied the accusation up and down. In truth, he had tried to buy their testimony. That was how he had got Jensen to testify against me, and that was how he had got Luna to make up his story about the jailhouse confession and the notes. In fact, it soon came to light that Luna's relationship with the police had always been very close. The detective investigating my case even became his friend. When Luna went back to prison to finish out his sentence, the detective used to write him every other week or so. He even promised to get Luna a job when he was paroled, and they became close associates.

Because he had cooperated with the police and testified against me, Luna applied to the governor for executive clemency. Evelle J. Younger, who would become the Los Angeles County District Attorney, Police Chief William Parker, and Joseph Busch, the special prosecutor in my

case, all signed the executive clemency papers for Robert Luna and had them sent to the governor, Edmund "Pat" Brown, Sr.

I don't know why in the world Governor Brown turned him down, but he did. He must have smelled something fishy or have been given information about the case, because Luna's recommendations were impeccable. When the clemency was denied, Younger, Parker, and Busch were afraid that Luna was going to turn against them. They wanted to keep him real close and real happy so that he wouldn't reverse his testimony.

Even after my trial, Luna continued with his career as a rat. He was transferred from San Quentin to Soledad and placed under special protection. Over the years he had made a great many enemies by being a snitch. I don't know what happened after his release, but I heard that he finally ended up getting killed.

Armed with Luna's bogus testimony, Busch tried to discount Winhoven's confession. As he was closing the case for the prosecution, he explained to the jury that Winhoven must have come forward because he was afraid of me. Somehow I had threatened him, and he was scared that his life would be in danger if he didn't testify as he had. Another of the district attorney's theories was that Winhoven was trying to make things easier for himself after he got to prison. He was going to be known as the good guy who got Ernie López off the hook, and in that way he would be a big shot when he got to the penitentiary. Busch reminded them that Winhoven had acted as his own attorney during the trial and had originally promised to prove to the jury that he was completely innocent of the MORE robbery.

He told the jury, "Winhoven either lied to you when he said he was innocent, or he is lying to you now when he says he is guilty. Either way, how can you trust this man, a convicted felon and a proven liar? He has told you nothing but lies, and he is not to be believed."

Busch also went on and on about my time on the Rock. "Ernie López was in Alcatraz, and his poor record there speaks for itself. He was constantly in trouble, getting sent to isolation, and he was often confined to the hole. He is all the way around an individual of bad character."

He presented the jury with all the reports that had been made against me. They documented all the fights I had had, the number of times I had been sent to the hole, and the times I had been put in isolation. He even suggested that Winhoven and I had plotted to commit the robbery while we were in Alcatraz. So we were guilty of conspiracy to commit a felony as well, though he had no proof to offer. Of course, when Red

and I were at Alcatraz, I had no idea that he would ever get out. He was not up for parole, and I didn't know when, or even if, he would be released. It was ridiculous to think that we were hatching plans together. By the time he was granted parole, he was on his way to McNeil Island and I was back in LA.

In any case, the prosecution rested after having hammered these ideas into the jurors' heads. The jury had been none too friendly toward me from the first, anyway. Throughout the trial, they laughed while waiting for the court to reconvene. They made little remarks to one another and then looked over at me. I could see that they didn't believe anything about my defense. It was simple to read the skepticism in their eyes.

After the prosecution rested, my attorney came to visit me in jail.

She said, "Ernie, Busch just stopped me in the hall and told me that the deal still goes, but after Monday, when your defense starts, the deal is off."

I told her, "You tell Busch thanks. But I'm not going to accept any deals."

On Monday, all my witnesses were in the hall waiting to testify, and I was brought in to the courtroom. My attorney was sitting in the empty jury box along with her husband — who was also an attorney — and they were talking over something with Busch.

Barbara came over and said, "Ernie, Busch has been talking to me again. Look, he's willing to make the deal."

"Well, Barbara, you know how I feel. I don't want to discuss it any more."

"Okay," she said. "I just thought I'd tell you."

In a little while, her husband came over to me. He gave me the same message from Busch, and I told him the same thing. No deal.

"Let's just start getting my people up on the witness stand."

Now, I have never seen a district attorney try to make a deal with someone after resting the case for the prosecution. Never before and never since have I seen anything like that. They were clearly worried about their chances.

Before the trial restarted, my attorney called me over once again. She read me a letter that she had typed. The letter said that my attorney had several times advised me that the district attorney wanted to cut a deal. The letter stated that I had refused and that I would rather take my chances with the jury.

Now I got a little mad at the way this letter was written. I had never

told her that I would take my chances with the jury. The phrasing made it sound as if I were guilty, that I would take a chance and try to beat the odds.

I told her, "Listen, I never said anything like that. I told you that I was not gonna plead guilty to a crime I never committed and that I'd rather go to the gas chamber."

"Oh no, that's no problem," she said. "I can change the wording there, and then you can sign the letter."

This signaled to me that she wanted me to make a deal so that she would get in good standing with Busch. I suppose she was thinking about her future career.

I finally told her that I would read the letter a little bit more carefully during recess and think it over.

I took the letter and held onto it for a long time. She kept trying to get it back from me, but I always managed to stall her with an excuse. She even asked Winhoven to try to get the letter back from me, but I never did return it.

Barbara presented the case for the defense by calling a witness who was a salesman at a shoe store in Pasadena. On the day of the MORE robbery, I had gone to buy two pairs of shoes and some other small items at the store, which was twenty-five miles from the scene of the crime. The salesman testified that he remembered me because I bought two pairs of the same shoes, something that was a little unusual. I had gone with my girl, and the three of us had made small talk, the usual little banter between customer and salesman.

He had entered the date of the sale in his books, and he could identify the shoes by the model numbers. I had worn one pair of the shoes to court, and I took them off right in front of the jury. The judge got quite angry at this stunt, and said that I would have to go shoeless because I had presented my shoes as evidence.

I told him, "That's fine, your honor. I'll go barefoot."

There was a little commotion in the courtroom until the judge finally relented and permitted the shoes to be entered as evidence by just the model number. I was allowed to wear my shoes again.

Next we called a police officer named Hector Garcia, who drew composite pictures from the descriptions of witnesses. He had no desire to serve as a witness for the defense, but we had subpoenaed him, and he had no choice. My attorney asked him if he had been at the scene right after the robbery, and he testified that he had been. He stated that

he had made a composite sketch of the second bandit, who was Winhoven, but that he wasn't able to make one of the first, because none of the witnesses could provide enough details for a reasonable likeness.

Garcia's testimony proved that nobody at the time could offer any kind of detail about the bandit's appearance. So no positive identification could be made, one way or another. Anyone who tried to come forward now with a description was simply manufacturing testimony.

We tried to call Leroy Caldwell, the large black man whose car had been commandeered on Sepulveda. After he testified initially, the authorities, it seems, had been to visit him numerous times. They were constantly coming around to his house and harassing him, telling him that they really wanted him to change his story and identify me. When he refused, they tore up his house while conducting a "search" for some supposedly stolen money. They confiscated his station wagon and towed it to the Fourth Street station. They even accused Caldwell of being in cahoots with the robbers and participating in the robbery. They badgered and scared him so badly that he ended up having a heart attack. To get as far from the LA police as he could, he quit his job and moved out of town. My investigator tried to find him after he moved, but he couldn't locate him in time for the trial.

When it came time for summation, Winhoven—who all along had been representing himself—told the jury that they would be doing a great injustice if they convicted me. He insisted that I was not with him during the robbery, that I had nothing to do with the planning of it, and that the only reason I was on trial with him was because I was his friend. He insisted again that Luna had told a bunch of lies and that he, Winhoven, was telling the truth.

The jury deliberated for several days. Finally, when the judge asked for a verdict, the judgment came down: guilty.

Then came the penalty phase. The jury deliberated again, and I heard the sentence they passed on me: death.

In the end, I believe that my being tried together with Winhoven hurt my case the most. If my case had been presented alone, I believe that I would not have been convicted, despite Luna's testimony against me. It looked very bad when Winhoven consulted with my attorney and tried to get advice from her during the trial. This made it appear as if the three of us were sharing strategies, and as if Winhoven's defense was closely tied to mine. That, plus Winhoven's confession, made me look guilty by association in the eyes of the jury.

Things were looking pretty bleak for me then, and I kept thinking over the details of my case. I came to realize something about the notes that Luna had passed on to the LA district attorney, the notes that detailed my supposed confession.

I told my attorney, "Look, Barbara, Luna's notes are proof that I couldn't have been in the tank with him during the time he claimed that I made those statements."

Luna had dated all the notes, and I remembered that on some of those dates I was in the hole in the Kern County jail. I remembered well because those were the days immediately before my preliminary hearing. I was in isolation, and it would have been impossible for me to converse with Luna.

Barbara kept telling me that she was going to subpoena the officers from Bakersfield to prove my point, but she never did. By now I was completely disenchanted with her representation, so right after I was sentenced to death, I fired her. But, as the saying goes, you only cover the well after somebody drowns.

I hired another attorney, a man by the name of Morris Lavine. He immediately put in a motion to vacate the conviction and the death sentence. A date was set for a hearing, and all the Bakersfield officers involved in the investigations of Luna, Winhoven, or me were subpoenaed. In addition, they were ordered to bring along all their records.

During this hearing, Busch instructed the officers to testify that they had seen me in the same tank with Luna. They were to add nothing more regarding the case. Most of the officers testified that they had seen me either in the tank with Luna or in the hole. Unfortunately, their records did not indicate the precise dates that I had been confined in isolation.

One officer offered a little more information than Busch wanted revealed. Lieutenant Matlock took the stand and said that I had been in the tank with Luna, and he knew this because he had ordered it. The LAPD had contacted his office and asked for Luna to be placed in the tank with me so that he could gather evidence. Lieutenant Matlock had not actually witnessed Luna being placed in the cell with me, but he had given the order to his officers, and when he gave an order, he expected it to be carried out. He went on to testify that he had told the LAPD that the plan had indeed been carried out.

Despite this testimony, Judge Walker denied the motion to vacate the conviction and the death sentence. He set a date for sentencing. We went to court and made a motion for a new trial on several grounds.

Lavine argued that the motion for severance should have been granted. Also, since Winhoven was representing himself, his conferring with my attorney had prejudiced the jury.

The trial had one more twist that I have not mentioned yet. I had subpoenaed a witness from Folsom to testify on my behalf. When he arrived from Folsom, he was held over in LA County Jail, from where he and thirteen other men escaped before the trial. The newspapers and television stations covered the story, and reported that I had subpoenaed this witness from Folsom for the sole purpose of helping him set up an escape.

During the trial, we made a motion for a new trial on the grounds that the jurors had been prejudiced by the newspaper and TV coverage of the escape. The judge asked the jury members if they had read about these events, and they all said that they had not read a word about it. They admitted to having heard something about the escape, but none of them had followed the case very closely.

After hearing arguments on all the points that had tainted my trial, Judge Walker still denied our motion for a new trial, and confirmed my death sentence. I remained in county jail for about ten more days before being transported to death row in San Quentin. Both Winhoven and I went at the same time. This was in April 1961.

CONDEMNED

They executed many men while I was on death row. I personally know of nineteen people who were executed in the gas chamber during my time on the row. The first man I knew was actually a young kid, about nineteen years old, named Alexander Robillard. He was executed just about the time I got to San Quentin, in April 1961. Then Ronny Rittger was executed around June 1961. Next they executed Jimmy Linden, in July. David Combes was executed around October, and Jimmy Kendrick in November.

I remember Jimmy Kendrick. He was so fed up with death row that he wanted to get his execution over with. His case had been delayed so long in the California Supreme Court that he wrote a letter and told them to get moving on his execution. He said he didn't want to have to send Christmas cards one more time. He urged them to rule one way or another, but to get going. The court did come down with its decision, and he was finally executed on November 3.

Soon after, Richard Lindsey and Billy Monk—who was in for kidnapping, not murder—were executed on November 21. Little Joe Gonzales (we called him Speedy) was executed on November 29. Rudolph Wright was executed in January 1962. Then Ray Lane in March. Lawrence Garner was executed on April 9, and Robert Hughes on April 18. Adolph Busch was executed in June. One of the men I knew pretty well was Augustine Baldonado, who was executed in August 1962.

He and Luis (Louie) Moya were partners in crime. The two of them had been approached by a woman named Elizabeth Duncan, whose son, Frank, was an attorney. She was completely infatuated with her

boy, and threw tantrums at the mere thought that he would ever leave her home. Even after he secretly married, Frank continued to sleep nights at his mother's. He finally had to confess that he was married when his wife became pregnant. Enraged, Elizabeth did what she could to break up her son's marriage. Finally she offered Moya and Baldonado $10,000 to kill her son's wife. The two men kidnapped the pregnant woman, drove along the coast, and threw her off a high cliff to her death.

When the pair went to collect their money, Duncan balked. Apparently she had become paranoid, and didn't want to turn over the cash in case Moya and Baldonado used it as proof of her involvement in the murder. Angry and out for revenge, the two men went to the authorities and told them the whole story. Their testimony convicted Duncan, but it didn't save them from the gas chamber. All three were executed on the same day, August 8, 1962. Elizabeth Duncan had to be bused in all the way from a prison in Pomona. She was killed first. Then Moya and Baldonado were placed in chair A and chair B of the gas chamber and killed at the same time.

Melvin Darling was next to be executed, in October. And Allen Ditson was executed in November 1962. One thing that not many people know: Allen Ditson was executed illegally. He had had a writ of *certiorari* pending with the U.S. Supreme Court. The court agreed to hear his case, which should have automatically stayed his execution. Well, it was claimed that, for some reason or other, the government did not get back to the California Supreme Court about the stay. The state court claimed that the stay was lost. Though his case was going to be reviewed by the high court, Ditson had already been taken downstairs and killed. When the U.S. Supreme Court granted *certiorari*, they asked the California Supreme Court to forward Ditson's records. At that point, for the first time, the state had to admit that he had already been executed. Though the case did not receive a lot of attention, the story was carried in some papers. I remember one headline: "A Dark Cloud in California Justice."

There were several inmates on death row whom I hated. They were a bunch of rats, or they had killed little kids for sexual pleasure. I hated them because I used to like kids an awful lot. I would give these guys a hard time because I wanted them to stay far away from me. Most of them never came around, anyway, because they knew better, and most of the other guys ignored these men as well. Often they didn't even

bother to leave their cells, figuring that they would be safer alone than with the rest of us during recreation.

There were all different types of people on death row. There were many who were not bad guys or career criminals, but had just gotten themselves into a mess. One guy, Alex Robillard—the first person I knew who was executed—was a nice kid, and had just run into more trouble than he expected. Alex used to call himself Alexander XIV; he was young, tall, and good-looking. In his case, he drove through a police blockade while fleeing a robbery. The police opened fire, and he shot back wildly as he was driving by. He happened to hit one of the policemen, and killed him. Because he had killed a cop, all the guards really wanted to take Robillard down. When they took him to be executed, the bulls kept asking, "Is he dead yet? Is the son of a bitch dead yet?"

I recall a number of fellows who became pretty good friends of mine. Two were John Vlahovich ("Big John," who stood six nine) and his co-defendant Donald Franklin. They had another codefendant, whom I never did like, named Joseph Rosoto. But Vlahovich and Franklin were my good friends, and they were innocent of the crimes for which they had been convicted and sentenced to death.

These three had already said their good-byes and been taken down for execution. When they take you for execution, you go down the day before, around 4:30 p.m., to what they call a strip cell. They bring your last meal to you down there, and you can eat your meal at any time, from 4:30 in the afternoon until the morning of your execution.

There are two or three strip cells down by the gas chamber, and they are completely empty except for a mattress on the floor and a toilet. Outside the cell there's a little space where an officer stays and keeps a deathwatch on you. The guard has a little stove close by, and when you want your last meal, he warms it up and gives it to you. You are kept there until ten o'clock the next morning, which is the hour of execution.

These three guys—Vlahovich, Franklin, and Rosoto—were down in the strip cells on the morning of their execution. At nine or nine thirty, they heard over the radio that Supreme Court Justice William O. Douglas had issued a stay of execution for them. So the three were brought back upstairs to the living.

Franklin was pretty funny, though he could be a serious guy, too. He had consistently proclaimed his innocence throughout the trial and appeals. If you were to read his case, you would start wondering how the hell he was ever convicted. Even the state supreme court said he had been convicted on very flimsy evidence, though it was enough evidence

for them to uphold the conviction. This is because the justices of the high court will not rule on any conflicting evidence. Their only interest is with questions of law. Any conflicting testimony must be dealt with by the jury system. If the jury believes or disbelieves certain witnesses, that's how the matter stands. The high court — or any appellate court, for that matter — will not involve itself with the credibility or testimony of witnesses.

As I said, old Franklin was kind of a funny guy. He used to say about the execution, "Let's get going. Either piss or get off the pot."

So when he came back from the holding cell downstairs, he made a lot of commotion. He was yelling, "Goddamn, I told 'em to get going, one way or the other."

He was shouting and really making a racket. One of my buddies said, "Eh, Frank, don't give me that bull. You were scared to death. When you went by last night shaking hands good-bye, your hand was soaking wet!"

Franklin joined in the laughter with everyone else.

The reason the case against Franklin, Vlahovich, and Rosoto was so flimsy was because the DA in Orange County, Cecil Hicks, had used a jailhouse informant to falsify testimony against Vlahovich and the others in 1962. Because of this perjured testimony, Vlahovich was convicted and sentenced to die. This seems to have become a common practice for prosecutors to win a conviction at all costs. I know this firsthand because it happened to me. These informants used by the police are planted to gather (or fabricate) information in exchange for having the charges against them reduced or dismissed. Some are even paid in cash. The common *modus operandi* of an informant is to testify that the defendant, over the informant's protestations, began talking about the crime he had committed. You would be surprised how many times in court you will hear someone testify, "I told him he should be careful about what he says, but the defendant just kept on going."

When a prosecutor asks an informant if anybody has promised him any kind of reward or better treatment for his testimony, he, of course, answers no. Informants get very good at making up the kind of conversation that he knows will be music to the prosecution's ears.

The informant who testified in John Vlahovich's case was a man named Charles Harrelson. He is the father of the actor Woody Harrelson, who played the role of Mickey Knox, the psychopathic killer in Oliver Stone's film *Natural Born Killers*. Charles Harrelson had been imprisoned in Orange County Jail for robbery, rape, and burglary.

Hicks ordered Harrelson to be wired with a transmitter. Hicks knew

ahead of time that the continual slamming of cell doors and the constant noise made by the other prisoners would make it almost impossible to get a clear recording from inside the jail. Of course, the recordings Harrelson made, which were presented in court, were completely unintelligible. They were entered as evidence, nevertheless, to suggest to the jury the legitimacy of the case made against Vlahovich.

Harrelson went on to fabricate a story, claiming that Vlahovich had made incriminating statements, which was completely untrue. His testimony was the main evidence that persuaded a jury to convict Vlahovich and condemn him to death. The California Supreme Court eventually reversed Vlahovich's conviction, and he was given a new trial. In the end, he was released from prison as a free man.

Meanwhile, in 1973, Harrelson was convicted for the contract killing of a businessman in Texas. After being released, he was again convicted of murder, this time for killing federal judge "Maximum John" Woods in San Antonio, Texas, in 1979. On December 21, 1982, the *Los Angeles Times* ran an article by Rone Tempest about Harrelson's case; the headline was "Texas Hit Man Charged with Killing Judge; Says He Helped California Police Build Murder Case." The article went on to report that Harrelson had been wired for sound to help win a conviction in an Orange County murder case in 1962. The story reports that neither Harrelson nor his attorney would name the murder case, but of course I know it was Vlahovich. As the article notes, "Harrelson's alleged cooperation was ironic because much of the case against him and his two co-defendants in the Woods slaying was based on Federal wiretaps of Harrelson's friends, jail associates, and attorneys. In his defense, Harrelson has contended that the wiretaps were illegally and improperly obtained." When his own attorney asked him what he did for a living, according to the article, Harrelson answered, "Gamble and make tapes for the government."

In any case, Harrelson was convicted and sentenced to prison. The man he killed, John Woods, was the first federal judge in more than a century to be assassinated.

I will try to run down for you the procedure they take when they are going to execute a man.

About twenty days before your execution, they keep a closer watch on you. During the nighttime, especially, they check your cell more often and more carefully than they do the others.

When you come down to about fifteen days, they give you a form to

fill out. They want to know where you want your body to be sent or if anybody is going to come claim you. If there is no one to claim your body, they take it to Marin County for cremation. They also want to know your clothes size because a lot of men on death row gain weight. There isn't much to do but eat and sit around, so men outgrow their clothes, and the authorities want to know what size pants to get you for your execution. They also ask you what you want for your last meal. For the first — and usually last — time in prison, they give you whatever you want to eat. Many people may think that they will give you everything you want, but they don't. They just give you what they claim is reasonable. You can request quite a bit of whatever you want, but they will not order an amount that they know you can't finish. Finally, they want to know if anybody is going to come and see you before the execution.

When you have seven days left, they let you have sole use of the TV. The TV was normally on the freeway, the area where we could walk up and down for exercise in the morning. There was one TV on death row, at least at that time. The TV was on a low table with wheels, and at seven days before execution, around two thirty in the afternoon, after you came in from exercise, they would put the TV in front of your cell. You got to have it there for your last seven evenings on death row. You could watch TV anytime from three thirty in the afternoon until five o'clock the next morning. They would have you make out a little schedule of the programs you wanted to watch and give it to the sergeant. Every so often, when one program went off, the sergeant would be there to change the station to the next program.

They would even push the little TV right against the bars of your cell if you wanted them to. That way they could plug your earphones in, and you wouldn't disturb the other prisoners. If a guy near you was watching the TV, you could get your own earphones and run a fine little wire to his line in order to make a hookup. You could connect your earphones to his so that both of you could listen to the TV. We always used a fine wire so that the guard wouldn't see it, but I'm sure that the bull knew exactly what we were doing. He didn't really care one way or the other as long as we weren't disturbing anybody.

Later on they put TVs in front of every third cell on death row. They had them mounted on the gun gallery, about ten feet up and maybe five feet away from the front of the cells. The TVs were tilted down so you could see them pretty well. The men in the three cells would watch the same TV, and everybody had earphones that they could plug directly into their TV. You changed the stations by remote control. The

three guys who were going to watch the one television had to agree on what programs to watch. The two men near me, Winhoven and another friend of mine, usually came to some agreeable arrangement. We liked pretty much the same programs, but overall we really didn't care all that much what program we would watch.

The day before your execution, after dinner, which is finished around three thirty, they leave the deadlock-bar unhooked and open your cell. You're the only one allowed outside on the runway, and you go and take a shower. All this time a guard on the gun gallery with a shotgun and a pistol is watching you shower and shave. By that time, you wouldn't have very much left in your cell. All of your personal property, which wouldn't have amounted to too much anyway, would have already been sent home. Usually the only thing left is a razor blade and soap. So you shower and shave and return to your cell.

You probably get back to your cell about four o'clock. They lock your door. At exactly four thirty you can hear a little commotion from way in front of the row, over by the way you first came in. When you come into the row, there's a solid-steel door that leads to an enclosure with bars. Once you are in there, they close the steel door, and you're caged in. You can't go anywhere until they open the second door, which leads into the row. You can hear the double set of doors being unlocked and locked, and by the time the officers have opened all these doors to get in, you have heard all the locks clicking and the bars banging and the keys jangling. So everybody on the row knows that they're coming for you.

When the officers come in, they come five strong: four bulls and one lieutenant. When I was there, the lieutenant was a real short, real fat old bastard by the name of Fred Bartlett. He stood about five five and weighed some 250 pounds. He really enjoyed this procedure. He would come into the row, a cigar clamped in his mouth, followed by four bulls. The cigar wasn't lit; he just liked to chew on it. He would march down to your cell and stand right in front of it, just looking at you. The four bulls would gather around him, and the man with the shotgun in the gun gallery would be right in front of your cell. At a given moment, still looking at you, he would raise his hand in a really dramatic motion, as if he were playing the part of the executioner, and bring it down real fast. There was no good reason to do all that bull, but he really enjoyed putting on a show. You could tell he was getting a kick out of the whole process.

His dropped hand was a signal for the other bulls way down at the entrance, outside the doors at the end of the tier, to pull the deadlock-bar. This is an old-fashioned deadlock-bar that binds the top of the

door. An unlocked door wouldn't open if the bar was binding it. So the guards would first have to unlock your door with the key. Then Bartlett would raise his arm, giving the signal to pull the bar and release the door.

That's when you would come out of your cell. If you happened to be in the front or middle of the row, you would go all the way down to the end, around cell 34. All the bulls follow you while you shake hands with the guys, going all the way down to the front of the row. Then they take you out the double doors and put what they call a restraining belt on you. This serves the same purpose as handcuffs, only it is made out of leather. They put this leather belt around your waist, bind your wrists to it, and take you out of the row.

They open another door, put you on an elevator, and take you down six stories to the first floor. As you come out of the elevator, you make a right turn, walk about eight feet, and run into a solid-steel door with rivets. They open this door and take you in. As soon as you are inside that door, you come to the holding cells. They place you in one of the strip cells, which contains just a toilet and a mattress. The only thing that you are allowed to have is a short little pencil. The officer gives it to you in case you want to write a last letter. You are also permitted to bring a little record player with you. The guard puts it outside, against the bars, so that you can put on the records you want and listen to music.

In the meantime, your last meal, ordered a couple weeks before, is available any time after four thirty. You can eat it a bit at a time or take the whole meal, depending on what you want. You just need to ask the bull, and he warms up whatever you requested.

You stay in that cell until the next morning. People like the chaplain and others come in and out during the night and morning, until the doctor shows up a bit before ten o'clock. He straps a stethoscope on your chest close to your heart and secures the rubber tube running from it to your back.

At almost exactly ten o'clock, they open the door of the holding cell. As you are led out, there is another solid door with rivets to your right. They open that door, the door to the gas chamber.

You see a narrow rug running all the way to the back of the gas chamber. You aren't wearing any shoes, just socks. As soon as they open that steel door, two guards grab you by the shoulders and arms. They hustle you all the way from that last door to the back of the gas chamber. You are taken in at a run, as if you would be in a hell of a hurry to get to the chair.

They take you into the chamber, and they strap you down into the

chair real fast. They screw the rubber tube running from the stetho-scope to the back wall of the chamber. On the other side of the wall, the doctor screws his end of the stethoscope into that same part where the stethoscope connects on the inside. This is how he can listen to your heart and know when to pronounce you dead. Meanwhile, the bulls, who are mostly wise guys, are patting you on the back and wishing you all kinds of good luck.

They close the high-pressure door of the chamber. Below you, under the chair, the cyanide is in a bag, like a little tobacco bag, that is sus-pended above a bucket containing sulfuric acid. The bag is hooked to a wire, which is connected to the executioner's lever. At the warden's signal, the executioner drops the bag of cyanide into the sulfuric acid. When the cyanide hits the sulfuric acid, fumes start coming up from underneath the chair; fine holes drilled through the chair allow the gas to get to you. Twelve to fifteen minutes later, the doctor pronounces you dead.

I understand that when you breathe in the gas, it produces a strong burning sensation. Apparently it is a pretty painful experience, and you are conscious the entire time. I know that you are still conscious because of Caryl Chessman.

Before he was executed, Chessman worked out a series of hand signals with a newspaper reporter with whom he had gotten pretty friendly. They had decided that when Chessman was in the chamber, he would signal with his thumbs. The right thumb meant that he was ex-periencing one thing, the left thumb meant another. If he was suffering, he would signal with one of his thumbs, and if he was still conscious but not in pain, he would signal with the other. When Chessman was finally executed, the reporter read the signals he had given. He saw that Chessman was suffering all the way through the execution, which took thirteen to fourteen minutes. So all the men who were executed by the State of California suffered a great deal for a quarter of an hour before their deaths in the gas chamber.

All executions are viewed by witnesses, who watch through the glass of the chamber. The body is left in the chamber until they vacuum out all the deadly fumes. You hear the motors starting, then you hear the suction sound coming from beneath the floor. You can hear this all the way up to the sixth floor, where death row is located.

On the ceiling of the gas chamber there are two lights, one red and one green. When they are pumping the fumes out of the gas chamber, they turn the red light on, which means danger. They vacuum the gas

chamber until it is clear, when the green light goes on. Then they go in and take the body out. If some relative has claimed the body, there is usually a hearse waiting. But if there are no relatives to claim you and you are to be cremated over in Marin County, things take a bit longer, and they keep the body in the prison until the paperwork is completed.

As I mentioned before, Lieutenant Fred Bartlett, the guard with the cigar in his mouth, used to really enjoy playing the role of executioner. I would glare at him when he was putting on this show because I hated him so much. He had been working for the Department of Corrections at San Quentin for about ten years when I arrived. During the time that I was there, he was arrested and later convicted for child molestation. It turned out that Bartlett was a child molester, one of the lowest forms of life. They gave him thirty days in prison, and he ended up being fired from his job.

After this happened, I used to make real loud comments so that the other bulls could hear me. I would holler over at my friends while look-ing up at the man on the gunrail, "Oh God, Joe, there's another child molester, right in the goddamn gun gallery!"

All the prisoners would bust out laughing.

"Look," I'd say, "he's got a shotgun. He's got protection now!"

The guards who worked on death row were generally a really sick breed who enjoyed the idea of putting men to death. Many of the guards hated me because I would often say all kinds of insulting things to them. I didn't do this on a whim. Every comment they got, they deserved, and more.

We had several disturbances on the row, demonstrations and little riots that sprang up because of the ill treatment we received. For ex-ample, a guard would come and shake your cell down. When they shook your cell down, they would make you come out and walk away. Meanwhile, the guards would turn over all the things in your cell, tear your pictures off the wall and throw them on the floor, really rip up the whole cell for no other reason than to mess with you. Not all the guards acted like that, but many bulls loved to do those things.

Several times we started a jamboree. Once we made a commotion because we were supposed to get out of our cell for exercise at ten thirty. Well, the guards running the row in the morning would take their sweet time—they would be talking to each other about their vacations or about ball games and scores—and sometimes we wouldn't be let out until eleven or eleven thirty. Whatever time they let us out, we had to

be back in our cells at two thirty sharp. So we raised hell about this. We banged the doors and made so much commotion by banging on the bars and rattling the cots that finally the deputy warden came up to find out what was going on. We explained the situation, and told him that the guards were intentionally stalling before letting us out for exercise. He finally agreed with us, and gave strict orders that our cells were to be opened at exactly ten thirty, regardless of what the guards had to do. This was often the only way that we could get anything changed.

One of the ways we passed the time on the row was to take up strenuous physical exercise. We would do anything that could be done without a weight set: chin-ups, push-ups, sit-ups—we would do them all. So I formed a little group that exercised together, and I asked the authorities to give us some benches so that we could work out. After I made the request a few times, they finally agreed to have some benches made. The shops would put the benches together if I drew up a diagram of what we needed, so I set about drawing up plans.

I designed an inclined bench for sit-ups. Another, for bench presses, lay flat. Since we had so little equipment, we had to be resourceful. The inclined bench had a wooden bar on the end, like a handle. We used to put the inclined bench on top of a table. If you lay on the flat bench and had somebody sit on top of the inclined bench, you could hold that wooden bar and push the inclined bench with the guy sitting on top. This was the way we did bench presses. If you wanted to do squats, you took the flat bench away from the table, had two guys sit on the inclined bench, and pushed up the bench from a squat. If you wanted to work your arms, you could do the same thing for a military press. We also used to work with a medicine ball. We developed all kinds of exercises, and we used to work out every day. We started to get into pretty good shape, and many of the guys really developed their physiques.

Of course, all the bulls on the gun gallery had their little remarks to make. They used to say things like, "Those guys sure will have nice bodies when they go down to the gas chamber. They're sure gonna make nice-looking corpses."

Not everything on the row stayed quiet for long.

In the summer of 1962, six inmates made a desperate attempt to escape from death row. Louie Moya and Augustine Baldonado—convicted for killing the daughter-in-law of Elizabeth Duncan—were involved, along with Charlie Bickley, Manny Chavez, Clyde Bates, and my old friend Red Winhoven. As far as I know, this escape attempt has never been

made public, and there was at the time a strong effort to hush up any stories of the attempt.

The escape began shortly after midnight on July 2, 1962. The men had used a hacksaw to cut the bars of their cells almost all the way through. They had also cut the bars at the far end of the freeway, the corridor where we exercised during the day. Since we were often alone in our cells, it was possible to work on the bars a little at a time without being noticed. Cutting the bars along the freeway was more difficult because the guards were constantly on watch while we were out exercising.

The men put a little table with a blanket over it at the far end of the freeway. While four men sat around the table playing dominoes, another guy would slip under the table and quietly cut the bars. A sixth man, meanwhile, would walk up and down the freeway to make sure that the gunrail guard wasn't getting too close to them. Usually the gunrail guard stayed up toward the front of the row when we were exercising. Every once in a while he would walk down the gunrail to the back end and take a look around before walking back to the front. The lookout signaled the other guys if the gunrail guard came around too close, and the man under the table stopped cutting until the guard had turned and walked back. The bottoms of the bars were cut completely through, but the tops were cut only part way. Before the men were called back into the cells, they covered up the cuts with soap and soot.

According to the plan, the men would, at a given moment, push the bars open, come out of the cells, and escape through the back of the freeway and into the gunrail. From there they would climb up to a row of large windows that rose high over the row. Long steel bars spaced fairly far apart protected the windows. If only one bar could be cut and pulled open, the men would get through the window and make their way out onto the roof. From there they would scramble over the roof to a section of the prison near the bay. This section jutted in toward the prison, so it formed a blind spot that the tower guards couldn't see. The men would drop down at this spot and make their way into the bay. From there it was simply a matter of swimming away before the alarm was sounded.

In fact, a friend of mine in the general population launched his own escape from San Quentin from this exact spot. He and another inmate had crafted a kayak out of leather, made their way onto the roof, and dropped down into the blind spot by the bay. They carried the kayak with them, then rowed away in it. Paddling was pretty rough, but they managed to get quite a distance from the prison walls. As they were

struggling out on the water, a sailboat came over, and someone on board asked them if they needed help. They just smiled, waved, and said that they were fine, just taking some exercise. The boat sailed off. This friend remained free for twenty-five years. It wasn't until the late 1990s that they finally caught up with him, in Florida, where he had been robbing a series of banks.

Just after midnight on July 2nd, Augie Baldonado got the attention of the officer on the gunrail, a guard by the name of C. L. Deatrick.

"The water in my toilet is running, and I can't get it to stop. The button's stuck."

I could hear Deatrick answer him back. "Keep pushing the button, Baldonado. That'll get it unstuck."

Augie made a big act of pushing it and hitting it. Of course, the button would not come out because he had intentionally jammed it. The plan was to convince the officer in the gun gallery to go all the way into the plumbing corridor that ran behind the cells so that he would try to unhook the button of the toilet from the inside. As luck would have it, Deatrick didn't need to be persuaded; he decided on his own that the only way he could fix that button was to go into the corridor. Baldonado's cell was about the tenth one in, so Deatrick had a ways to go inside the corridor before he got to the right cell.

Once he entered the corridor, the other inmates pulled back the partially cut bars and came out of their cells. They went over to the bars that they had cut at the back of the freeway — the ones leading into the gunrail — and worked those bars free, too.

While Baldonado remained in his cell, the other five inmates walked around the gunrail and gathered at the entrance to the plumbing corridor, where Deatrick had gone in. While Deatrick was inside, trying to fix the toilet, Augie was in his cell, making sure that the water kept running. When his partners were in place, Baldonado unjammed the button and shouted through the wall that everything was okay, the button had come out, and the toilet had stopped running.

Deatrick came out of the plumbing corridor, and just as he stepped out the door, the five men grabbed him. Deatrick kept struggling, trying to grab his whistle or fire off his shotgun to alert the other guards. The men had to hit Deatrick over the head with one of the bars they had taken from the gunrail in order to quiet him down. Manny Chavez took Deatrick's pistol, and Bates put on his uniform. Toting the shotgun, Bates walked down to the gunrail to cover the entrance to the row.

Chavez went down the gunrail toward the front, and found Sergeant

Roy Kardell walking out of his office. The sergeant hadn't heard Deatrick return to his position in the gunrail, and was coming out to investigate. Chavez turned the gun on him and ordered him to lie down.

"Sergeant," Chavez said, "this is it. Do as I say or I'll kill you. You know I've nothing to lose. Lie down on the floor and keep quiet."

Kardell couldn't believe that some inmate had a pistol, and he tried to tackle Chavez. Manny clobbered him with the pistol and knocked him flat. Kardell looked up and saw Bates holding a shotgun. Thinking that Bates was Deatrick, he hollered to him to turn his shotgun on Chavez, not realizing that the man in the gunrail was an inmate too.

Bates shouted back at him, "Lie down, you son of a bitch, or I'll blow your goddamn brains out!"

Bleeding and dazed from the blow, he lay down. Their hands tied behind their backs and bleeding, Kardell and Deatrick were shoved into the office. Bates wet a towel and tried to wipe some of the blood from the two guards' faces while the other men took their keys.

It was now midnight, when Sergeant Kardell was supposed to make his regular count to the sergeant in the control room. Since they celled near Kardell's office, Louie Moya and Manny Chavez were well aware of this routine. Every midnight they would hear him call the control room. Kardell would say, "Calling control room for the count. Count's all clear." Then he would hang up.

So in the office Moya dialed 251, the extension number to Sergeant McCarthy in the control room. Chavez had the pistol trained on Sergeant Kardell, and Moya held the phone up to his ear when the connection was made. He instructed Kardell to say the count was all right. But when Kardell heard McCarthy's voice, he hesitated.

McCarthy asked him, "Is there any trouble on the row?"

Kardell knew Moya couldn't hear what McCarthy was asking, so he answered, "Yeah, yeah, that's right."

In the meantime the prison operator, sensing that something was wrong, had tipped off Warden Dickson. The warden called together the off-duty guards and notified the state militia. Their plan of action was to saturate the row with tear gas and flush the escapees out. If that plan failed, Dickson authorized a battalion of heavily armed guards to storm the row and kill all the prisoners, if necessary.

Not long after 1:00 a.m., a group of guards and militia members scrambled up to the roof. They opened the skylights above death row and dropped canister after canister of tear gas down into the row. They bored holes through the concrete roof and shot canisters through there

as well. We could hear the clatter of the canisters as they hit the bars, and the tear gas kept pouring in, spreading its choking smoke everywhere. The rest of us on the row tried our best to protect ourselves from the burning gas by wrapping wet towels around our faces and lying on the floor.

The escapees did not surrender, despite the tear gas that had filled the row. The guards decided that their only option was to storm the row and shoot as many inmates as they could. They figured that all of us were as desperate as hell and that this was their only hope of recapturing the row and possibly rescuing a few of the hostages, even if it meant killing everyone else, whether we were involved in the break or not.

By this time, however, the six guys realized that they had no chance of escaping, and they got on the phone with the warden to begin negotiating their surrender. Finally, sometime after four in the morning, the guys set the guns, keys, and ammunition down in front of the access door. The guards outside, armed to the teeth, could see all this through the window leading into the row. The six then went to the bathroom area and locked themselves in the showers. Only then did the guards come in from the outside and release Kardell and Deatrick. So ended the attempted escape from death row.

The whole row was locked down for a long time while the guards conducted their investigation and cleaned up the row. The six men involved in the plot were placed in the hole for several weeks. Moya and Baldonado, however, were coming up close to their execution date. So after about two weeks they were let out of isolation and brought back to their cells. They waited out their sentences, and were finally gassed on August 8, 1962. The other men involved weren't punished while their various appeals were pending or their execution dates approached. In the end, none of them were taken to the gas chamber, however, because of what happened next.

MY FIGHT FOR LIFE

For the entire four and a half years that I sat on death row, I worked doggedly through my appeals. I labored over my case almost every day, poring over law books and providing information to my attorney. In our opening brief to the Supreme Court of California, we first drew their attention to all the errors that were prejudicial to my case during my trial, and we followed up by pointing out problems in the proceedings themselves.

We brought up the issue of the lineup, the illegal search and seizure, and the exclusion of Mexican Americans from the jury panels. We brought up everything that we had claimed in the motion for a new trial filed with Judge Walker, and presented all of it to the state supreme court. We also made an issue of the disciplinary reports that had been brought into evidence during the penalty phase of my trial. The record clerk brought down from Alcatraz testified that he had found between sixty and eighty reports that had been made against me during my stay in the prison. The files were very complicated: some of the reports dealt with minor infractions, some were falsified, and some were exaggerated. All of these reports were present in the files together. We argued that to include these reports without bringing in the officers to testify about the specific infractions of the rules each report detailed was a violation of my constitutional rights. By presenting only the reports and not bringing in the officers, they had denied me my right to cross-examine the officers. On this point the state supreme court overruled us.

We noted as well that during my trial a guard from McNeil Island, John Harris, was brought all the way from Washington to testify against

me. He recounted how he had been assaulted when Dillon and I made our escape from the island, an event that had happened almost twenty years before. In my trial he testified about things that were not in the original records or that had never happened. In his testimony he recalled all kinds of events that cast me in the worst possible light. The testimony should never have been allowed: Harris, obviously prejudiced against me, would have testified to anything that worked against me. It was clear that he fabricated events or recalled things that he had not raised at my trial in Tacoma.

One key point we made had to do with the jury instructions during the penalty phase of the proceedings. The prosecution had informed the jury that even if it handed down a death sentence, the sentence would not necessarily be carried out. This was part of the stock instructions that all district attorneys in California gave to juries in death penalty cases. Busch told the jurors that if they sentenced me to death, Judge Walker could reduce the sentence to life, or the Supreme Court of California could reverse or modify the death sentence, or the governor could commute the sentence. By issuing a death sentence, the jury was not necessarily condemning me to die, and Busch repeatedly emphasized this point.

We claimed that providing the jury with this information was a violation of my constitutional rights. The jury had no way to know what another judicial department or the executive branch might do if it reviewed my case. Thus, the stock instruction prejudiced the penalty phase of my trial. In my time on death row, I found in the law books a 1958 case, *New Jersey v. White* (27 N.J. 158, 142 A.2d 65), in which the petitioner claimed the same legal point I was trying to make.

In addition, we argued that since the LAPD and the district attorney had planted Robert Luna in my cell, he acted as an agent of the police. There were rulings from other states that lent authority to our point. Those states had ruled that anybody planted by the police becomes an agent of the police. So my constitutional right to consult with counsel before speaking to the authorities had been denied. Joseph Busch had unquestionably planted Luna in my tank, so I thought that this was a very strong point: their entire case rested largely on Luna's fabricated testimony.

Together, Winhoven and I worked pretty hard up on death row to bring all these points to the attention of my attorney, Morris Lavine. In fact, we drew up a document like a regular brief, raising what we thought were good points for a new trial. We did all the research and,

after putting it in proper form, sent it to Morris Lavine. Later on, Lavine wanted to take credit for these points. In actuality, he did nothing but receive our brief, argue the case before the court, and mimeograph the required eleven copies. Red and I put in all the work.

After all the briefs were filed by my attorney and by the attorney general, the California Supreme Court finally heard my case in August 1963. They affirmed my conviction by a unanimous vote and denied all my allegations in a long opinion written by Justice Rey Schauer. According to the opinion, I did not have a right to have counsel present during the lineup; Luna's testimony was admissible; the products of the illegal search and seizure were admissible; the disciplinary documents from Alcatraz could be introduced without having the officers present for cross-examination; and we had not proven that the exclusion of Mexican Americans from the jury was intentional and systematic. The opinion denied every one of my allegations, all the way down the line.

The justices did not comment on a few points, one of them being the issue of the stock instruction to the jury. On this and a few other points we raised, the justices made no comment except to say they were devoid of merit. Justice Schauer wrote that any mistakes that had been made at my trial were harmless, and had not affected the deliberation or outcome of my case. So the court denied my motion for reversal and affirmed my conviction.

The opinion, I felt, was an example of the court's shoddy judicial work. On the point of there being no Mexicans on the jury-selection panels, the court argued that I had not proved systematic exclusion. In 1955, the U.S. Supreme Court ruled—in *Reece v. Georgia* (350 U.S. 85)—that the burden of proof was on the state to show that there had been no discrimination in jury selection. They ruled that it would be *impossible* for a defendant to prove discrimination, so the onus was on the state to provide substantial evidence showing that there was no discrimination. The California Supreme Court unjustly put the burden of proof on me.

I should say that one of the justices, Marshall McComb, was a notorious judge on the state supreme court. Some years after the denial of my motion, McComb was arrested for wandering around an airport, dressed as a security guard and acting rather oddly. The police did not know who he was. McComb refused to appear in court and was sentenced to five days in jail for contempt. When he died in 1981, I heard that he had left his wife one dollar and given the rest of his money to

a law library. In order to contest the will, Mrs. McComb had to air details of McComb's mental instability throughout his adult life. Her testimony documented that his bizarre behavior began well before he joined the majority opinion in my case. Unfortunately, he helped decide whether I lived or died.

After the state supreme court denied my motions, I started preparing petitions to be filed in the U.S. Supreme Court. Petitions for a writ of *certiorari* were eventually filed, and in the meantime I continued working on my case.

In 1961 the U.S. Supreme Court had handed down a decision — *Mapp v. Ohio* (367 U.S. 643) — regarding illegal search and seizure. It ruled for the first time that the states would have to abide by federal law as far as illegal searches and seizures were concerned. Before *Mapp v. Ohio,* the Supreme Court had ruled that Fourth Amendment protections against unlawful searches and seizures did not apply to the states, and therefore the state could search your house or your car without a warrant. A petitioner's only recourse in such a case was to sue the state for not having a warrant. But the evidence obtained through these illegal searches could be used in court.

In *Mapp v. Ohio,* the court ruled that the Fourth Amendment should be considered in conjunction with the Fourteenth Amendment, which prohibits the states from abridging the privileges or immunities of citizens of the United States. Therefore, any evidence obtained from an illegal search or seizure could not be used in court. In other words, they applied what they call "the exclusionary rule" to the states. The court decided that previous rulings that had allowed the use of evidence from illegal searches were unfair. After investigating the matter, the justices found that evidence obtained from illegal searches was used primarily against the poor, since the poor lacked the resources to sue the state. So the U.S. Supreme Court reversed its previous decision.

In 1964, the Supreme Court handed down two decisions that pertained to the right to counsel: *Massiah v. United States* (377 U.S. 201) and *Escobedo v. Illinois* (378 U.S. 478). This was several years before the famous 1967 *Miranda* decision in which the court ruled that a suspect had to be informed of his rights before being questioned. The *Massiah* case involved some men who were transporting heroin aboard ships. Two defendants — Massiah and Colson — were arrested, but the authorities didn't have enough evidence to prove their guilt. So they planted a microphone on Massiah's codefendant, Colson, to overhear him and Massiah discussing the heroin smuggling operation. Detectives about

a block away were recording the transmission. In that case, the justices ruled that Colson was, effectively, an agent of the police because he had been used for the purpose of obtaining evidence against Massiah. Any taped conversation introduced during Massiah's trial had been unconstitutionally obtained, since he hadn't been advised that he could have counsel present when he spoke to Colson. This case seemed quite pertinent to my own, given the manner in which the cops had used Luna to obtain information.

The *Escobedo* case broadened the *Massiah* decision. The justices ruled that before a defendant already accused of a crime could be questioned, he had the right to have counsel present. Moreover, the defendant had to be advised that he didn't have to say anything to the police without counsel present. Those two decisions covered all four corners of my case, as they say in legal parlance.

In denying our appeal, the California Supreme Court ruled that I had voluntarily offered information during my alleged conversations with Luna. Supposedly, I had, of my own free will, told him about the crime, and like a good prisoner, he had reported it to the officials. The court based its decision on the fact that if information about a crime is revealed in conversation, the conversation can be used as testimony in a trial.

I argued that since the police had planted Luna for the sole purpose of gathering evidence, that made him an agent of the police, and I should have been advised of my right to counsel. So *Massiah* and *Escobedo* were decisions directly applicable to my case.

While the U.S. Supreme Court was deciding these cases, I was on death row, preparing a writ of *certiorari*. During that time, I got to know a young guy on the row named Joseph Morse. He was about nineteen years old, and had been sentenced to death for killing his sister and his mother.

Morse was preparing his appeal, and he asked me if I would read his opening brief. After I read it, I told him, "Joe, I don't think you have a chance in hell. You haven't argued any points of law."

He seemed pretty downcast, but I told him, "Listen, Joe, I've got a point here that I raised, though the state supreme court shot me down. It's a point the court didn't mention in their opinion, and it's worth raising in your case."

The point concerned the district attorney's stock instruction of telling the jury that if it imposed a death sentence, the sentence would not necessarily be carried out. This was the point that I had raised

in my own opening brief. In fact, I still remember the page number: page 166.

My help perked Joe up a bit. I told him, "This is what I'll do: I'll copy it, and I'll have you send this point to your attorney. Tell him to include it in his closing brief and see if it helps."

So he sent the argument to his attorney, who included it in the closing brief of his appeal. The California Supreme Court, when it ruled on his appeal in 1964, declared that he had indeed been denied a fair trial in the penalty phase.

The decision in Joe Morse's case became a landmark, *People v. Morse* (60 Cal.2d 631), and most of the men on death row at the time took advantage of it. Almost all of them got a reversal on the penalty phase of their trials because the stock instruction read to all their juries was declared unconstitutional. Because of the legal point I gave to Joe, all the guys on death row had their sentences reversed.

In the meantime, the state supreme court had denied me a rehearing. Thirty days went by, then the court sent my case back to the Los Angeles trial court, which would set an execution date. Under the law, once the state supreme court has decided your case and a rehearing has been denied, they send what they call the "remittitur" down to the trial court. ("Remittitur" transfers jurisdiction over matters in the case from the appellate court to the trial court.) The judge who sentenced you is then required to set a date of execution not less than sixty but no more than ninety days away.

As soon as the remittitur was sent down in early October, a deputy district attorney named Marshall Schulman asked Judge Walker to set an early date of execution. My attorney told me that because Schulman was so persistent and bothered the judge so much about setting an early date, the judge wound up bawling him out in court. In the end, Judge Walker set an execution date for seventy-two days later — December 11, 1963.

I asked the state supreme court to grant me a stay. They denied me with a little procurement decision: "forthwith the stay of execution was denied." My next move was to file a writ of *certiorari* with the U.S. Supreme Court.

The days, in the meantime, were ticking down. It would soon be a week before my execution date. By that time I had been on death row for a few years, and I had shaken hands with many men who had been taken down to the gas chamber. I had come to accept that I, too, could

very well be put to death. In fact, they had already measured me for the clothes that I would wear in the gas chamber, and I had placed the order for my last meal.

Because of the writ of *certiorari*, Justice William O. Douglas granted me a stay of execution. His decision came on December 8, 1963, three days before my scheduled execution.

Immediately I filed a writ of *error coram nobis* ("the error before us") with the California Supreme Court, alleging that the inclusion of Luna's testimony was unconstitutional and illegal under the *Massiah* and *Escobedo* decisions. Because I filed a writ of *error coram nobis*, the state attorney general, not the district attorney, was required to provide testimony about Luna in relation to my case. In the writ, I noted that the question decided in the Joseph Morse case was on a point that I had raised in my opening brief before the California Supreme Court, a point the court had denied without comment. Under these rulings, I argued, I was entitled to a new trial.

In his reply, the state attorney general conceded that the district attorney of Los Angeles, with the aid of the LA Police Department, had placed Robert Luna in my cell for the purpose of gathering evidence. The attorney general admitted that Luna was a plant, but he claimed that the plant had worked and that Luna had gathered incriminating statements from me. He went on to argue that this had been a very difficult case and that without the use of Luna, the necessary evidence could never have been gathered.

After considering the reply of the attorney general, the state supreme court ruled on my case. First, they ruled that Luna's conversation was admissible because both *Massiah* and *Escobedo* were decided after the court had affirmed my conviction. The decision in those cases could not be applied retroactively to mine. Although they ruled that the holdings of *Escobedo* and *Massiah* covered the four corners of my complaint, they decided that my case, as far as they were concerned, was final. They would not give me the advantage of those two decisions.

The court went on to address my point about the unconstitutionality of the stock jury instruction. The justices ruled that the making of such comments to the jury had tainted the integrity of the penalty phase and that, therefore, they *would* retroactively apply *People v. Morse*. In so doing, they reversed the penalty phase, but not the innocence-or-guilt phase, of the trial.

My death sentence was finally reversed in 1965.

After all those hours of poring over law books, all the effort of filing

writs and arguing points of law, the work paid off. Still and all, I didn't feel that justice had truly been served. After all, the reversal overturned the death sentence for a crime I never committed in the first place.

Sixteen of the men with whom I had lived under the constant threat of death in San Quentin won reversals because of the *Morse* decision. Many of the men never did go back to death row. In fact, many served out their sentences and are now free men. And I'm glad to say that many were grateful to me because they knew that I was the one who had given the point to little Joe Morse. They used to shake my hand and pat me on the back when they saw me. They were real happy about the way things turned out in the end, and I have to admit, so was I. My death sentence was commuted to life, and eventually I served out enough years to earn release.

I later read that some time after these reversals had been granted, a number of high-powered lawyers got together for a seminar that concluded with an elegant dinner. My attorney, Morris Lavine, was there, and he rose on that occasion to give a brief speech.

He began, "You know, in this profession you win some and you lose some."

He then went on to describe how he had tried to use the precedent of *New Jersey v. White* to argue the unconstitutionality of the stock jury instruction before the California Supreme Court. He went on to cite *Massiah* and *Escobedo* as precedents concerning a defendant's right to consult with counsel before speaking to an agent of the police.

"I took these points—the unconstitutionality of the stock instruction and the right to counsel—before the state supreme court in order to reverse my client's sentence. Well, the writ was shot down. But we kept at it, and, finally, my client received a reversal."

He went on and on like that. After the dinner, as all the lawyers were leaving the hall, I heard that Joe Morse's attorney confronted Lavine.

"Listen, you dirty son-of-a-bitch, that was my case that I argued before the U.S. Supreme Court! I presented the *New Jersey v. White* case as precedent."

These two respectable, powerful lawyers nearly came to blows over whose case and whose client had first made the points that won the reversals.

When he heard about it, Joe Morse got mad as well. He told me that he wrote to his attorney: "You lying punk. It was Ernie who came up with the argument, and don't you forget it!"

In the meantime, as I said, my death sentence had been commuted to life. In 1966 I was transferred from San Quentin to Folsom prison. Some weeks after I arrived, a few guys came around to my cell.

"C'mon, Ernie, we got something for ya!"

I followed them down to a storage room. A group of guys who had had their death sentences reversed had organized a little party for me. They set up chairs and tables and served ice cream they had bought from the canteen. The party was in gratitude for my having helped save their lives.

I can't help thinking about the group of us—convicted felons, accused murders, hard-core inmates—sitting around eating ice cream and congratulating each other on our success. On the outside, hundreds of miles away in some fancy ballroom, two high-powered lawyers nearly came to blows over the very same issue that we were quietly celebrating in a Folsom prison storage room.

EPILOGUE

Of course, I've been no angel in my life. This is still no reason to have been tried, convicted, and sentenced to death for a crime that I didn't commit. The death penalty is a politically motivated punishment that has little to do with ensuring justice or preventing crime. I've known several men who were executed unjustly by the state. I came within days of being one of them myself.

I spent five years in Folsom, from 1965 to 1970. The authorities considered me and several of my friends—Joe Morgan, Big Zeke, and others—troublemakers because we didn't bow down to their power. For this, the guards placed us "behind the screen." We were locked down every evening around five and kept in Building 2, which was a kind of high-security section of Folsom. The doors had metal screens on them; that's where the phrase came from. Even so, I spent a number of good years at Folsom because I was surrounded by my friends, and no matter what happened or how hard times got, we knew we would stick up for each other and stick together.

My time in Folsom came to an end when I hurt my back while working in the industries. The medical staff at Folsom couldn't adequately treat a back problem, but the correctional authorities refused to transfer me to another facility. I ended up suing the state correctional system to get it done, but I was finally transferred to the California Medical Correction Facility at Vacaville in 1970. There I could receive better medical treatment for my back.

Though I would end up spending nine years at Vacaville, I was once transferred for three months to San Luis Obispo for "stress therapy."

This program was set up to provide counseling and therapy to help prisoners manage stress and anger. The authorities believed that the therapy was successful when a prisoner expressed remorse for the crimes he had committed. Once the therapy was deemed a success, he was eligible for parole.

In my case, I explained that I could not feel remorse for something that I had not done. I had all along insisted on my innocence, and I would not lie now, even to earn early parole. So I was sent back to Vacaville, where I remained until my parole in 1979. By that time I had spent eighteen years of my life, four of them on death row, for a crime that I had not committed.

No sooner was I discharged from parole in 1982 than I was arrested again the following year. In 1984 I was tried and convicted for extortion and robbery. I don't need to go into the details about my trial, but it's enough to say there was a great deal of contradictory testimony and half-truths told (in fact, some outright lies) that got me sent to federal prison in Lompoc, California. In 1990, the authorities transferred me to a prison in Phoenix, Arizona, where I stayed until 1994. For six months after my release I stayed in a halfway house. I was granted parole, and finally discharged in 1998. I am now a free man, living in Los Angeles.

Just one last note: I returned to Alcatraz in 1999, forty years after my release. Believe me, I'd rather see Alcatraz as a tourist than as a prisoner any day. Still, it was nice to see the place that I called home all those years ago.

In the end, I don't think that there is any lesson to be learned from my story. Any kind of easy moral would probably be silly and simplistic. I've stated a number of times that crime *does* pay, if you don't get caught. You have to look only at the Rockefellers, the Kennedys, or many other millionaires in American history whose wealth came from breaking the law. So, no, I don't think there is some lesson that you can take from my life. It's been my life, and, for what it's worth, I share my story with you.

AFTERWORD

Whoever destroys a soul, it is considered as if he destroyed an entire world. And whoever saves a life, it is considered as if he saved an entire world.
— JERUSALEM TALMUD, SANHEDRIN 4:1 (22A)

The story Ernie López tells about his life leaves one in an ambiguous position. On the one hand, it is easy to admire his skill and cunning, his cleverness and his rigid refusal to capitulate to the brutality of the U.S. correctional system. On the other hand, his life of crime is certainly not heroic, and he hints at having done things that are, at best, morally questionable. As the person to whom it has come to translate his anecdotes into a story, I find myself in an even more ambiguous position.

My involvement in the writing of Ernie's story came about completely by accident. My uncle, Carlos Torres, had known Ernie when the two were kids in East LA, before Ernie was sent to Preston. After his return, Ernie would sometimes ask my uncle to let him copy his homework or his tests so that Ernie could stay in school. One of Ernie's few joys in his hardscrabble young life was being able to play on the junior high school football team. Though he is not physically large, his exploits on the field—especially his ability to hit and take a hit—were legendary. However, because his education had been so severely disrupted, Ernie's only chance to receive passing grades and remain on the team was with the "extracurricular" help of my uncle and other friends. In the end, Ernie never did finish high school.

As his career in crime developed, Ernie's fame (and infamy) grew among his home neighborhoods in East LA. His exploits, along with those of his even more notorious compatriot, Joe Morgan, soon became part of East LA folklore. Over time my uncle lost track of Ernie, and did not hear of him for several decades.

Quite by coincidence, he and Ernie ran across each other again in 1998. The two caught up on old times, and Ernie told my uncle about his time on Alcatraz and in San Quentin. He even produced a roughly typed manuscript that recounted a section of the events told here. My uncle thought that I would be interested in the story and showed me a copy. A friend of Ernie's had produced the original manuscript, laboriously typing out the stories Ernie told him as the two sat together in the library of Vacaville.

Even in its rough form, the story I read felt special. Aside from the excitement, adventure, and danger that it describes, it struck me as the expression of a powerful fighting spirit. My uncle arranged a meeting at a small home-style restaurant in East LA, and so began a process of talking, taping, and transcribing that lasted well over a year.

Ernie conveyed his story to me as an oral narrative, with interruptions, repetitions, pauses, and ellipses. His are stories that have been developed over years of jailhouse tellings, and they form a part of lost literary tableau: the stories that prisoners tell to entertain one another and pass time. These stories are one of the means by which prisoners endure the deadly monotony of their sentences.

Though the tapes of our sessions were transcribed with the exceptional help of Lynn Itagaki (to whom I am exceedingly grateful for both her transcription skills and her legal research), what you have read here is not a transcript. Rather, the book is a kind of ventriloquism. On paper, Ernie's oral narrative can at times sound flat and repetitious. When heard, however, the story is compelling and vivid. In order to convey on paper the sense of excitement and anticipation his stories create, I have had to form a narrative that conforms to literary convention.

My writing tries to imitate the tone and flavor of Ernie's voice without reproducing it word for word. It is an attempt—not always successful—to convey as simply and truthfully the spirit of Ernie's own storytelling. The aesthetic of his stories is inflected by a sense of *rasquachismo,* a term defined by cultural critic Tomás Ybarra-Frausto as "an outsider viewpoint" stemming from an "irreverent stance that debunks convention" (155). The content and direction of these stories are entirely his, the words are mostly mine, and the effect is something that I hope readers find valuable and interesting.

One thing readers may note is a lack of affect or feeling conveyed by the narrative. This gives a clue, I suspect, to the nature of Ernie's narrative. It is, in a sense, a staging of a life rather than a strict autobio-

graphical account. In part, this is due to the experiences Ernie has had in the legal system. One constructs one's story and sticks to it. In part, Ernie has approached his life in a very pragmatic way. For example, Uncle Carlos, Ernie, and I took a trip to Alcatraz to return to his site of incarceration. As we walked up the steep road leading from the dock to the prison, I asked Ernie how he had felt the first time he made that ascent in 1944, knowing that he would spend at least eleven years on the Rock. He told me that he had felt nothing; it was just something he had to do. It is this cold-blooded quality that served him well in his dealings with the penal system. However, this lack of feeling may also distance him from others, especially strangers who are reading about his life. Rather than try to "correct" this tone in the story, or to delve into more personal feelings and emotions, I have let this lack of affect stand as part of Ernie's own story and experience.

In short, I have sought to give voice to Ernie's story from his point of view, allowing him to construct his own character. All along, it seemed clear to me that he was—of course—offering a partial view. This was, possibly, a means of protecting himself from further prosecution. Ernie is a smart man, and he would be unlikely to offer potentially incriminating evidence of criminal behavior in a public forum such as this. However, I think the self-serving quality of some of his story has more to do with his experience. One of the prime lessons learned in prison is to be always guarded, wary, and reserved. And, of course, never to admit anything.

This forms, to my mind, part of the pleasure of the narrative. Ernie represents himself as a tough and laconic antihero. Although he is interested in issues of justice and fairness, it is clear that he also delights— horrible and vicious as parts of his life are—in the adventure of the whole thing. In no small part, my motivation for writing this book had less to do with the issue of objective veracity than with the power of narrative. The manuscript is certainly an oral history, but it is also a narrative that seeks to give voice in both style and point of view to a man who has experienced the most horrible conditions of the American penal system. As an oral history, the story challenges the idea of objectivity and transparency in oral histories, and this is both troubling and intriguing.

The text presents a particular problem as an oral history because it is so clearly biased. For this reason, I tend to think of my collaboration with Ernie as something akin to Latin American testimonial literature. By this, I mean that the problems of "truth" and "represen-

tation," as well as those of "author" and "speaker," can never be fully resolved. Generally speaking, testimonial literature seeks to challenge official versions of history and to give voice to the underprivileged and repressed. This book is motivated in part by a desire to share a view of the world that would otherwise be completely unfamiliar or unseen. Ultimately, readers must take the story for what it is and come to terms with what they find valuable, what they find entertaining, and what they simply find unbelievable.

Throughout his story, Ernie displays a firm sense of honor, a strong pride in work, and a belief in a moral code. Though this code is one that those of us outside prison may not appreciate, there is at work a very clear ethical system in which integrity in one's actions and faith in one's friends is foremost. When pressed on an issue like jailhouse homosexuality, Ernie expresses his disapproval of such behavior, but does not dwell on the topic. His disdain for homosexual behavior is matched by his disregard for formal religious belief. Like his father, Ernie rejects any kind of organized religion. His is a wholly existential world, one where salvation and morality are founded on behavior, not faith. Salvation has more to do with survival than spiritual rebirth, and so too does morality.

This pragmatic and materialist worldview manifests itself in the obvious pride that Ernie takes in the quality of the work he did in the prison shops. At one point in our discussions, he offered me an elaborate explanation of how he and others had helped found the broommaking industry on Alcatraz, and how their efforts had helped streamline and expand the production. His skill at manual labor came at a cost: as a result of a woodworking accident at Alcatraz, Ernie lost half a finger of his left hand. Nevertheless, years after this loss, he spent laborious hours making grandfather clocks while serving time at Vacaville. His clocks even won awards for their beauty and craftsmanship. Like many people in the outside world, Ernie clearly took pride in the day-to-day work that made up the majority of the time he spent behind bars.

In addition to the personal element at the heart of these stories, there is a historical scope to the form of Ernie's life. Beginning in East Los Angeles during the Great Depression, the life of crime that Ernie falls into is born as much out of necessity as ambition. As we were preparing this narrative, Ernie recounted a story about a time he and a friend stopped for gas at a station in East LA. They were quickly surrounded

by a group of little kids. They eagerly asked if they could help with the oil or tires or gasoline in return for small change.

His friend turned to him.

"Ernie," he said, "these are the next generation of criminals."

This comment, made as a joke, reveals a truth: need and ambition are a lethal combination. How are these young kids to get ahead in society when there are no legitimate opportunities available to them? Ernie's friend undoubtedly saw in those children's eager eyes a reflection of his and Ernie's own childhood. Their hopes and dreams (Ernie often talks about having wanted to be a football player when young) run head-on into an unforgiving wall of limited possibilities.

The story of Ernie López plays out against a backdrop of great historical change in the United States. The community of East Los Angeles was in transition, going from being populated by poor Jewish immigrants to one largely comprising poor Mexican families fleeing the ravages of the Mexican Revolution (1911–1920). Historian Rodolfo Acuña estimates that as much as one-eighth of the Mexican population immigrated to the United States between 1910 and 1930 (123ff.). This movement led, as Douglas Monroy explains in his study of early Mexican American communities in Los Angeles, to an unprecedented growth in the Mexican population in the United States—what he calls the "First Great Migration" (2). Previously, the Mexican presence in California was a small remnant of the original Californio population, the community established under Spanish, and later Mexican, rule before the U.S.-Mexican War (1846–1848). David Gutiérrez notes that an average of 25,000 Mexican immigrants entered the United States each year between 1920 and 1929 (69). What work opportunities had arisen in industrial Los Angeles as a result of World War I and the Roaring Twenties quickly dissipated following the stock market crash of 1929, leaving East LA struggling with poverty and little expectation of improved conditions. The Great Depression provided some of the original impetus for Ernie's life of necessity and crime, since East LA was hit particularly hard by the downturn in the world economy.

Though subject to the harsh economic conditions of the time, people of Mexican ancestry were beginning to forge a new sense of belonging in the United States. Though his parents' lives were firmly rooted in Mexican thought and culture, Ernie is a part of a second generation of Mexican Americans, who created a new binational cultural identity, one that made a profound social and political impact in the years to

come. This was a generation that, as George Sánchez has noted, had to cope with the knowledge of being members of a society in which equality and justice were not experienced equally by all citizens (272–273).

This new identity and understanding of citizenship came to bear fruit as a result of World War II. As John Chávez and others explain, so many members of this new Mexican American generation were involved in the war that they came to develop an earned sense of U.S. citizenship, with all the rights and privileges thereof. This sentiment is expressed well by Raúl Morín, a veteran of World War II: "We felt this was an opportunity to show the rest of the nation that we too were also ready to fight for our nation. It did not matter that we were looked upon as Mexicans; the war soon made us all genuine Americans, eligible and available immediately . . . to defend our country, the United States of America" (15). The war afforded them the opportunity to prove their loyalty to a country that tended to view Mexican migrants and Mexican Americans alike as foreign outsiders.

While this social and political presence unfolded, a social counter-current arose. On the one hand, World War II led to a new wave of Mexican migration, since the war effort increased demands for industrial, agricultural, and manual labor. This growth triggered a backlash and a tightening of immigration controls. The perceived invasion by Mexican outsiders was matched by a suspicion of the foreign element within the national borders: the Mexican American, especially Mexican American youth who donned the foppish zoot suits.

A well-known example of how powerful this suspicion could be was the infamous Sleepy Lagoon murder trial. On the night of August 2, 1942, a young man by the name of José Díaz was found dead near a gravel pit used by local children as a swimming hole. The police ascribed his death to a fight that had broken out the night before between two Mexican gangs, the Downey Boys and the 38th Street Club, at a party near the pond. Because Díaz was associated with the Downey Boys, the police arrested twenty-two members of the 38th Street Club on charges of murder and conspiracy (Gutiérrez, 124). Among the arrested was the purported ringleader of the club, Henry Leyvas.

As George Sánchez explains, the 38th Street Club was one of thirty-five youth clubs that were termed "gangs" by the media and the police (266–267). These clubs often met in public schools, in police substations, and under official supervision. Nevertheless, these organizations were all soon viewed as part of an increasingly dangerous threat to social stability.

The press had a field day with the arrest of the 38th Street Club members as an example of Mexican American hooliganism. They sensationalized the murder as well as the trial, going so far as to romantically dub the swimming hole the Sleepy Lagoon, after a popular Harry James tune.

The media were not alone in inflaming public passion against Mexican American youth. The Los Angeles police, notorious throughout their history for their strong-arm tactics, became the apparatus by which powerful anti-Mexican feelings were manifest in brutal social action. People of Mexican descent in the United States found themselves cast as outsiders, dangerous foreigners ready to infiltrate and undo American society. In some ways, the wave of patriotic fervor that overtook the nation as a result of World War II negatively altered the political and social landscape of the country. Mexican Americans faced numerous conflicts and contradictions as they dealt with issues of national, cultural, and personal identity. The central dilemma was how to remain true to a distinct sense of cultural and binational identity and yet be an American citizen. The antiforeign sentiment in the country created a distinct problem for ethnic "others" in the United States.

The Sleepy Lagoon trial stands as a prime example of how a perceived foreign presence in the United States was systematically dehumanized. As a part of this dehumanization, the young defendants had to endure a number of humiliating and damning experiences. From the time of their arrest until two weeks into the trial, the presiding judge, Charles Fricke, ordered that the defendants not be allowed to cut their hair or change their clothes, reasoning that only hoodlums wore zoot suits. Their shabby appearance thus served as evidence of their guilt.

There were other irregularities with the trial, including the fact that all twenty-two defendants were tried together, seated as a group apart from their lawyers, with whom they were prohibited to sit or consult in court. At the trial the Los Angeles police also submitted a report that declared Mexicans were by nature violent and likely to engage in criminal activity (Sánchez, 266).

Xenophobia had before this time led to the appointment of E. Duran Ayres as head of the Los Angeles County Sheriff's Department Foreign Relations Bureau. He was charged with investigating the role of Mexican Americans in any social unrest. Ayres concluded that Mexicans, being descendants of Indians, were actually Asian, and therefore had less concern for human life. This, of course, allowed for an easy equivalence between the Mexican presence in the United States and the per-

ceived threat to state security represented by the Japanese American population on the West Coast, recently interned as a result of President Roosevelt's signing of Executive Order 9066 in February 1942.

Ayres suggested as well that Mexicans had inherited the violent tendencies that their Aztec forebearers made manifest in the form of human sacrifice. His view was that "utter disregard for the value of life" was universal throughout the Indian population of the Americas. This, Ayres concluded, "of course is well known to everyone" (Gutiérrez, 125). Judge Fricke had E. Duran Ayres testify as an expert witness against the Sleepy Lagoon defendants.

By mid-January 1943, seventeen of the defendants had been found guilty on charges ranging from assault to first-degree murder and given prison terms running from five years to life. The most serious offenders were sent to San Quentin to serve out their sentences. After a great effort by concerned activists, Hollywood celebrities, and others, the Second District Court of Appeals finally overturned the guilty verdicts on October 4, 1944.

Anti-Mexican sentiment was not restricted to specific individuals accused of criminal activity. The so-called zoot suit or pachuco "riots" in the summer of 1943 revealed a general resentment and violent rejection of Mexican Americans. The "riots" consisted of gangs of U.S. servicemen rampaging through numerous Chicano communities in and around Los Angeles, beating Mexican American youths and spreading terror. Over the course of several days, large groups of servicemen would commandeer taxi cabs—whose drivers often offered their services for free—and roam the streets of East LA in search of young men decked out in their finest zoot suits. The sailors and soldiers set upon their victims, beating them and tearing apart their clothes, leaving them bloody, beaten, and mostly naked in the streets of their community. As a result of these attacks, in an all-too-familiar perversion of justice, many Mexican American youth were arrested. None of the servicemen was ever charged (McWilliams, 244–254).

In his study of the riots, Mauricio Mazón sees several causes for the violence. The servicemen who took part were often new recruits, unused to the authoritarianism of the military. Their sense of frustration and rebellion found an easy target among civilians. In this sense, the zoot-suiters were a perfect target, since their individualism and freedom was the antithesis of the regimented life of the servicemen. Carey McWilliams notes that clothing like zoot suits is "often used as a badge of defiance by the rejected against the outside world and, at the same

time, as a symbol of belonging to the inner group. It is at once a sign of rebellion and a mark of belonging. It carries prestige" (McWilliams, 243). Combined with the psychological elements of resentment and antiauthoritarian rage, the police mobilization of anti-Mexican feelings proved a formidable force (Mazón, 67–72).

In response, some Mexican American youth turned away from mainstream American identity and values. The image of the zoot-suited pachuco became, for many Mexican American youth, an icon of resistance or counterculture. Joe and Clairece Feagin explain that in the United States "some subordinated racial and ethnic groups have drawn on their well-developed cultures to resist discrimination and slavish assimilation to the dominant Anglo-Protestant culture. . . . They not only foster a sense of identity and pride but also facilitate the group's survival and enhance its ability to resist oppression" (15).

Pachucos (and pachucas) personify rebellion, with their stylized clothes, their gangster image, and their fluency in *caló*, the street language associated with a Mexican criminal underclass. Pachucos represented for many youth the quintessence of nonconformity and resistance. Octavio Paz, in a 1950 essay on the pachuco, argued that the pachuco, standing outside both U.S. and Mexican society, "actually flaunts his differences. The purpose of his grotesque dandyism and anarchic behavior is not so much to point out the injustice and incapacity of a society that has failed to assimilate him as it is to demonstrate his personal will to remain different" (14–15). Rather than highlight the failure to properly assimilate to the dominant society, the pachuco celebrates the cultural and social difference he embodies.

Young Chicanos began to glamorize the pachucos as Robin Hood figures rather than as criminals, and caló become an important part of colloquial language rather than underworld slang. It came "to symbolize the ways and attitudes of the pachucos and of Mexican American youth in general" (Paz, 23). The pachuco became a cultural icon, and caló became a means by which a group identity was forged and maintained. At this level of cultural distinction, the pachuco became a figure who helped define an assertively distinct Mexican American identity.

It is this quality that cultural critics like Octavio Romano-V. celebrate. He argues that the "Pachuco *movement was one of the few truly separatist movements in American History. . . .* The Pachuco indulged in a self-separation from history, created his own reality as he went along even to the extent of creating his own language" (83, emphasis in the original). Though this description may be excessively celebra-

tory, it does point how that the image of the pachuco allowed for the expression of a unique identity in the face of social rejection.

This is not to deny the connection between the pachuco and a criminal underclass. The term "pachuco" was a colloquial way of referring to someone from El Paso, and the jargon of the El Paso underworld provided much of the pachuco's vocabulary. Rosaura Sánchez in *Chicano Discourse* notes that the origins of caló have been traced back to Spain, where heavily hispanicized gypsy language had mingled with the speech of Spanish delinquents (84–85). It is thought that early Spanish explorers and settlers brought the familiar street language of Spain to the New World. Caló, from its inception, has been associated with a marginal demimonde.

Caló and its speakers followed the tracks of the Southern Pacific railroad to Los Angeles, where a large group of young Chicanos from El Paso settled in 1942 (Baker, 22). Their petty criminal activities continued, and though the popularity of their dress and speech spread, the pachuco remained marginal to the law as well as the community until World War II and immediately following. The pachucos and their drapes—long coats, pancake hats, baggy pants with narrow cuffs— represented a compelling image of nonconformity for Mexican American youth at a time when their identity as American citizens came into question.

As the Sleepy Lagoon trial and the zoot suit riots indicate, to the official world of Los Angeles—the sheriff's office, the police department, the justice system—there was no discernible difference between criminals and rebellious youth. The early experiences of Ernie López become emblematic of the way in which Mexican American young men were viewed and treated by the authorities. But even before these events, the authorities viewed the Mexican American community as a breeding ground for crime, an attitude that continues to inform both public opinion and public policy today.

In our shared social imagination, we fear the danger and threat presented by youthful gangs of African American and Latino (and increasingly Asian American and even Armenian) youth. In Ernie's case, he had to deal with a legal and penal system that effectively created a perpetual criminal underclass. In Los Angeles before World War II, this underclass was comprised of primarily Mexican youth.

Ernie's story reflects the sense of persecution and injustice felt by many Americans of Mexican descent during this period of U.S. history. As a

thirteen-year-old in 1935, his first major criminal infraction was for joy-riding and evading arrest. His first punishment was to be beaten by the arresting police, brutality that landed him in a hospital with a ruptured appendix. Later, while three of his compatriots were granted probation and a fourth was sentenced to a school for boys, Ernie was sent to the Preston School of Industry. He spent his two-year sentence learning to survive among the most hard-core juvenile criminals in the state. The excessive punishment he received set a pattern that was to hound him the rest of his career.

It is against the backdrop of battles fought at home and abroad during World War II that Ernie's early criminal life unfolds. The war offered Ernie the opportunity to advance economically and socially through inventive, perhaps sometimes brutal, criminal activity. It was his robbery of valuable B and C gasoline stamps that afforded Ernie access to a world he could only have dreamed about. By virtue of his ill-gotten gains, he gained status and influence. He was introduced to many celebrities from all walks of life: motion picture stars, professional football players, directors, nightclub owners, even politicians. The other shoe was sure to drop, and after a year of the high life, Ernie was tried for possession of and conspiracy to distribute federal property. World War II did, however, provide him with an undreamed-of opportunity.

There is one historical aspect of this story that many readers might not have readily perceived. At various moments in this narrative, Ernie mentions his close friendship with Joe Morgan. Though Joe appears as a kind of minor character in these stories, he and Ernie were quite good friends throughout their lives. For reasons that should become readily apparent, there is a reticence on Ernie's part to discuss too extensively his friendship with Joe. The two grew up together in East LA, got into trouble together, served time together, and became as bonded as brothers. Later in life, as is recounted in Ernie's story, they were accused of committing the same bank robbery together.

During his life, Joe "Pegleg" Morgan was recognized as the de facto leader of the prison gang "La Eme," the Mexican Mafia. Though Slavic American, Joe felt himself to be a Chicano through and through. He was raised in the same neighborhood and among the same influences as Ernie. Like Ernie, he got into trouble early with the law. In fact, Joe lost his right leg after being shot by the Los Angeles police in an escape attempt from jail. Like Ernie, Joe became involved with women at a young age. In 1946, at the age of sixteen, he took a thirty-two-year-old lover. The first time he served a sentence in prison was for murdering

the husband of his lover. Though eventually released on that charge, Joe ended up spending forty of his sixty-four years behind bars. It was while serving a sentence for violating parole that Joe fell in with leaders of La Eme (Katz, B4). Eventually, through cunning, skill, and brutality, Joe rose to be recognized as the kingpin of the gang.

The Bureau of Prisons has termed La Eme the most active of the five major U.S. prison gangs (Trout, 62). It was formed in the Deuel Vocational Institution of the California prison system in Tracy, California, between 1957 and 1960, and became a major presence after 1967 in both the state and federal penal systems. Federal prosecutors have accused La Eme of organizing a criminal enterprise meant to control drug trafficking, prostitution, and gambling in Los Angeles, alleging in 1995 that several of its members violated the Racketeer Influenced and Corrupt Organizations (RICO) Act (Ramos, A18). State and federal law enforcement officials claim that La Eme is composed of at least 1,000 members, both in and out of prison, who use intimidation, extortion, and murder to control their enterprises (Ayres, A14).

Up until his death in November 1993, Joe Morgan had become among certain circles a legendary outlaw, an outsized antihero who represented for a number of young Chicanos a rejection of social convention and morality. Joe's exploits—from his escape from county jail using tools hidden in his prosthetic leg, to his organizational abilities in forming La Eme, to his well-honed skills at prison survival—added to his reputation. As one Drug Enforcement Administration agent put it, Joe Morgan "had his own sense of honor, whether you agreed with it or not, and he lived by it" (Katz, B4). He is to this day a larger-than-life character in the imagination of many who know of La Eme and its doings.

In 1993 Joe Morgan sued Edward James Olmos, Universal Studios, and several others for the fictionalized portrayal of La Eme in Olmos's film *American Me*. Morgan sought $500,000 in punitive damages; he claimed that the negative portrayal of a one-legged white boy who runs with young Chicano hoods, gets into trouble with the law, and helps found a Latino prison gang would harm his chances for parole. Apparently, displeasure with the film was expressed in ways other than lawsuits. Director, producer, and star of *American Me*, Edward James Olmos felt that his life was in danger as a result of the film.

The protagonist of the movie—a character based on Rudolfo (Cheyenne) Cadena, a member of La Eme slain by rival inmates in 1972—is sodomized in jail, proves impotent when having sex with a woman,

and is killed by members of his own brotherhood. None of these events, though portrayed in the movie, have any factual basis. Consequently, the depiction was perceived as a direct insult to La Eme.

In prison, respect means survival. The writer of the original screenplay for *American Me*, Floyd Mutrux, explains that the members of La Eme "joined together out of a need for dignity and respect. . . . If it weren't for [Rudolfo Cadena and Joe Morgan] — and what they stood for — I wouldn't have written the story" (Katz, A24).

Ultimately, three people who had served as advisors on the film were murdered. In 1996, several men reputed to be members of the gang were tried and convicted for the murders. Although Ernie strongly voiced his disdain for what he perceived as the lies told in *American Me*, he never told me whether he was involved with La Eme or not, whether he knew of their activities, or even if Joe Morgan was involved with the gang. And I never asked him directly.

My interest throughout has been in turning the stories Ernie wanted to tell into a narrative that was readable and interesting. I wasn't concerned about interrogating him or learning about areas of his life that he did not offer up. Though some of the material emerged as a result of my questions about particular events or people, Ernie controlled the content of this book. This is, in the end, Ernie's story.

In any event, La Eme did not achieve its influence or notoriety until just after the principal events covered in this book. Even so, the unspoken story of La Eme remains a powerful though silent subtext in these stories about Ernie's many exploits.

His experience forms a kind of prehistory to the development of contemporary prison gangs. It is heavily influenced by the dehumanizing conditions to which prisoners were (and are) regularly subjected in U.S. prisons. Given the exploding prison population in the United States (which increased by seventy percent between 1990 and 2000), the kinds of events Ernie endured are becoming more and more a part of the contemporary American social landscape. The prison conditions that have bred blood brotherhoods continue to affect more and more of our people, something with which every American should be concerned.

One salient point throughout this story, no matter how biased, is the pattern of injustice Ernie has endured. He is ready to acknowledge that, as he puts it, he has been no angel. However, he also knows that many of his actions were the unfair result of prejudice and persecution. There was little way out of the poverty into which he was born. Although a

small but growing Mexican American middle class did gradually develop in Los Angeles during the time of this story, the reality for most people of Mexican descent in the United States was one of hardship, hard work, and poor pay.

The exclusion and criminalization many Mexican Americans endured contrasted sharply with opportunities and luxuries seemingly promised by U.S. society. World War II offered for Ernie, as it did for many, the first opportunity to rise above the abjection and struggle of the Great Depression. The career path Ernie followed was as an outlaw. It is not possible to say how much this decision was due to a personal sense of rebellion, an individual reaction to brutal experiences endured at a tender age, or a burning sense of social outrage. Probably all three reasons played strong roles.

When I asked him why he thought it was important that his story be told, he thought for a while before responding.

"To show people that things aren't always fair."

Ernie's story gives insight into a world few of us have experienced. It testifies and bears witness to the brutality and injustice endured by many poor and disenfranchised citizens of the United States.

Ernie is a *veterano,* a veteran of a war fought at home that no one wins. Some of the weapons used in this war have been segregation, discrimination, and violence, all perpetrated in the name of the law. Other weapons have been gang membership, drug trafficking, and coldhearted cruelty. The struggles in the United States that many young men of color face are one legacy of the war that Ernie — like so many others — fought. Unlike so many others, Ernie has survived. His story presents us with the voice of one who — though subjected to a system meant to destroy his soul — not only endured but survived, and in surviving, prevailed.

WORKS CITED

Acuña, Rodolfo. *Occupied America: A History of Chicanos*. New York: Harper and Row, 1972.

Ayres Jr., B. Drummond. "Battle Against Mexican Mafia Opens New Front in Court." *New York Times*, 26 November 1996, A14.

Baker, George Carpenter. *Pachuco: An American-Spanish Argot and Its Social Functions in Tucson, Arizona*. Tucson: Univ. of Arizona Press, 1974.

Benjamin, Walter. "Theses on the Philosophy of History." In *Illuminations*, edited by Hannah Arendt and translated by Harry Zohn, 253–264. New York: Schocken Books, 1969.

Chávez, John R. *The Lost Land: The Chicano Image of the Southwest*. Albuquerque: Univ. of New Mexico Press, 1984.

Feagin, Joe R., and Clairece Booher Feagin. *Racial and Ethnic Relations*. 6th ed. Upper Saddle River, N.J.: Prentice Hall, 1998.

Gutiérrez, David G. *Walls and Mirrors: Mexican Americans, Mexican Immigrants, and the Politics of Ethnicity*. Berkeley and Los Angeles: Univ. of California Press, 1995.

Katz, Jesse. "Film Leaves a Legacy of Fear." *Los Angeles Times*, 13 June 1993, A1, A24.

———. "Reputed Mexican Mafia Leader Dies in Prison at 64." *Los Angeles Times*, 10 November 1993, B1, B4.

Mazón, Mauricio. *The Zoot-Suit Riots: The Psychology of Symbolic Annihilation*. Austin: Univ. of Texas Press, 1984.

McWilliams, Carey. *North from Mexico: The Spanish-Speaking People of the United States*. Westport, Conn.: Greenwood, 1968.

Monroy, Douglas. *Rebirth: Mexican Los Angeles from the Great Migration to the Great Depression*. Berkeley and Los Angeles: Univ. of California Press, 1999.

Morín, Raúl. *Among the Valiant: Mexican-Americans in World War II and Korea*. Alhambra, Calif.: Borden Publishing Company, 1963.

Paz, Octavio. *Labyrinth of Solitude*. Lysander Kemp, Yara Milos, and Rachel Phillips Belash, trans. New York: Grove Press, 1985.

Ramos, George. "U.S. Uses Racketeering Law to Fight Mexican Mafia." *Los Angeles Times*, 2 December 1996, A1, A18, A19.

Romano-V., Octavio, Ed. "The Historical and Intellectual Presence of Mexican-Americans." In *Voices: Readings from El Grito, a Journal of Contemporary Mexican American Thought, 1967–1973*. 2nd ed. Berkeley, Calif.: Quinto Sol Publications, 1973.

Sánchez, George J. *Becoming Mexican American: Ethnicity, Culture, and Identity in Chicano Los Angeles, 1900–1945*. New York: Oxford Univ. Press, 1993.

Sánchez, Rosaura. *Chicano Discourse: Socio-Historic Perspectives*. Rowley, Mass.: Newbury House Publishers, 1983.

Tempest, Rone. "Texas Hit Man Charged with Killing Judge; Says He Helped California Police Build Murder Case." *Los Angeles Times*, 21 November 1982, A15.

Trout, Craig H. "Taking a New Look at an Old Problem." *Corrections Today* 54, no. 5 (July 1992): 62, 64, 66.

Ybarra-Frausto, Tomás. "Rasquachismo: A Chicano Sensibility." In *CARA: Chicano Art: Resistance and Affirmation, 1965–1985*, edited by Richard Griswold del Castillo, Teresa McKenna, and Yvonne Yarbro-Bejarano, 155–162. Los Angeles: Wright Art Gallery and the University of California, Los Angeles, 1991.